Social Protection under Authoritarianism

Social Protection under Authoritarianism

Social Protection under Authoritarianism

Health Politics and Policy in China

XIAN HUANG

OXFORD
UNIVERSITY PRESS

OXFORD
UNIVERSITY PRESS

Oxford University Press is a department of the University of Oxford. It furthers the University's objective of excellence in research, scholarship, and education by publishing worldwide. Oxford is a registered trade mark of Oxford University Press in the UK and certain other countries.

Published in the United States of America by Oxford University Press
198 Madison Avenue, New York, NY 10016, United States of America.

Library of Congress Cataloging-in-Publication Data
Names: Huang, Xian (Professor of political science), author.
Title: Social protection under authoritarianism : health politics and policy in China / Xian Huang.
Description: New York, NY : Oxford University Press, 2020. | Includes bibliographical references and index.
Identifiers: LCCN 2020007997 (print) | LCCN 2020007998 (ebook) | ISBN 9780190073640 (hardback) | ISBN 9780190073671 (on-line) | ISBN 9780190073657 (updf) | ISBN 9780190073664 (epub) | ISBN 9780197642771 (paperback)
Subjects: LCSH: Welfare state—China. | China—Social policy. | Medical policy—China. | Health insurance—China. | Elite (Social sciences)—China. | Social stratification—China. | Authoritarianism—China.
Classification: LCC HN733.5 .H844 2020 (print) | LCC HN733.5 (ebook) | DDC 306.0951—dc23
LC record available at https://lccn.loc.gov/2020007997
LC ebook record available at https://lccn.loc.gov/2020007998

For my parents, Baihui Huang and Xingwu Xie

Contents

Acknowledgments   ix
List of Abbreviations   xiii

1. Introduction   1

2. A Theory of Stratified Expansion of Social Welfare   27

3. Overview of China's Social Health Insurance   57

4. The Center's Distributive Strategy and Fund Allocation   86

5. Local Motivation and Distributive Choices   111

6. Understanding Subnational Variation in Chinese Social Health
   Insurance   134

7. Who Gets What, When, and How from Chinese Social Health
   Insurance Expansion?   160

8. Conclusion   190

Appendix A: Data Sources   203
Appendix B: List of Interviewees Cited in Chapters   205
Notes   207
References   227
Index   243

Acknowledgments

The journey for this book began in the summer of 2009 when I finished my first year of PhD coursework at Columbia University and went back to China for two months of exploratory fieldwork on labor, wages, and social welfare topics. As I was interviewing managers and workers in Chinese enterprises, I became very aware of the remarkable disparities in social welfare benefits among different Chinese regions and social groups. I was so fascinated by this that I determined to study the political causes and consequences of these social welfare disparities and inequalities in China. Thus, the journey began.

The manuscript was initiated as my PhD dissertation. At that stage, I incurred many debts to those who generously provided intellectual help, emotional support, and friendship during the dissertation research and writing. First, I would like to thank my dissertation committee members. My greatest intellectual debt goes to Isabela Mares, my advisor at Columbia. Isabela has been a role model for my academic career: she has the most passion and devotion to academic research that I have ever seen and she sets a very high standard for academic research. Isabela encouraged me to pursue this research and generously offered advice and guidance at every stage of its development. I am also extremely grateful to Andrew Nathan, who provided critical help at every step of my professional development. Nathan read through many drafts of my work even though some of these were quite preliminary and rough. On each of these drafts, Nathan gave me thoughtful and extensive comments, which I have saved as treasures in my computer and I learn something new every time I read them again. Finally, Vicky Murillo and Kimuli Kasara offered tremendous help during my dissertation research and writing. Vicky was very generous with her time, allowing me to discuss my ideas for dissertation chapters with her and always offering helpful comments and suggestions. Kimuli was sharp in finding the weakness of my arguments and reasoning; her insightful comments always improved my work. I am lucky to have a group of wonderful professors, colleagues, and friends who constantly provided encouragement and help during the ups and downs of my graduate study at Columbia. I am deeply thankful to Ada Mui, Ali Cirone, Benjamin Liebman, Boliang Zhu, Brett Meyer, Chao-Yo Cheng, Elham Seyedsayamdost, Florence Larocque, Hanzhang Liu, Hiroaki Abe, Israel Marques, Jerome Doyon, Kay Shimizu, Jack Snyder, Johanna Rickne, Kui-min Chang, Leanne Tyler, Li An, Pierce O'Reilly, Pablo Pinto, Pavithra Suryanarayan,

Qingjie Zeng, Qiong Qin, Sung Eun Kim, Timothy Frye, Xiaobo Lü, Xiaodan Zhang, Xin Gong, Yuen Yuen Ang, and Yao Lin.

Much data and many insights for this book were gained from my fieldwork in China. Between 2009 and 2012, I visited the social welfare bureaus of 15 prefectural cities, 5 counties, and 4 townships in 16 provinces in mainland China. The fieldwork would not have been possible without the help of many colleagues and friends. Kay Shimizu opened the door for me to do fieldwork in rural China and kindly shared her fieldwork experiences and findings with me. I would also like to thank my Chinese colleagues who generously lent their connections to me for my fieldwork research: Tianbiao Zhu from Peking University, Jen Der Lue from National Chung Cheng University (Taiwan), Shaolong Wu and Yapeng Zhu from Sun Yat-Sen University, Baozhen Wang from Wuhan University, Ji Liu from Nankai University, Xiaofang Wu from South China Normal University, and Haiyan Duan from East China University of Political Science and Law. In the spring of 2012, I spent one month in data collection at the Universities Service Centre (USC) for China Studies at the Chinese University of Hong Kong. I would like to thank Qi Gao, Puzhou Wu, and other staff at USC who helped make my stay productive. Finally, I am extremely grateful to the government officials, workers, enterprise directors, health policy experts, and hospital and pharmacy managers whom I interviewed or who discussed the research topic with me. They generously spared time from their work to talk about policy, practice, and their experiences and opinions about social insurance in China. I benefited tremendously from these conversations.

In 2016, I became an assistant professor of political science at Rutgers University and began to revise my dissertation and transform it into this book. In this process, I received constructive comments and valuable help from my great colleagues at Rutgers: Beth Leech, Bingxiao Wu, Dan Kelemen, Eric Davis, Jack Levy, Ji Li, Kira Sanbonmatsu, Lei Lei, Mi Shih, Mingwei Liu, Mona Krook, Rick Lau, Robert Kaufman, Tanja Sargent, Tao Jiang, and Hannah Walker. I also greatly benefited from the help and encouragement of scholars outside Rutgers: Alastair Smith, Avery Goldstein, Cai Zuo, Dan Chen, Dorothy Solinger, Emily Hannum, Fubing Su, Jacques deLisle, Jane Duckett, Jean Hong, Jidong Chen, Jin Huang, Jing Zhan, John Yasuda, Linda Cook, Ling Chen, Mark Frazier, Mary Gallagher, Marshall Meyer, Maria Repnikova, Martin Dimitrov, Melani Cammett, Meina Cai, Natalia Forrat, Pablo Beramendi, Pierre Landry, Qin Gao, Ryan Manuel, Seung-Youn Oh, Sungmin Rho, Suzanne Scoggins, Thomas Remington, Wenfang Tang, William Hsiao, Xiaobo Lü, Yue Hou, and Yuhua Wang.

This research received generous financial support from the Weatherhead East Asian Institute, the Center for International Business Education and Research, and the Graduate School of Arts and Science of Columbia University, Center for the Study of Contemporary China at University of Pennsylvania, Chang Ching-Kuo Foundation, and Tokyo Foundation. This financial support was a tremendous help in allowing me to concentrate on my research.

Last, I would like to thank my family who have always been supportive. My husband, Shanglong, accompanied me throughout this journey and provided constant support. My first daughter Jiajia was born when the manuscript was finished as a dissertation; my second daughter Wenwen was born when the manuscript was revised into this book. They are gifts from God who have cheered me during this very long journey. My parents provided tremendous help with child care along the way. Most important, they worked hard to give me the best possible educational opportunities, without which I would never have been able to start and complete this journey. Hence, I dedicate this book to my parents with love.

Abbreviations

CCP	Chinese Communist Party
CGSS	China General Social Survey
CHNS	China Health and Nutrition Survey
CMS	Cooperative Medical Scheme
GDP	Gross Domestic Product
GIS	Government Insurance Scheme
LIS	Labor Insurance Scheme
MoF	Ministry of Finance
MoH	Ministry of Health
MoHRSS	Ministry of Human Resources and Social Security
NGO	Non-governmental Organizations
NRCMS	New Rural Cooperative Medical Scheme
PRC	People's Republic of China
RMB	Renminbi, or Chinese Yuan
SARS	Severe Acute Respiratory Syndrome
SOE	State Owned Enterprises
SPI	Social Protection Index
UEBMI	Urban Employee Basic Medical Insurance
URBMI	Urban Resident Basic Medical Insurance
URRBMI	Urban and Rural Resident Basic Medical Insurance
WTO	World Trade Organization

Social Protection under Authoritarianism

1

Introduction

Li Jing, a 26-year-old journal editor, and Wang Nan, a 31-year-old software engineer, were a couple working and living in Beijing. Like people of this age who were born in China's inland rural areas, they had a dream of settling down and starting a family in a large city, like Beijing, in China's economically advanced regions. Li and Wang's hard work since college had made their dream come closer than ever before: both of them had decent jobs in Beijing, and Wang Nan had finally paid off his student loans and his father's debts for medical treatment and long-term care for a serious stroke. For the first time in their lives, their savings had begun to accumulate. Everything with this couple, their income, family, and life seemed to be gradually improving until one day in 2011 when Wang Nan collapsed at work. A subsequent computed tomography (CT) exam made the doctor suspect that a tumor was growing in Wang Nan's brain. This led the young couple to embark on a long journey full of struggles with the city's health care system and social insurance bureau.[1] Compared to millions of peasant workers or informal employees in Beijing, Wang Nan was lucky: he had good health insurance—the social health insurance for urban (formal) employees. But still, he wasn't allowed to choose the best hospital and doctors for treatment. The hospitals and doctors that Wang Nan desperately needed to save his life were not the ones designated by his health insurance—they were considered "out-of-network." In a city like Beijing with over 20 million people, good hospitals and doctors are always scarce, even though the country's best medical professionals and resources are concentrated there. After pulling some strings, paying "red pockets" (informal payments to hospital employees), and being on the waiting list for quite a long time, Wang Nan was finally admitted to a preferred hospital for brain surgery to remove the tumor. The surgery, though successful, left Wang Nan frail and with a bleak prospect for full recovery. Meanwhile, financial problems were looming for this couple and their family. The medical tests and the surgery had wiped out all their savings before the more expensive and long-term chemotherapy began. Early on, Li Jing had not been worried because she assumed that "the health insurance [would] cover the costs." When their attempts to be reimbursed for the medical expenses after the operation were denied by the city's social health insurance bureau because "Wang Nan doesn't hold the local *hukou* (household registration)[2] in Beijing," Li Jing was completely outraged.

Social Protection under Authoritarianism. Xian Huang, Oxford University Press (2020). © Oxford University Press.
DOI: 10.1093/oso/9780190073640.001.0001

This young couple began to fight vigorously with this "unfair and unjust system." They began using social media to publish their real-life story to draw public attention to China's health care problems and the broader social protection system that has profound impacts on billions of citizens' livelihoods and well-being. Li Jing once wrote on her Weibo (equivalent of Twitter in China) that "when hearing the crack of my dream, I believe more than before that a just and fair system of social protection is crucial. We need public attention and we must shake the system so that they [the authority] understand our sufferings and the importance of us. . . . It [Wang Nan's disease] is just the beginning of the domino, bringing up a series of experiences about inequity, injustice, and inefficiency of the health care and health insurance systems. It made me see the distant and dark officialdom."

Li Jing and Wang Nan's story embodies the key themes of this book. Their experience provides several important observations about China's health system in the first decade of the 2000s. First, as migrants in Beijing they were incorporated into the city's social health insurance system through formal employment. Despite the city's later reluctance to cover his medical expenses after Wang Nan lost his ability to work, the preceding enrollment and coverage still signify major progress given the ubiquitous discriminations against non-local people in the decentralized social welfare system in China. Second, as ordinary people seeking better medical treatment and resources, Wang Nan and his wife encountered many barriers that demand personal payments, *guanxi* (personal connections), social status, and even luck in order to obtain the best possible opportunity for a cure. There are many people in China unable to overcome these barriers to receiving better or even necessary medical treatment due to their lower incomes, occupations, and social status. This reflects the long-lasting problems about health care accessibility and affordability ("*kan bing nan, kan bing gui*" or, getting medical care is difficult and expensive) in China in the reform era since 1978.

As a victim of a catastrophic disease, Wang Nan received financial protection and medical resources from social health insurance that were quite limited. It is probably not the disease but the injustice, inequity, and inconvenience the couple had experienced in dealing with the health system that have so stressed them. Li Jing and Wang Nan are an archetypal family of China's rising middle class in Beijing, and their resources are not the worst compared to some other social groups. But this couple's complaints and courageous articulation of their difficulties have revealed the hidden tensions behind the distribution of health care benefits in China in the reform era. Why do people with social health insurance still complain fiercely about the system? When and how did ordinary people, like Li Jing and Wang Nan, get covered by social health insurance? What are the benefits that the social health insurance offers to people like them and to others?

Before the disease struck Wang Nan in 2011, Chinese social health insurance had undergone a dramatic expansion. Taking power in 2002, the Hu Jintao administration pledged to build a "harmonious society" and adopt a "scientific development" perspective in governance, emphasizing the importance of balancing economic growth and social development. In the early 2000s, a social health insurance program for urban employees, the so-called Urban Employee Basic Medical Insurance (UEBMI, *chengzhen zhigong jiben yiliao baoxian*) was fully established in all Chinese cities. In the following years, social health insurance was rapidly expanded to reach rural China through the New Rural Cooperative Medical Scheme (NRCMS, *xin nongcun hezuo yiliao baoxian*) that was officially launched in 2003. Four years later in 2007, urban non-working populations such as dependents, elders, and students were incorporated into the social insurance system through another social health insurance program, Urban Resident Basic Medical Insurance (URBMI, *chengzhen jumin jiben yiliao baoxian*). In 2009, 60 years after the People's Republic of China (PRC) was founded by the Chinese Communist Party (CCP), the party central leadership announced comprehensive health reform to provide "safe, effective, convenient, and affordable" health care to all.

Prior to the expansion of social health insurance in 2004, less than one third of the Chinese population was covered by health insurance. By the end of 2011, over 90% had some form of social health insurance. The expenditure for urban social health insurance was 353.81 billion RMB in 2010, more than four times the level of spending in 2004.[3] People without local *hukou* (or residency), like Wang Nan, were insured either through employment-based social health insurance in the city where they work (e.g., UEBMI) or residency (*hukou*)-based social health insurance in their hometowns (e.g., URBMI, NRCMS). Similarly, expansive trends can be found in the provision of other social insurance benefits in China. Figure 1.1 shows that the number of beneficiaries for major urban social insurance programs, including pension, medical, and unemployment insurance, grew rapidly in China between 2007 and 2011. Among these programs, social health insurance is the largest and has increased the most significantly and rapidly. Hence, in this book I will focus on social health insurance programs to investigate the social welfare expansion in China during the first decade of the 2000s.

China is not unique among the middle-income developing countries in dramatically expanding social welfare provision. As early as the 1990s, China's East Asian neighbors South Korea and Taiwan had notably increased social welfare provision and were providing national pension or health insurance programs (Wong 2004). Likewise, in Latin American countries such as Mexico, Argentina, Brazil, and Chile, old-age pensions and health services previously restricted to formal-sector insiders also began to be extended to outsiders such as rural workers, the self-employed, the unemployed, and informal-sector workers in the

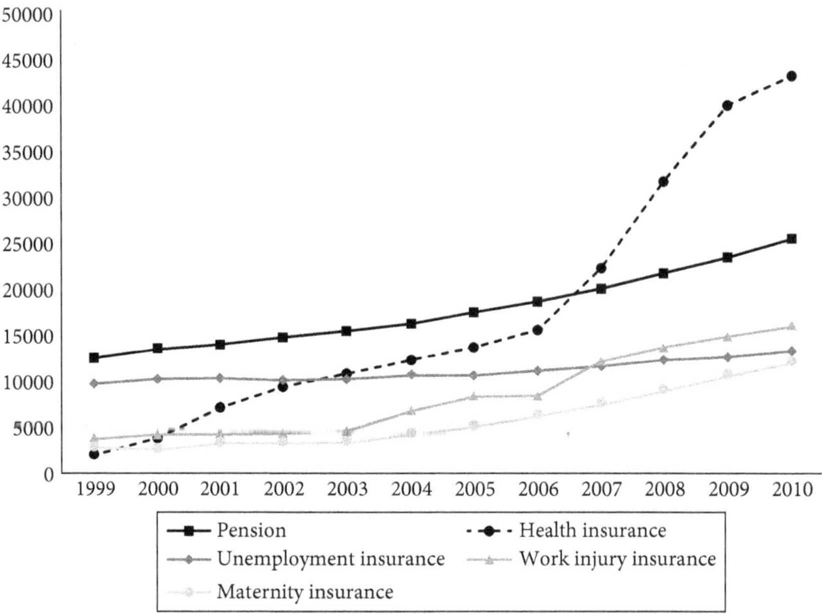

Figure 1.1 Individuals Covered by Urban Social Insurance Programs in China (Unit: 10,000)

Data source: China Labor Statistical Yearbook (2000–2011).

2000s (Garay 2016; Diaz-Cayeros et al. 2016). However, in most of these East Asian and Latin American countries, the expansion of social welfare was associated with democratization or the development of democratic institutions. The adoption of democratic regimes by these countries allows for competitive election and political participation, inaugurating channels for the expression of interests and demands for social benefits. Given the absence of democratization or significant political reforms in China, its attempts to expand social welfare are puzzling.

Besides the absence of democratization, China's unprecedented expansion of social welfare is puzzling for two other reasons. First, the expanded benefits have not only maintained the privileges of elite groups such as government and party officials, civil servants, public-sector employees, and formal workers of privileged state-owned enterprises (SOEs), but they have also reached the most vulnerable and disempowered social groups such as peasants and the urban poor. Rural residents, urban unemployed or self-employed people, even some rural-to-urban migrants who were previously excluded from the social welfare system, are now covered by separate social health insurance programs in China. This expansion of social insurance coverage runs counter to the intuition that these marginalized social groups have less capacity to exert political influence and are thus more likely to be left out in benefit expansion in an authoritarian country.

Second, despite the national progress made toward increasing the overall amount of social welfare beneficiaries and expenditures, the expansion of social welfare is far from a uniform practice and shows remarkable subnational variation across Chinese regions. These variations reveal four distinct models of social welfare expansion in subnational China: (1) a generous and inclusive model: giving more people more benefits; (2) a generous yet exclusive model: giving certain social groups more benefits; (3) a strict yet inclusive model: giving meager benefits to more people; and (4) a strict and exclusive model: giving only meager benefits to only certain groups. These variations appear particularly puzzling given that China is a unitary state whose institutions are identical across the country. One might ask what political or economic factors can account for the remarkable regional variation in China's social welfare expansion.

This book addresses these puzzles about the social welfare expansion in China from 1999 to 2011 and explains its distributive variations across social groups as well as geographic units. More generally, it seeks to answer the following questions regarding social welfare provision in an authoritarian country: Why would authoritarian leaders expand social welfare provision in the absence of democratization? What are the distributive features and implications of social welfare expansion in an authoritarian country? How do authoritarian leaders design and enforce social welfare expansion in the decentralized multilevel governance setting?

I contend that in social welfare provision, authoritarian leaders face a trade-off of effectively balancing benefits between elites and the masses to maximize the regime's survival prospects. When authoritarian leaders concentrate too many benefits on elites, they become vulnerable not only to unrest from the discontented masses but also to threats from within the empowered elites who can replace the incumbent leaders. Yet when authoritarian leaders reduce the privileges of elites and empower the masses by universalizing benefits, they risk betraying the very elites on whom they rely for political survival.[4] Hence, the distributive pattern of social welfare provision results from the strategic choice made by the authoritarian leaders to balance the benefits between elites and masses. The Chinese authoritarian leaders choose to manage the distributive trade-off by establishing an expansive yet stratified social welfare system, perpetuating a particularly privileged provision for the elites while developing an essentially modest provision for the masses. The stratified social welfare expansion in China serves the central leaders' (the Center) interests in maintaining regime stability by enlarging the beneficiary groups while privileging the politically connected and important groups in the social welfare system. In China's decentralized multilevel governance setting, however, the stratified expansion of social welfare is implemented by local leaders, who attempt to meet the Center's expectations for career advancement but confront various constraints in vastly different local circumstances. The decentralized implementation brings about great regional variation in the distribution of social welfare benefits in China.

Local political economies account for a substantial part of the regional variation in China's social welfare expansion. Chinese local leaders encounter different constellations of constraints in social policy implementation, namely, fiscal stringency and social risks. High social risks without adequate fiscal resources at local governments' disposal motivate the local leaders to focus their expansion efforts on enlarging the risk pooling of social health insurance, resulting in a strict yet inclusive model of health insurance expansion (i.e., giving meager benefits to more people); on the contrary, abundant fiscal revenues (whether locally sourced revenues or fiscal transfers from the central government) combined with low social risks encourage local leaders to enhance the benefits of social health insurance exclusively, leading to a generous yet exclusive model of health insurance expansion (i.e., giving certain groups more benefits). In contrast, a combination of both high fiscal revenues and social risks gives rise to a generous and inclusive expansion of social health insurance (i.e., giving more people generous benefits); by the same logic, a combination of both low fiscal revenues and social risks is conducive to a strict and exclusive expansion (i.e., only giving certain people meager benefits) which is basically to maintain the status quo of social health insurance characterized by low coverage and meager generosity.

The Center tolerates such wide regional variation in social health insurance expansion as long as welfare privileges of the elite groups (i.e., government and party officials, civil servants, public-sector employees, SOE formal workers) are maintained. But the balance between elites and masses in benefit distribution is delicate and volatile in China's authoritarian and decentralized multilevel governance setting. The dynamics of central-local relation in enforcing the stratified social welfare expansion stands at the core of the politics of social welfare provision in China during the 2000s.

1.1. The Puzzle: Stratified Expansion of Social Health Insurance in China

Social health insurance is the primary component of social protection and health benefits provision in China. The Chinese social health insurance in the 2000s is puzzling in two ways: dramatic expansion and prominent stratification. The number of people covered by Chinese social health insurance drastically increased as the system began to enroll not only the working population but also urban and rural non-working residents in the first decade of the 2000s (Figure 1.2). In 2004, only 34.4% of the Chinese population were covered by social health insurance programs; by 2010, the coverage rate had increased to around 90% of the population. Meanwhile, the growth of health insurance generosity is substantial. From 2008 to 2001, the per capita expenditure of social health insurance has tripled.

A closer look at the social health insurance expansion, however, reveals that the expansion is remarkably uneven across subnational regions. Both the generosity and population coverage have differed remarkably across provinces during the expansion. Figure 1.3 shows that between 2007 and 2010, the coverage of social health

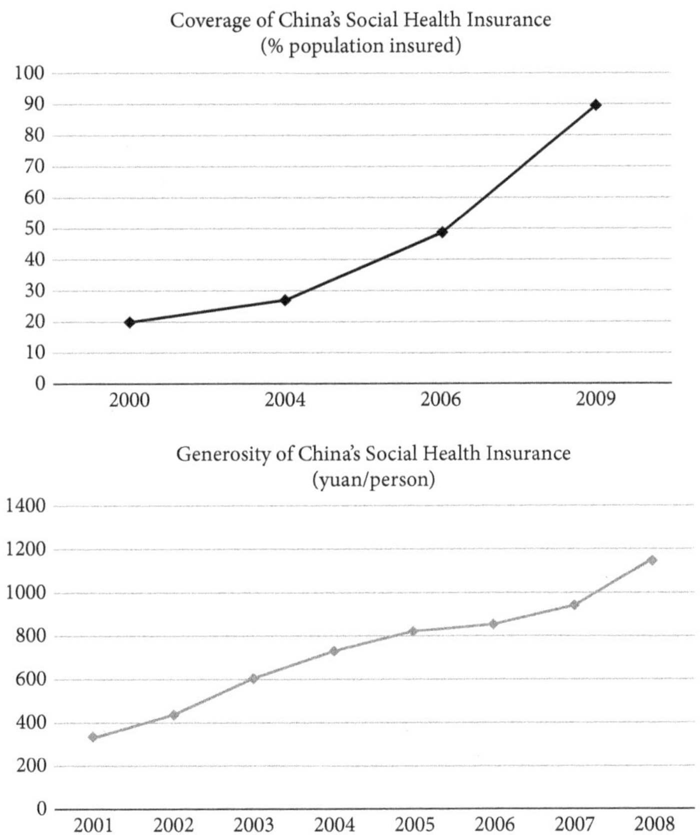

Figure 1.2 Expansion of Social Health Insurance in China (2000–2009)

Note: Coverage of social health insurance is measured by the percentage of people covered by social health insurance in the total population. Generosity of social health insurance is measured by the annual social health insurance expenditure per beneficiary.

Data source: China Labor Statistical Yearbook, China Human Resources and Social Security Yearbook, 2001–2010.

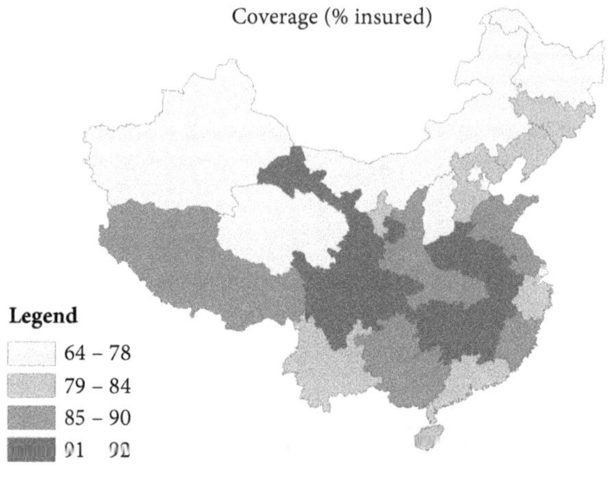

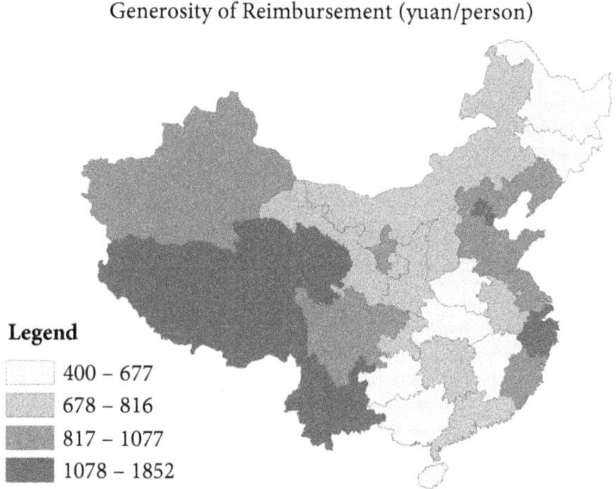

Figure 1.3 Subnational Variation in China's Social Health Insurance (2007–2010)
Data source: China Human Resources and Social Security Yearbook, 2008–2011.

insurance was much higher in the central and coastal regions than in the northeast and western regions; in contrast, the generosity of social health insurance was significantly higher in the western and coastal regions than in the central and northeastern regions. In 2010, up to one quarter of the urban population in northern provinces such as Qinghai, Shanxi, and Heilongjiang were still unprotected by social health insurance, while over 90% of the urban population was covered in the provinces along the Yangtze River such as Sichuan, Chongqing, Hunan, and Jiangxi. In terms of generosity, the per capita expenditure of urban social health insurance in Beijing, the capital city of China, was 1,852 yuan/person (averaged from 2007 through 2010), more than four times that of Jiangxi province in inland China.

Moreover, the stratification of social health insurance is manifest at the societal (group) level. Provincial health insurance statistics, presented in Figure 1.4, shows that peasants and their dependents were the largest beneficiary group in Chinese social health insurance expansion throughout 2007–2010. From 2007 onward, urban non-working residents, including urban unemployed,

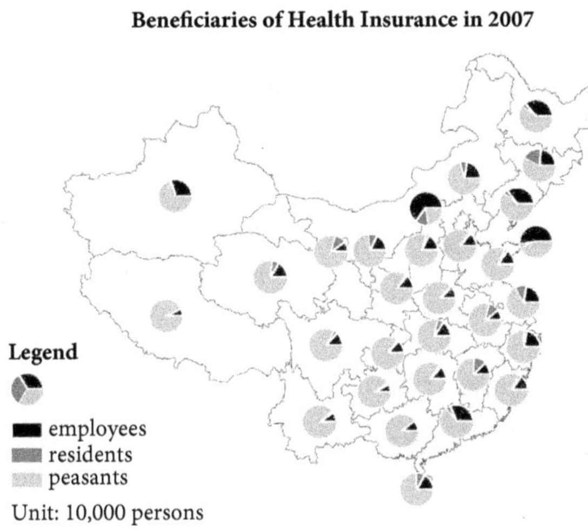

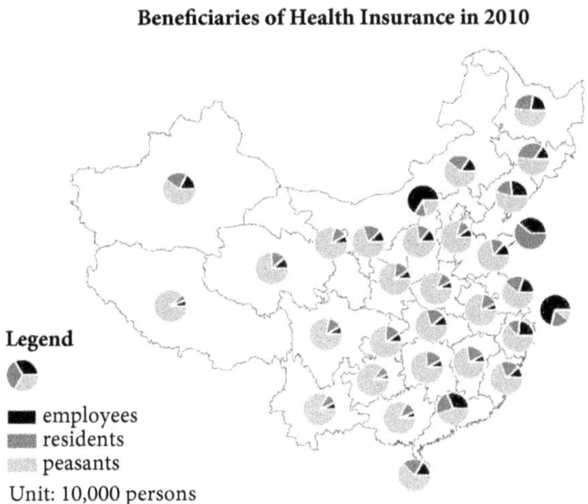

Figure 1.4 Social Health Insurance Beneficiary Groups by Province (2007 & 2010)

Data source: China Health Statistical Yearbook, various years; China Human Resources and Social Security Yearbook, various years.

self-employed, elderly, and students, were increasingly insured through the newly established URBMI program, becoming the second largest group of beneficiaries of social health insurance in most provinces by 2010. In contrast, the percentage of employees in social health insurance declined by 4% from 2007 to 2010. Only in the coastal metropolises (e.g., Beijing, Shanghai, and Tianjin), more than half of social health insurance beneficiaries were urban employees.

However, it would be wrong to conclude that urban employees, who are the primary beneficiaries of the UEBMI program, have lost out in the social health insurance expansion. On the contrary, a comparison of the per capita expenditures of UEBMI, URBMI, and NRCMS programs, respectively, in 2007 and 2010 suggests that in both years, the health insurance generosity for urban employees was remarkably higher than the ones for the urban non-working and rural populations (Figure 1.5). In 2010, the expenditure of the UEBMI program was thirteen times the combined expenditures of the URBMI and NRCMS programs. This indicates that the smallest group of social health insurance beneficiaries—urban employees—enjoyed the lion's share of social health insurance benefits. This indicates that the Chinese social health insurance in the 2000s was not only expansive but also highly stratified.

The prominent disparity between the size of beneficiary groups and the benefit level of their respective health insurance programs urges us to look carefully into the enrollment of social health insurance in China. Given that there are various social health insurance programs with distinct contribution and benefit rates in China, do citizens get to choose which program to join? Figure 1.6 shows a typical scene at a local social insurance administration center in China where citizens register for social insurance including pensions, health, unemployment, and work injury insurance. Individuals are instructed (guided by the overhead digital signboard) to go to different windows or stand in different lines for social insurance registration according to their socioeconomic status, including *hukou*, employment status, and employment sector. Since Chinese social health insurance programs are designed and organized around social groups (i.e., civil servants, public-sector employees, urban formal workers, urban non-working residents, and rural residents fall under different programs with distinct contribution and benefit rates), low-status groups cannot join the programs designed for higher-status groups (e.g., rural people cannot join urban programs; dependents cannot join employee health insurance).

All this evidence highlights the puzzling feature of China's social health insurance in the 2000s: the impressive growth of social health insurance enrollments and the increased number of social health insurance programs do not reduce, but rather reinforce, health inequalities across social groups and subnational regions. Instead of leveling the social playing field, the expansion of social health

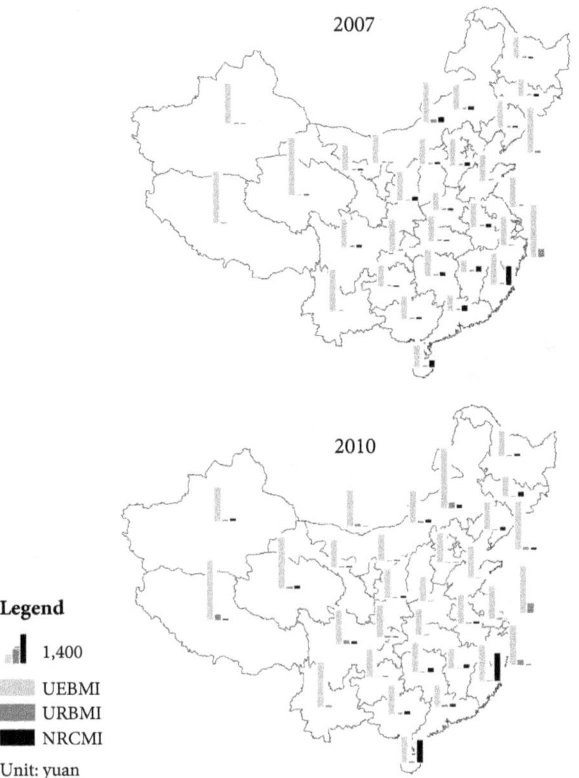

Figure 1.5 Generosity of Social Health Insurance Benefits by Program
(2007 & 2010)
Urban Employee Basic Medical Insurance (UEBMI); Urban Resident Basic Medical
Insurance (URBMI); New Rural Cooperative Medical Scheme (NRCMS).

Data source: China Health Statistical Yearbook, various years; *China Human Resources and Social
Security Yearbook*, various years.

insurance in the 2000s has continued to link welfare benefits to citizens' social
status, employment, and residency.

1.2. The Intellectual Lineages: Social Welfare Provision in Authoritarian Countries

The study of social welfare provision in non-democracies has been growing
(Mares and Carnes 2009; Cammett and Sasmaz 2016). Unlike social policy in
democracies—which usually results from the activities of social movements,
organized interests, unions, and labor parties—social policy in authoritarian

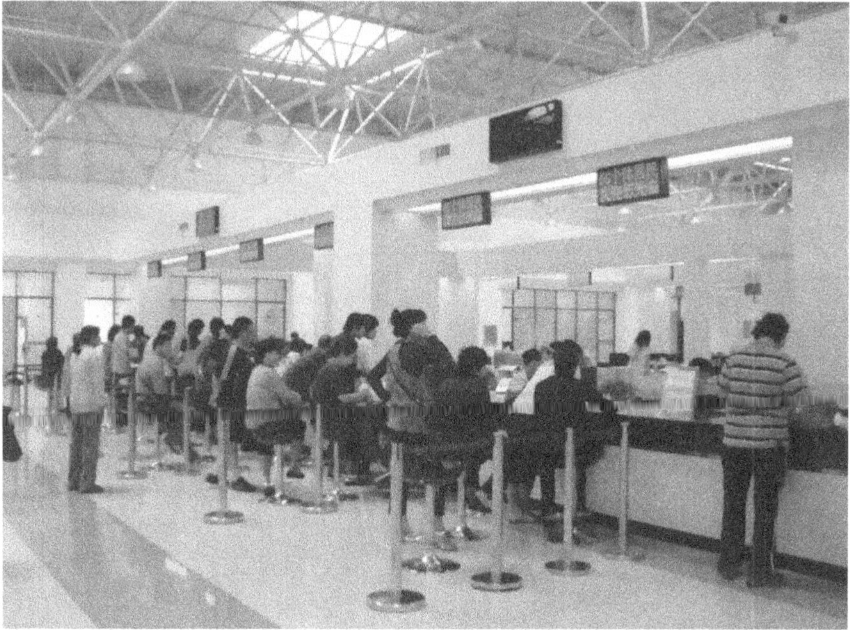

Figure 1.6 Stratification of Chinese Social Health Insurance
Note: Picture showing people waiting to register for social health insurance; taken by the author in the social insurance administration building, Shenyang city, June 14, 2012.

countries is believed to be largely based on the proactive role of leaders who take preventive actions to deter future problems (Forrat 2012). To minimize potential threats to regime stability, authoritarian leaders must manage relations on two fronts in particular: the elites and the masses (Boix 2003; Acemoglu and Robinson 2006; Svolik 2012). As threats to regime stability can emerge from either front (Haggard and Kaufman 2016), choosing to distribute rents and goods only to elites or only to the masses is not an optimal strategy for authoritarian leaders. Authoritarian leaders must balance to their advantage the distribution of resources and benefits between elites and masses (Magaloni and Kricheli, 2010).

Extant studies suggest that authoritarian leaders provide welfare benefits to achieve multiple goals: they use social welfare policy to reward the loyalties of winning coalitions (Haber 2007; Bueno de Mesquita et al. 2003), to buy off dissidents (Gandhi 2008), or to engender human capital for economic growth (Wintrobe 1998). Based on these insights, I assume that authoritarian leaders are influenced by the multiple functions of social welfare; and more important, they factor the distributive trade-off between elites and masses into their policy choices in social welfare provision.

Extant studies also help to account for the differences in social welfare provision across political regimes or countries. Bueno de Mesquita and colleagues (2003) connected political leaders' policy choices about social welfare provision to a regime's institutions for selecting rulers (the "selectorate").[5] More specifically, Mares and Carnes (2009) contended that the specific profile of social policy that autocracies pursue is premised on their political strategy for survival such as cooptation, purge, or organizational proliferation.[6] While extant studies provide a solid foundation for understanding the political motivations of social welfare provision in the authoritarian regime, some important questions remain unaddressed in the literature.

First, beyond the macro-level association of authoritarian leaders' political strategies and their social policy choices, previous studies do not fully consider the trade-off of balancing social benefits between elites and masses, a political dilemma that authoritarian leaders constantly encounter and must resolve in order to maintain regime stability. When authoritarian leaders concentrate too many benefits on elites, they become vulnerable not only to threats from within the empowered elites who might replace the incumbent leaders, but also to unrest from the discontented masses. Yet when authoritarian leaders reduce the privileges of elites and empower the masses through universalizing benefits, they risk angering the very elites on whom they rely to ensure their political survival. How can authoritarian leaders design social welfare policies to strike a balance between the interests of elites and masses? What are the institutional and political conditions that facilitate such a balance? Is the strategic balancing in social welfare provision sustainable in the authoritarian setting? This book will pick up where previous research has left off. Analytically, I develop an argument that directly exposes the trade-off facing authoritarian leaders when allocating welfare benefits among different social groups, and I explain the stratified expansion strategy that authoritarian leaders may adopt in response to the trade-off. Empirically, I test the distributive implications of that strategy and explicitly examine the distribution of welfare benefits under Chinese authoritarianism.

Second, the influence of subnational politicians on the design and implementation of welfare programs has been absent in most discussions to date, because previous studies of authoritarian social welfare systems largely focus on policymaking at the regime level. However, subnational politicians have a crucial role to play in social welfare provision under authoritarianism. As many countries turn to various forms of decentralization, particularly in the developing world where state capacity is weak and the monitoring of policy enforcement is costly, national leaders often leave most of the decision making regarding welfare provision to localities (Diaz-Cayeros et al. 2016; Lü 2014; Niedzwiecki 2018). Local leaders' incentive structures and policy choices concerning social welfare provision thus merit closer attention. Theoretically, as most studies presume a nexus between democracy and decentralization (Riker 1964), intergovernmental interactions (including cooperation, bargaining, and conflicts) are often studied in the contexts of electoral, partisan, and congressional or parliamentary politics (Wibbels 2005; Diaz-Cyeros 2006; Beramendi 2012). Nonetheless, we know relatively little about how central leaders operating within an authoritarian yet decentralized political system ensure that local social welfare provision will lend support to their paramount goal of maintaining regime stability. By examining local incentives and policy choices for social welfare provision as well as central-local interactions in the course of Chinese social welfare expansion, this book theorizes on policymaking and implementation in an authoritarian country where the state structure is characterized by decentralization and multilevel governance.

Third, even though the institutional design of welfare programs is typically multidimensional, many existing studies of social welfare focus on only one of its dimensions, usually levels of government spending. Examining levels of welfare spending, however, provides insufficient insight into the actual distribution of welfare benefits. This book focuses on the distribution of social welfare benefits and disaggregates it into three dimensions: generosity, coverage, and stratification. Generosity refers to the average level of benefits that beneficiaries receive. Coverage represents the percentage of the total population that has access to welfare benefits. Stratification captures the difference or inequality in levels of benefits received by different beneficiary groups or regions. This book demonstrates that the multidimensional conceptualization of welfare distribution can provide a more fine-grained and comprehensive framework for understanding authoritarian leaders' strategy and policy choices in social welfare provision.

This book develops a theory of social welfare expansion in the authoritarian setting. In this theory, authoritarian leaders are fundamentally interested in regime survival and stability.[7] As threats to the regime can come from both elites and masses, authoritarian leaders must distribute resources between them in a strategic manner. Doing so in a way that efficiently balances the distribution of benefits between elites and masses to maximize the leaders' survival prospects entails making choices with potential costs. Therefore, authoritarian leaders may try to expand a modest provision of welfare benefits to the masses while preserving a particularly privileged provision of welfare benefits for elites. I call this the "stratified expansion strategy" for social welfare provision. This strategy is manifested in the three dimensions of social welfare distribution in the following ways: (1) stratification: a hierarchy is established and maintained in the social welfare system in which welfare entitlements and benefits are linked to individuals' socioeconomic status or their relationships with the political authority; (2) expansion of coverage and generosity: on the condition that the hierarchy or stratification is maintained, social welfare provision is expanded to incorporate non-elite groups and even to raise the benefit levels for these groups.

1.3. The Subject and Argument: Social Welfare Expansion in China

This book examines the institutional design, distributive characteristics and outcomes of social welfare provision in the authoritarian setting through a detailed study of the Chinese social health insurance system between the years of 1999 and 2011. In terms of regime type, China is a one-party (or single-party) autocracy. Compared to other mid-income one-party autocracies (e.g., Cuba, Vietnam, Laos, Uzbekistan, Turkmenistan) that have spent, on average, 5.85% of gross domestic product (GDP) on health care in the first decade of the 2000s, China has a more modest health expenditure—about 4.77% of GDP.[8] The Chinese level of total health expenditure in GDP is significantly lower than those of other autocratic regimes, such as monarchy (6.71%) and multi-party (5.44%), but higher than those of military regimes (3.51%). As shown in Figure 1.7, despite relatively low health expenditure as a share of GDP (meaning that generally fewer resources are allocated to health services), China's public health expenditure (including social health insurance expenditure and other government health spending) as a share of total government expenditure is 10.06%—higher than the average of one-party authoritarian countries (9.26%) and of the other types of autocracies such as multi-party (9.56%) and military (7.43%). Among all types of autocracies, only monarchy and no-party regimes on average devote more of total government spending to health services than China does. A conclusion that can be drawn from this comparison between China and the other mid-income countries, especially autocracies, in the 2000s, is that despite limited resources, the Chinese authoritarian regime has attached a relatively high priority to providing health care compared to its counterparts with similar political regime types on average.

The Chinese case offers several advantages for studying the distributive politics and policies in an authoritarian setting. First, China is one of the largest and most enduring authoritarian regimes in the world. The regime has proved to be notably resilient despite domestic political turmoil (e.g., the 1989 Tiananmen Square incident) in the past decades and the global collapse of many autocracies during the "third wave" of democratization and the "Arab Spring." The longevity of the Chinese authoritarian regime gives us opportunities to examine the formation, evolution, and outcome of the regime's distributive strategy for social welfare development. Second, China's authoritarian system is decentralized, which provides a rare and ideal laboratory to explore how local incentives and

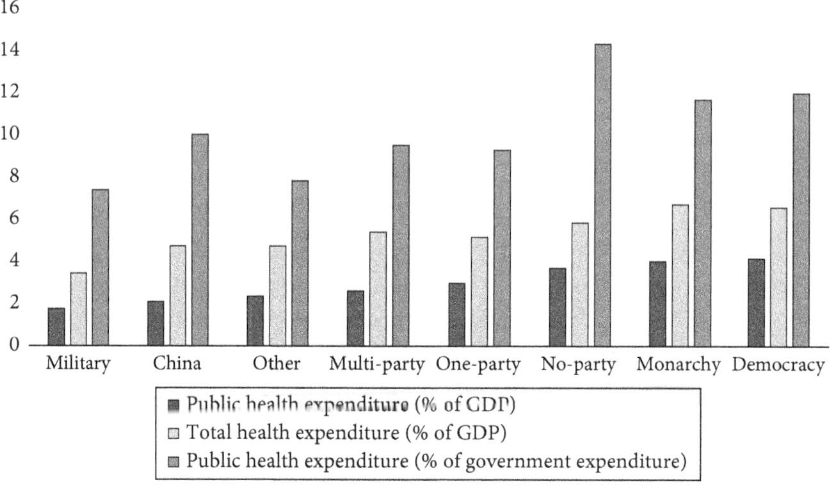

Figure 1.7 China's Health Expenditures in Comparison to Mid-Income Countries by Political Regime

Notes:

1. Data cover 106 middle-income countries (MICs) from 2000 to 2012. MICs are defined by the World Bank as having a per capita gross national income of US $1,026 to $12,475 (2011). Tuvalu and Nauru are excluded from the sample due to unavailability of data.

2. The first cut of regime types is democracy/autocracy, based on Freedom House and Polity scales; among autocracies, regime types are specified as monarchy, military, one-party, multi-party, no-party, and other (that does not fit under any other regime type). China belongs to the one-party (autocracy) regime.

Data sources: Health expenditure data from World Development Indicators Dataset (World Bank); regime categorization data from Authoritarian Regimes Dataset (Hadenius and Teorell, 2007; Wahman et al. 2013).

central-local interactions shape policy implementation in the authoritarian, multilevel governance setting. Third, China offers considerable heterogeneity across space, time, and social strata. The Chinese social health insurance system has experienced dramatic expansion and reform in the past decades since 1998. The wide variations in social welfare provision across regions and social strata in China allow us to test the implications of the theory in a context with relatively large sample for study while controlling for historical and institutional factors.

To explain China's stratified expansion of social welfare provision, I argue that the Chinese authoritarian leaders aim to ensure regime survival and stability by establishing and maintaining a particularly privileged welfare provision for the elites—government and party officials, civil servants, and formal employees of the public sector and SOEs—while providing essentially modest social welfare for the other social groups. Specifically, under China's politically centralized and fiscally decentralized system, the central leaders, on the one hand, establish and control a highly stratified social welfare system to "divide and rule" society, privileging certain groups over others; on the other hand, the central leaders seek to accommodate diverse and broad social needs by delegating discretionary power to local leaders in expanding the coverage and generosity of social welfare programs. Given the Center's strategy, Chinese local leaders have both mandate and discretion in social welfare expansion. They aim to meet the Center's expectations of social welfare expansion in order to advance their political careers. Since social instability is an veto point in China's official evaluation and promotion qualification, local leaders try to provide welfare benefits in ways that can address the salient social needs in their jurisdictions to prevent social unrest. However, local leaders must work within the context of local constraints and resources. In some circumstances, they make policy choices that diverge from the distributive strategy most preferred by the Center. The dynamics of central-local interactions, including control and evasion of control, is at the core of the politics of social welfare expansion in China.

In China's decentralized multilevel governance system, local fiscal resources (or constraints) and social risks are two prominent factors that shape local leaders' policy choices for social health insurance expansion. The local political economy, especially the variations in local fiscal resources and social risks, accounts for a considerable part of the subnational variations in China's social health insurance expansion. All other things being equal, regions with higher social risks tend to cover more people in their social health insurance to obtain large risk pooling, while regions with more fiscal resources tend to provide more generous health insurance benefits. The distinct models of social health insurance expansion chosen by local leaders according to the local political economy result in different distributive patterns of social health insurance in subnational China.

Specifically, high social risks without adequate fiscal resources at the local governments' disposal motivate local leaders to focus their expansion efforts on enlarging the risk pooling of social health insurance, resulting in a strict yet inclusive model of health insurance expansion (i.e., giving meager benefits to more people); on the contrary, abundant fiscal revenues (whether locally sourced revenues or fiscal transfers from the central government) combined with low social risks incentivize local leaders to enhance the benefits of social health insurance exclusively, leading to a generous yet exclusive model of health insurance expansion (i.e., giving certain people more benefits). In contrast, a combination of both high fiscal revenues and social risks gives rise to a generous and inclusive expansion of social health insurance (i.e., giving generous benefits to more people), while a combination of both low fiscal revenues and social risks is conducive to a strict and exclusive expansion (i.e., only giving certain people meager benefits) which is basically to maintain the status quo of social health insurance characterized by low coverage and generosity.

These arguments generate two sets of observable implications under China's authoritarianism. The first set concerns the distributive behaviors of political actors (i.e., central and local leaders); the second set pertains to the distributive characteristics of social health insurance. Specifically, the central leaders intentionally control and maintain a uniform and persistent pattern of stratification in social health insurance while promoting an expansion of social health insurance coverage and generosity at the local level; local leaders' policy choices in the implementation of the stratified social health insurance expansion vary remarkably with the local political economy. As for the distribution of social health insurance benefits, the expansion of social health insurance is constantly biased in favor of the elite groups, though it has modestly extended benefits to the masses; moreover, coverage and generosity of social health insurance systematically correlate with conditions of the local political economy such as local fiscal resources and social risks.

1.4. Research Design

To test the observable implications of my argument about China's stratified expansion of social welfare provision, I employed a multi-method approach that combines quantitative analysis and qualitative studies. While the quantitative analysis examined the distributive characteristics and outcomes of Chinese social health insurance expansion, the qualitative studies revealed the distributive process and policies of governments at various levels in the expansion. Table 1.1 summarizes the observable implications about the stratified expansion of social health insurance in China and the empirical tests of these implications. Details about the qualitative and quantitative data used in the empirical analysis are provided in the appendixes.

First, I made use of archival and primary documents to probe and uncover the policy deliberation and political calculation at the central level about allocation and expansion of health care benefits during the late 1990s and the first decade of the 2000s. Relying on these primary documents in Chinese, such as central government directives, central leaders' speeches, and central work conference and ministerial meeting memos regarding social health insurance, I found that the Center tries to maintain the stratification of social health insurance via fiscal transfers to local governments in addition to social legislation and centralized personnel control. To further test this finding, I collected and analyzed data on the central-to-local fiscal transfers from 1999 to 2010, finding evidence indicating that the Center has allocated more fiscal transfers to the provinces with more elite groups (e.g., civil servants, public-sector employees, SOE formal workers) to maintain these groups' welfare privileges.

Table 1.1 Observable Implications and Empirical Tests

Observable Implications	Empirical Tests
1a. The Center intentionally embeds and maintains stratification of social health insurance benefits during social health insurance expansion.	• Close reading of primary documents such as the central government's directives, the central leaders' speeches, and central work conference and ministerial meeting memos regarding social health insurance expansion • Statistical analysis of the central-to-local fiscal transfers during social health insurance expansion
1b. Local implementation of the stratified social health insurance expansion differs remarkably across provinces.	• Descriptive and cluster analyses of government statistics on local social health insurance • Evidence drawn from interviews with national and local social insurance administrations, health care providers, and health insurance beneficiaries
2a. Coverage and generosity of social health insurance systematically correlate with local socioeconomic conditions.	• Analysis of provincial panel data on social health insurance and local socioeconomic conditions • Case studies of social health insurance reforms in different localities based on interviews with local officials and stakeholders of social insurance
2b. The dramatic expansion of social health insurance is constantly biased in favor of the elites, though benefits have generally been extended to the masses.	• Analysis of government statistics on social health insurance benefits across social groups over time • Analysis of individual-level survey data on social health insurance participation and benefits over time

Second, I carried out 68 in-depth interviews with government officials in 16 Chinese provinces between 2009 and 2013; most of these officials are from the social insurance bureau at various levels of government (i.e., national, provincial, prefectural, county, and township levels) in charge of policy specification and implementation for social health insurance. These interviews gave me knowledge of social health insurance administration and reform in the respective localities. More important, in these interviews I gained in-depth understanding of the regional variation in social health insurance and the causes of the variation in local leaders' policy choices for social health insurance expansion. My field interviews with other stakeholders of social health insurance, including beneficiaries, hospital directors, medical professionals, pharmaceutical companies, public health experts, labor nongovernmental organizations (NGOs), and enterprises of different ownerships, complement the official interviews by identifying different perspectives and sources of information to assess the distributive pattern and the underlying politics of Chinese social health insurance expansion.

Third, I conducted a detailed subnational comparative study on Chinese social health insurance. This study has three components. First, I characterized the local models of social health insurance expansion through a cluster analysis using government statistics on social health insurance expenditure and population coverage, and the socioeconomic conditions of provincial units in mainland China (including four provincial municipalities) from 1999 to 2010. The results suggest that there are four significantly different models of social health insurance expansion among Chinese provinces. Some provinces tend to expand both the coverage and generosity of social health insurance, providing generous benefits to more people, while other provinces expand coverage or generosity only, giving more people meager benefits or giving certain people generous benefits; a few other provinces have maintained low levels of generosity and coverage throughout the course of social welfare expansion. The 31 Chinese provincial units can thus be classified into four clusters with distinct political economies. Then, I demonstrated with detailed subnational comparative case studies the different dynamics of central-local interactions in the four clusters of Chinese provinces. The case studies drawn from my field interviews reconstructed local considerations and policy choices, and identified the conditions under which local leaders may (or may not) develop policy preferences different from the central leaders' regarding social health insurance expansion. Last, I used the provincial-level dataset to systematically examine the correlations between the local political economy and subnational variations of social health insurance.

Finally, I used rich quantitative data at the individual level, including the China General Social Survey (CGSS) and the China Health and Nutrition Survey (CHNS), to examine the distributive patterns of social health insurance benefits both across social strata and across regions in China during the first decade of the 2000s. Unlike some existing studies of social welfare that rely on aggregated government social spending, I developed and adopted multidimensional conceptualizations and measurement of social welfare distribution that better reveal the trade-off facing authoritarian politicians in distributing benefits and the combination of policy choices they accordingly make in different dimensions.

1.5. Alternative Explanations

The political economy literature offers a variety of explanations for redistribution in general and social welfare expansion specifically. Three paradigms or approaches stand out as possible alternative explanations of Chinese social welfare expansion: economic, social, and leader or agent-centered approaches.

The economic paradigm posits that economic changes such as industrialization, modernization, and globalization give rise to the development of a welfare state (Cameron, 1978; Flora and Heidenheimer 1981; Rimlinger 1971; Rodrik 1998). In this perspective, a welfare state or expanded social welfare provision is a functionalist response to social problems resulting from economic transition or structural change, such as poverty, unemployment, and inequality. In advanced industrialized economies, generous social policies are also made to encourage investment in learning and adopting specific skills (Estevez-Abe, Iversen, and Soskice 2001). The economic paradigm emphasizes the economic origin and interest in explaining the momentum for social welfare development. The underlying assumption is that the welfare state is a state response to citizens who turn to the state for security and protection when being exposed to economic risk and market dislocation. This assumption might be less proper in non-democracies that usually lack direct accountability or electoral linkage between citizens and the government. Nonetheless, economic conditions certainly play a role, even in autocratic countries, in shaping the trends of a welfare state. The social welfare expansion accompanying remarkable economic growth in China in the first decade of the 2000s, as demonstrated in Chapter 3, is an affirmative example. However, the economic paradigm is less successful in explaining the distributive strategy and outcome of social welfare provision for it treats the welfare state as a reaction to economic changes. I argue that economic factors (e.g., GDP, trade openness) should be considered as factors that condition social welfare expansion but not necessarily predetermine it.

Another possible explanation of social welfare expansion is from the social perspective that views the welfare state as a reaction to class struggle or distributive conflicts among social groups (Esping-Andersen 1985; Korpi 1983; Meltzer and Richard 1981; Stephens 1979). According to this perspective, the power of social movements, labor or left-wing parties, and trade unions predicts social welfare expansion. The social perspective is good at predicting the dynamics of social policies: generous social policies are likely to emerge when the left-wing political forces gain the upper hand. Nonetheless, the limitation of this perspective is noticeable in explaining the social welfare expansion in non-democracies where social movements and civil society are often repressed, if existing at all. As discussed earlier in this chapter, a generous welfare state is not exclusive to democracies and certainly not every democracy is a generous welfare state. The explanatory power of the social perspective is also limited in accounting for the nuanced differences of social policies across countries or subnational regions with the same regime type and political partisanship.

Recent studies about "consultative authoritarianism" (He and Thøgersen 2010; Truex 2017) and "government responsiveness" (Meng et al. 2017; Chen et al. 2016; Truex 2016) in China suggest that there seems to be some room for policy entrepreneurs, activists, and even ordinary citizens to participate in government policymaking. Some researchers (Duckett 2018; Huang 2015) have found a significant role played by international organizations and ideas that account for the timing and content of NRCMS policies. These findings jointly portray a counterintuitive picture of policymaking in China that was commonly believed to be closed, non-transparent, and autocratic. However, these findings should not be overinterpreted or misunderstood to suggest that societal forces, whether civil society groups or individual actors, have become dominant in policymaking in China. On the contrary, both "consultative authoritarianism" and "government responsiveness" are mostly conditional on the proactive and strategic soliciting of social feedback or experiment-based policy initiatives by the Chinese authoritarian regime (Heilmann 2008; He and Thøgersen 2010). Based on my research including over 100 field interviews with government officials, social insurance administrators, and stakeholders of social health insurance in China, I found that the making and planning of Chinese social health insurance policy in the 2000s was undoubtedly dominated by the state.

The third possible explanation of social welfare expansion puts the emphasis on individual leaders, their values, visions, power, and inter-personal relations. The initiation and adoption of social insurance are often traced back to pioneering leaders such as Bismarck in Germany, von Taaffe in Austria, and Napoleon III in France (Esping-Andersen 1990; Beck 1997; Rimlinger 1971). The leader-centered explanation can also be found in studies of economic, financial, fiscal, and social policies in China (Li, 2005; Guo, 2009; Shih, 2007; Zhu & Zhang, 2016). A prominent example of the leader-centered paradigm or perspective is the factional explanation of policy shifts in China's reform era (Shih 2004, 2007). The main strength of this paradigm is its ability to account for policy dynamics in the authoritarian setting—short-term or dramatic policy turns. Nonetheless, it works less well to explain the long-term trends of social welfare provision, such as policy continuity. The overview of social welfare development in contemporary China, provided in Chapter 3, shows that the stratification of social welfare provision biased in favor of elites has been quite persistent. The social welfare expansion in China during the first decade of the 2000s, which this book focuses on, was initiated under the Jiang Zemin administration in the late 1990s and extensively implemented under the Hu Jintao administration from 2003 to 2012. There was no sign of significant change in the stratified social welfare expansion when Xi Jinping, the new general party secretary, officially took power in 2013. The persistence of stratified social welfare in China is puzzling given the distinct ruling priorities and ideological claims of the different leaders throughout the 2000s.[9]

An extension of the leader-centered perspective is the agent-centered approach that adopts a more fluid conception of "leaders," focusing on bureaucratic actors and institutional arrangements (e.g., systems of rank, functional divisions of authority, and decentralization). Bureaucratic actors are also found to play a large role in making and implementing social welfare policies in Latin American countries (Niedzwiecki 2018), Russia, and Eastern European countries (Cook 2007). A prominent example of the agent-centered approach in the Chinese context is the "fragmented authoritarianism" paradigm in which policy outcomes are considered to be strongly influenced by bargaining among competing bureaucratic agencies (Liberthal and Oksenberg, 1988; Mertha, 2009). According to this paradigm, policymaking in China is influenced by interests of the implementing agencies, such as central ministries and provincial governments charged with enforcing the policy. The fragmented authoritarianism paradigm certainly helps to explain the policy process of Chinese social welfare provision. As shown in Chapter 3, given the fragmented and decentralized institutional arrangements of policymaking and implementation for social health insurance in China, the competition among bureaucratic agencies with similar ranks (e.g., Ministry of Health, Ministry of Human Resources and Social Security) is inevitable; consequently the policy for social health insurance expansion is usually incremental and the process is protracted. But fragmented authoritarianism cannot explain the distributive profile and outcome of Chinese social welfare provision properly, especially at the subnational level.

The explanation of Chinese social welfare expansion this book provides incorporates both the economic paradigm and the agent-centered perspective to construct a more comprehensive framework that takes into account the diverse local political economy and the decentralized multilevel governance setting in China. As such, this book complements these approaches by explaining not only the trend of Chinese social welfare expansion but also its distributive patterns and subnational variation. Moreover, as discussed in Section 1.2, the theory of stratified social welfare expansion developed in this book emphasizes the authoritarian leaders' distributive trade-off to explain the political constraints that influence social welfare expansion in China. This constitutes a stark contrast to the social or class-struggle perspective that emphasizes the power of social movements, labor or left-wing parties, and trade unions in explaining social welfare expansion in other countries.

1.6. Plan of the Book

To preview the chapters, Chapter 2 presents the theory of this book that explains the political logic and distributive characteristics of social welfare provision in the Chinese authoritarian setting. The theory takes into account the logic of authoritarian regime survival, multilevel governance, and local political economy, and specifies the main political actors and their interests and strategies in Chinese social welfare provision. I argue that authoritarian leaders, whose basic interest lies in regime survival and stability, use stratifying and expansive social welfare policies to privilege elites and placate the masses. To explain social welfare expansion in the Chinese authoritarian yet decentralized setting, it is necessary to disaggregate the authoritarian state and to examine divergences in policy preferences among different levels of the authoritarian state and the factors that shape the dynamics of interaction among them, ultimately with an eye toward the impact of these divergences and interactions on policy implementation and outcomes. This argument generates some predictions about the distributive behaviors of political leaders and the distributive characteristics of social welfare provision in the Chinese authoritarian and multilevel governance setting. I also propose a set of local political economy conditions, including local fiscal resources and social risks, which predict the likelihood of divergence between central and local leaders in policy preferences and choices for social welfare expansion in China.

Chapter 3 draws from secondary literature to review the history and evolution of social health insurance in contemporary China (since 1949), providing the historical background and the economic context of China's social health insurance expansion in the 2000s. I show that throughout the history of contemporary China, social welfare was never considered a basic social right for citizens. Despite dramatic changes in the coverage and generosity of social health insurance across different developmental periods in China, the stratification pattern of Chinese social health insurance was persistent and reinforced during the social health insurance expansion between 1999 and 2011.[10] Moreover, the economic transition and the diversification of regional economies in China constitute the economic context where the Chinese central and local leaders' motivations for and differential responses to social health insurance expansion take shape.

Chapter 4 focuses on the Chinese central leaders (the Center) and their distributive strategy and behaviors in social welfare provision. The deliberations and calculations reflected in the central leaders' speeches between 1998 and 2011 show that the stratified expansion of Chinese social welfare was the Center's most preferred model for social welfare provision in this period. Both central leaders and ministerial technocrats, in various internal speeches and communication, revealed their hidden concern and the measures they took to maintain the elites' welfare privileges and benefits during the welfare expansion. Careful reading of the primary materials also suggests that the Center's fiscal transfers to local governments were an important means of maintaining the welfare privileges of elite groups (e.g., civil servants, public-sector, and formal employees of state-owned enterprises). This chapter later analyzes the central-to-local fiscal transfers from 1999 to 2010 and shows that the larger the elite groups in a province, the more fiscal transfers the province received from the Center.

Chapter 5 focuses on the local leaders' distributive motivations and policy choices in social welfare provision. The combination of political centralization and fiscal decentralization compels Chinese local leaders to specify major policies in local circumstances while balancing the Center's various mandates and directives with local resources and constraints. Drawn from the qualitative evidence collected from my fieldwork in China between 2009 and 2012, this chapter not only demonstrates the regional variation in local policy responses to the Center's directive for stratified expansion of social health insurance, but also provides examples of the local calculations and policy choices in implementing the health insurance expansion. The causes for the differences in local policy choices for social health insurance expansion are a result not only of the regional disparities in socioeconomic conditions and resources, but also the contradiction embedded in the Chinese authoritarian regime's distributive strategy: expanding basic benefits to the masses while maintaining the welfare privilege for the elites.

Chapter 6 investigates the coverage and generosity dimensions of Chinese social health insurance in the first decade of the 2000s, with a focus on the regional (i.e., cross-provincial) variation using a cross-sectional time-series research design. First, the cluster analysis provides supportive evidence for the existence of four models or types of social health insurance expansion in China: (1) the risk-pooling model (i.e., giving meager benefits to more people); (2) the privileging model (i.e., giving certain groups more benefits); (3) the dual model (i.e., giving generous benefits to more people); and (4) the status-quo model (i.e., giving only meager benefits to only certain groups). The clustering of Chinese provinces in social health insurance expansion also corresponds to the differences in local political economies. Second, the chapter makes detailed inter-regional comparisons and intra-regional studies to reconstruct the mechanism linking a local political economy to the local distributive patterns of health insurance benefits, that is, local socioeconomic conditions shape local leaders' policy preferences and choices for allocating social health insurance benefits in their jurisdictions. Finally, the regression analysis demonstrates significant statistical correlations between local social risks and expansion of social health insurance coverage, and between local fiscal resources and expansion of social health insurance generosity. The three empirical analyses combined provide a political economic explanation of the subnational variations in the expansion of Chinese social health insurance.

Chapter 7 examines the stratification dimension of Chinese social health insurance in the first decade of the 2000s. Based on the analyses of national social survey data, it examines the variation of social welfare benefits across social strata, addressing who got what benefits, when, and how as a result of China's social health insurance expansion between the years of 2003 and 2011. It shows that social health insurance expansion did significantly broaden Chinese citizens' access to basic health care. However, the expansion, which entails health insurance fragmentation and increasing benefit disparities, not only reinforced existing social cleavages such as the urban-rural divide, but also generated new divisions within both urban and rural groups. After expansion, Chinese social health insurance was highly stratified across three cleavage lines: (1) urban versus rural; (2) labor market insiders versus outsiders; and (3) public versus private sectors. These social cleavages are interwoven in such a way as to fragment society and privilege elite groups over others without fracturing society along a single and deep class line.

Chapter 8 summarizes the main findings and contributions of the book. After a speculative note on the prospect of health reform in China after 2012 when the new leader, Xi Jinping, took power, this chapter discusses the implications of this study for both Chinese social welfare development and its authoritarianism. Finally, the book concludes with a deliberation of the conditions for applying the argument about stratified expansion of social welfare provision beyond China.

2

A Theory of Stratified Expansion of Social Welfare

A welfare state is typically considered to be associated with democracies (Marshall 1950, 10–11; Bulmer et al. 1989, 73–74; Heclo 1981, 390). According to conventional wisdom, democracies are better than nondemocracies in providing public goods, including social welfare, for two reasons. A top-down explanation holds that democratic leaders need to garner a large share of the popular vote in order to win elections, so they have a stronger interest in providing public goods to secure broad support. Alternatively, a bottom-up explanation argues that democracies permit interest group organizations that increase social pressure, allowing public demand for social welfare to drive government spending and policy decisions. Many quantitative studies find empirical support for the contention that democracies spend more than non-democracies on social welfare (Przeworski et al. 2000; Lake and Baum 2001; Brown 2004).

However, some studies note that significant variations exist in public goods provision and social welfare spending within both democracies and non-democracies (Mulligan et al. 2004; Charron and Lapuente 2011; Haggard and Kaufman 2008). Scholars have also noticed that many welfare programs have been adopted by non-democratic governments (Esping-Andersen 1990; Mares and Carnes 2009; Knutsen and Rasmussen 2018) and that some autocracies spend more than democracies on social welfare benefits (Haggard and Kaufman 2008). Motivated by this puzzle, researchers have paid more attention to social welfare in non-democracies (Forrat 2012; Cammett and Sasmaz 2016; Mares and Carnes 2009). But certain intriguing questions are still unanswered: What is the core concern of autocrats in their distributive policies and measures? Why do autocratic leaders need to maintain a balance between elites and the masses in distribution? How can they achieve balance between these two? As autocracies try to satisfy both elites and the masses, what impact does this strategy have on the distribution of welfare benefits in an autocratic society?

My overarching argument for these questions is that some authoritarian leaders extend welfare benefits to the masses after a privileged welfare provision for elites is established, striking a strategic balance between the interests of the two groups to prevent threats to the regime. The distributive pattern of social welfare provision in authoritarian countries is a result of the strategic

Social Protection under Authoritarianism. Xian Huang, Oxford University Press (2020). © Oxford University Press.
DOI: 10.1093/oso/9780190073640.001.0001

choice made by authoritarian leaders who must keep both groups reasonably satisfied to ensure the regime's survival. When authoritarian leaders concentrate too many benefits on the elites, they are vulnerable not only to unrest from the discontented masses but also to threats from within the empowered elites who might replace the incumbent leaders. Yet when authoritarian leaders reduce the privileges of elites and empower the masses by universalizing benefits, they risk betraying the very elites on whom they rely to ensure political survival. One solution to this trade-off for authoritarian leaders is to establish an expansive yet stratified social welfare system, perpetuating a particularly privileged provision for the elites while developing an essentially modest provision for the masses. I call it the "stratified expansion strategy" for social welfare provision.

To study the distributive impacts of autocracies' stratified expansion strategy for social welfare provision and lay out its observable implications, I developed a multidimensional conceptualization of social welfare provision by disaggregating the distribution of social welfare benefits along three dimensions: generosity, coverage, and stratification. Generosity captures the depth of social welfare provision, or the average level of benefits that individuals receive. Coverage, defined as the proportion of people who receive welfare benefits out of the total population, represents the breadth of social welfare provision. Stratification concerns the inequality of benefits received by different groups of beneficiaries or regions. These three dimensions may be correlated in a predicable way under specific conditions. For example, when the total amount of social welfare benefits (e.g., budget for social welfare) is fixed, broad coverage might lead to lower generosity. For another example, all other things being equal, low coverage combined with high generosity indicates high stratification (inequality) of social welfare provision.

To substantiate the stratified expansion strategy of autocracies in social welfare provision, I focused on the politics and policies of social welfare provision under the Chinese authoritarian regime. The remainder of this chapter is structured as follows. Section 2.1 explains the trade-off autocratic leaders face in distribution of benefits between elites and masses. I articulate the "stratified expansion strategy" autocratic leaders may adopt to manage the trade-off in social welfare provision and discuss the alternative option and its applicable condition. Section 2.2 contextualizes the autocracies' stratified expansion of social welfare in the setting of Chinese political economy. The following two sections, 2.3 and 2.4, further specify the political actors, their interests, strategies, and policy choices for social welfare provision in China. Section 2.5 links together all these elements—structure, actors, and strategies/policy choices—and summarizes the predicted distributive outcome of social welfare provision in China.

2.1. Social Welfare Provision in Authoritarian Countries

2.1.1. The Trade-Off

Autocrats' fundamental interest is to stay in power. To do so, they need supporters. There are basically two instruments with which autocrats can garner regime support: sticks (e.g., coercion, repression, terror) and carrots (e.g., distribution of rents, benefits, patronage). The focus here is on the carrots—cooptation, more specifically, social welfare policy as a key policy tool that autocrats employ to retain power. Unlike public policy in democracies, which usually results from the activities of social movements, organized interests, unions, and parties, social policy in autocracies is largely a result of the proactive role of autocrats taking preventive actions in anticipation of future problems that could undermine regime survival and stability (Forrat 2012). The political economy literature of autocracies suggests that autocratic leaders often use cooptation, such as privileged access to social services and benefits, among many other private goods and payments, to buy support for the regime (Gallagher and Hanson 2009; Gandhi 2008; Wallace 2014; Harris 2017; Albertus 2015). Wintrobe (1998) argues that dictators provide public goods mainly for two purposes: (1) to increase the loyalty of the population, and (2) to promote general economic growth on which the dictator's budget depends. With a more political emphasis, the selectorate theory (Bueno de Mesquita et al. 2003) connects the motivation for public or private goods provision to the size of winning coalitions within the selectorate that leaders need to please to stay in power. When the leaders need a large winning coalition in the selectorate for political survival, they have more incentives to provide public goods to ensure that more people will stand on their side against the opposition forces.

The political economy literature on autocracies is better at disclosing autocrats' motivations for providing public goods than in explaining the distinct policy profiles and strategies in benefit provisions or resource allocation found among autocracies. A few cross-national studies of social welfare policy have shed light on the connections between the specific profile of social welfare policy that autocracies pursue and their political strategy for survival. According to Haber (2007), the survival strategies of autocrats can be summarized into three types: terror, cooptation, and organizational proliferation. Based on this, Mares and Carnes (2009) contend that if the autocracy counts on terror, torture, and purges to survive politically, one should see little or no social policy legislation in the regime. Conversely, if the autocracy relies on cooptation of a small group of critical supporters, its leaders will enact "restrictive" social policies characterized by narrow coverage and generous benefits. And if the autocrat is brought to power by a broad coalition of interests and chooses a strategy based on organizational proliferation, social policy will be characterized by high levels of institutional fragmentation, on the one hand, and broader coverage, on the other. In a similar vein, Haggard and Kaufman (2008) point to "critical realignments" in the first half of the twentieth century: strategies of political survival with respect to working-class and peasant organizations (e.g., incorporation or exclusion of organized labor in ruling coalitions), in addition to economic development strategies, to account for the differences in social welfare policies (e.g., focus on social spending, population coverage of benefits) across East Asian, East European, and Latin American countries.

Although these studies have identified a correlation between autocratic leaders' political strategies and their social policy choices, they do not pay enough attention to the imperative that autocratic leaders need to efficiently balance the benefits between elites and masses for maximizing their survival prospects. Many studies of authoritarian politics focus on either the relation between autocratic leaders and elites or the relation between the leaders and the masses. Few studies have paid enough attention to the struggle, tension, and trade-off that autocratic leaders encounter in balancing between the elites and the masses in distributing benefits and resources.[1] The elite-mass balancing in distribution affects the survival and stability of autocracies for three reasons.

First, to minimize potential threats to regime stability, autocratic leaders who are fundamentally interested in their survival in power must manage relations on both fronts: with elites and with masses. Steven Haggard and Robert Kaufman's studies of democratization and regime change demonstrate that roughly half of regime changes were triggered by mass mobilization based on redistributive grievances and the other half by elite-led transitions (Haggard and Kaufman 2016).[2] Since threats to the survival and stability of autocracies can come from either front, choosing to distribute rents and goods only to the elites or only to the masses is not an optimal strategy from the autocratic leaders' perspective. With the uncertainty of potential threats such as riots, insurrection, military coups, assassination, intra-party revolt, and so on, autocratic leaders must distribute benefits or allocate resources between elites and masses in a strategic manner to maximize the prospects of regime survival and stability. When autocratic leaders concentrate too many benefits on elites, they become vulnerable not only to threats from within the empowered elites who can replace the incumbent leaders, but also to unrest from the discontented masses. Yet when autocratic leaders reduce the privileges of elites and empower masses through universalizing benefits, they risk betraying the very elites on whom they rely to ensure political survival. Thus, the risk of losing the balance between the elites and the masses characterizes the distributive politics in autocracies.

Second, autocratic leaders make distributive decisions and policies under constraints posed by their economic, fiscal, and political resources. These constraints make the strategic balancing in distribution—calculatedly distributing resources between elites and masses—more imperative to autocratic leaders who can't afford overspending on either of the groups. A considerable part of revenues or resources autocratic leaders collect or generate will be privatively consumed by themselves; the remaining revenues or resources will be distributed to please elites and placate masses for regime survival and stability. Although economic growth and natural resource windfalls can generate more resources or revenues, autocratic leaders always desire more for their private consumption. Hence, resources for social distribution are always scarce, and the trade-off between elites and masses must be handled strategically.

Third, given the risk of losing the balance in distribution and having to work within the resource constraints, autocratic leaders must target specific groups and provide different benefits to divide and rule. The elites, depending on the country's context, may consist of soldiers, landowners, civil servants, veterans, salaried professionals, business owners, and/or industrial workers; these are the "critical supporters" (Knutsen and Rasmussen 2018) or "selectorate" (Bueno de Mesquita et al. 2003) whose support is critical for the autocracies to survive. Autocratic leaders attempt to please the elites with privileged entitlements, health care, pensions, and access to scarce resources. The masses, who consist of politically unconnected groups such as peasants, urban and rural poor, low-skilled and informally employed people, while politically marginalized, can also be influential to social and economic stability. Collective actions by these mass groups, even just scattered and individualized incidents, can cost autocratic leaders considerable material and administrative resources, potential foreign investment, and public support. Accordingly, it is not uncommon for autocratic leaders to attempt to placate masses by extending to them social welfare provisions such as basic health care, minimum livelihood allowance, and public housing. The key in social welfare provision of autocracies is to differentiate and target specific social groups (i.e., elites, masses) to efficiently maximize prospects of regime survival and stability. Accordingly, autocratic leaders might exploit existing or create new social cleavages (e.g., urban-rural divide, state/nonstate sectoral cleavage, formal/informal employees) in social policies to achieve the "divide and rule" outcome.

2.1.2. Possible Solutions

To address the needed trade-off in resource allocation or benefit distribution, one option autocratic leaders can adopt in social policy is to maintain a particularly privileged welfare provision for the elites while expanding an essentially modest provision for the masses, the so-called stratified expansion strategy in social welfare provision. It serves the autocratic leaders' interests in maintaining regime stability by consolidating divisions among social groups and privileging the politically connected or important groups to reward their loyalties to the regime while balancing the gaps between the haves and the have-nots. This strategy is evident in the three dimensions of distribution of social welfare benefits: (1) on the stratification dimension: a hierarchy is established and maintained in a social welfare system in which social entitlements and benefits are linked to people's sociopolitical and socioeconomic status (e.g., administrative rank, employment sector, and residency); (2) on the coverage and generosity dimensions: keeping the stratification, social welfare provision is expanded to incorporate as many social groups as possible and even to raise the level of benefits for them.

For autocracies to maintain stability and survival, the necessary condition is that the welfare commitment—privileged benefits for the elites as well as the basic welfare provision to the masses—must be credible to those groups. Autocratic leaders constantly face the "dictator's dilemma" (Wintrobe 1998): autocrats strong enough to co-opt by preferential distribution of rents, benefits, and resources are also strong enough to breach such commitments. Existing studies of authoritarian regimes have focused on formal institutions such as political parties, elections, legislatures, and judicial institutions that authoritarian leaders employ to alleviate the commitment problem (Brownlee 2007, Magaloni 2007; Levitsky and Way 2010; Gandhi 2008; Gandhi and Przeworski 2006; Blaydes 2010). The design of distributive policies or measures is another important approach for understanding why social welfare programs, such as social insurance, can mitigate the dictator's dilemma and enhance regime support and survival (Knutsen and Rasmussen 2018; Diaz-Cayeros et al. 2016; Huang and Gao 2018).

Social insurance programs such as pensions and health insurance have clear fixed criteria for determining eligibility and payments. Compared to the particularistic or clientelistic transfer programs under which politicians have much discretion in determining who gets what, when, and how, the nondiscretionary feature of social insurance programs by design reduces recipients' concern about the credibility of these programs. Establishing social insurance programs is costly for autocratic leaders (e.g., requiring initial investment in administrative and monitoring infrastructure such as hiring and training state agents, building information and bookkeeping systems, collecting contributions from employers and individuals, and so on), and this reduces the reversibility of these programs (Knutsen and Rasmussen 2018). Also, social insurance programs are inclusive in the sense that the larger the insurance pool, the better the risk sharing, so they tend to expand by including anyone who qualifies; but they still can be controlled because the eligibility rules can be adjusted by autocratic leaders. These features in policy design make social insurance programs a particularly attractive and effective tool to realize autocrats' stratified expansion strategy for social welfare provision.

An alternative strategy that autocratic leaders can adopt to address the trade-off between elites and masses is to develop policies that play one group off the other or that use cooptation of one group to weaken or threaten the other. A paradigmatic case of this strategy is the land redistribution launched in some Latin American countries that serves the regime leaders' interest of weakening or even destroying landed elites who pose potential threats to the regime while placating the rural poor and undercutting the threat of instability from below by redistributing land to them (Albertus 2015). Another case exemplifying this distributive strategy in autocracies is the "martyrs' welfare state" established by the Islamic Republic in Iran after the 1979 revolution. The Islamic Republic inherited and used the corporatist welfare organizations of the Pahlavi monarchy which were limited in reach to a circumscribed segment of the population; additionally, the Islamic Republic created a second set of postrevolutionary welfare organizations that directly targeted those segments of the population excluded from the previous system. Given the wide and intense elite competition that the Islamic Republic failed to channel into an enduring single-party apparatus in the post-revolution period, the regime leaders decided to constrain the political elites' technocratic, top-down welfare projects by relying upon the second set of welfare institutions that capitalized on the popular mobilization of the 1979 revolution and the eight-year war with Iraq to build up state capacity and consolidate power (Harris 2017).

It is noteworthy that a key condition for autocratic leaders to adopt this strategy in distribution is that there is a coalitional split between regime leaders and (some subset of) elites that incentivizes the leaders to turn on the elites and disempower them while mobilizing the masses (Albertus 2015). In contrast to the "stratified expansion strategy" that resembles a win-win game in distribution between elites and masses, the "play-off strategy" of mobilizing one group to weaken the other is more like a zero-sum game that creates absolute winners and losers in the distribution.

China remains largely outside the studies of distributive politics and policies in authoritarian countries.[3] This book attempts to specifically examine the distributive trade-offs and corresponding strategic balancing between elites and masses in social welfare provision by the Chinese authoritarian regime. I argue that the Chinese leaders have adopted the stratified expansion strategy in social welfare provision especially since the late 1990s: perpetuating a particularly privileged provision for the elites while developing an essentially modest provision for the masses. Although China can't represent all the authoritarian countries, probably not even the single-party authoritarian regime specifically, an in-depth study of the distributive trade-off, strategies, and policies of the Chinese authoritarian regime in social welfare provision will significantly enhance our knowledge and understanding of the authoritarian welfare state and the elite-mass trade-off in authoritarian distributive politics.

2.2. Political Economy of Social Welfare Provision in China

As China is one of the largest and most enduring authoritarian countries in the world, the politics of social welfare provision in this country bears both similarity and distinction compared to that of other authoritarian countries. The authoritarian nature of the Chinese regime makes it share autocrats' common concern about the trade-off in distributing resources within and between elites and masses; the large size and distinct features of the Chinese political economy create a different political structure and constellation of actors and strategies in the realm of social welfare policy.

2.2.1. Structure

Three basic features define the formation and enforcement of the Chinese regime's distributive strategy. First, China is a large country with vast regional variations in population, resources, and economic development. The huge regional disparities mean that this country is a collection of the third, second, and first worlds. As of 2015, Chinese administrative units, from high to low levels, comprised 31 mainland provincial units (including 22 provinces, 5 ethnic autonomous regions, and 4 provincial-level municipalities), 334 prefectural units (291 prefectural cities, 40 prefectures, and 3 leagues), 2,852 county-level units and 41,039 township-level units. Because of the wide heterogeneity of Chinese subnational regions, there is extreme complexity and difficulty when it comes to central rule. This basic condition is related to and probably gives rise to the second feature of Chinese political economy: decentralization.

China has one of the most administratively decentralized systems in the world. Localities account for over 80% of all government spending and most of the social welfare and service provisions; many local governments are eager to take policy initiatives and experimentation to achieve economic development and various other goals (Montinola, et al. 1995; Heilmann 2008). Moreover, each of the administrative units governs the next lower level units in its jurisdiction. This constitutes a hierarchical power relation among the governments of different levels, and decentralization takes place from top to bottom of the hierarchy. The top-down hierarchy is intrinsically related to the third and foremost feature of Chinese political economy: authoritarianism.

China is a large decentralized country, but it is also an authoritarian country. The unusual combination of decentralization and authoritarianism in China is difficult for outsiders to grasp (Gibson 2004; Landry 2008). The authoritarian nature of the Chinese regime is manifested in, at least, three aspects. First, the CCP, the single ruling party of China, has been in power since 1949, exerting a tight rein on almost every important state policy and decision. The party and the state are fused deliberately: many leaders hold concurrent party and state positions and are transferred seamlessly between the two hierarchies (Ang 2016). Second, none of the political leaders are publicly elected: local leaders and government officials are appointed by superiors at the next higher level; central top leaders (i.e., General Secretary of CCP, Premier) are selected and groomed in advance by previous top leaderships. Hence, political leaders look upward to their superiors rather than downward to their constituencies for accountability. Third, public participation in political decisions and policymaking is forbidden or strictly controlled. Although public opinion and social inputs are sometimes solicited for policy consultation and deliberation, the power and influence of the party-state far surpasses that of society in decision making.

The social welfare strategy adopted by the Chinese authoritarian regime is to maintain a particularly privileged welfare provision for the elites— including party and government officials, civil servants, and public sector and SOE formal employees—while establishing an essentially modest social provision for the other groups. To enforce this strategy in the Chinese political economy, the regime must rely on agents it can trust and control. This is where the dynamics of central-local relation and interaction enter the picture and where local political leaders prove crucial to social welfare provision in China's authoritarian and decentralized multilevel governance setting in which electoral and accountable relationships between constituencies and local leaders have been lacking.

2.2.2. Agency

Before explaining the central-local interaction that constitutes the core of welfare politics on the supply side in China, we need to clarify who the central leaders and local leaders are; and who the elites and masses are in the Chinese context. The central leaders (or the Center) are the party and government heads at the national level, including the general secretary of the CCP, the premier of the State Council (i.e., central government), and the top leaders of the party central standing committees and organs. Although it is not a secret that there are several factions within the Center or top leadership (Shih and Liu 2012; Shih 2004), it is considered a unity with a relatively coherent set of interests throughout this book for two reasons. First, the time period under study falls largely within the

Hu Jintao administration (2002–2011). Since the conflicts between factions are more palpable during leadership successions it is reasonable to assume that the Center or top leadership was a coherent political actor in the social welfare policies of this particular time period under study. Second, our focus on social welfare politics on the supply side lies in the central-local interactions rather than within the Center. It is noteworthy that the Center defined here doesn't include the bureaucrats of various government ministries at the national level. The ministerial officials and bureaucrats, including their subordinates at the local levels, are considered part of the elites whose interests and welfare privileges are protected by the Center.

Similarly, the term "local leaders" refers to the party and government heads at the local (province, city, or prefecture, and county) levels. These positions are on the Center's *nomenklatura* list (Laundry 2008, Manion 1984, Lieberthal 2004)[4] and they will be held accountable by the Center if there is severe failure in implementing the Center's decrees and policies, such as mass protests due to official malpractice in their jurisdictions. The local leaders themselves are part of the elites as they have been given better and more benefits and entitlements than the other social groups. But the local leaders are different from the rest of elites (e.g., bureaucrats or civil servants, public-sector employees, SOE formal employees) as they are given power and responsibility by the Center to distribute benefits and allocate resources among the masses. Hence, from the perspective of personal interests, local leaders share the interests of other elites who benefit from the Center's preferential welfare treatment and protection. Nonetheless, from the perspective of public interests, local leaders are the primary actors who are held responsible for specifying and executing the Center's mandate of social welfare expansion and development for the broader social groups in their jurisdictions.

One might inquire about the roles played by societal groups such as elites and masses when theoretically reconstructing the authoritarian leaders' distributive interests and strategies. Some existing studies found that bureaucratic interests and conflicts influence the adoption and reform of social insurance in China (Duckett 2003; Hsiao 2007; Huang, 2013; Remington 2019; Muller 2017). A growing strand of literature argues that the discontent among marginalized groups and looming social unrest can explain various Chinese distributive policies and measures including minimum livelihood allowance, pensions, and land rights since the late 1990s (Pan 2015; Hurst 2009; Frazier 2010; Wallace 2014; Heurlin 2016). The study in this book, despite focusing on the supply side of Chinese social welfare—mainly central and local leaders' interests and strategies—does not dismiss the influence of social demand and specific social groups including elites and masses. Instead, the supply-side perspective and argument embraces the potential recipient-side influence to account for leaders' political calculation, distributive strategy, and policies.

From time to time during China's social welfare reforms, the government introduced various forms of policy consultation and limited deliberation, soliciting inputs and feedback of both elite and grassroots groups (Kornreich et al. 2012; Karindi 2008). In this sense, the supply and demand sides of social welfare policies cannot be easily separated. The approach adopted in this study is to focus on the government (hence, the "supply side" of social welfare provision), especially the political leaders or main decision makers within the government, to explain the distributive rationale, pattern, and outcome of Chinese social welfare expansion in the 2000s.

On the recipient side of social welfare, I intentionally distinguish elites and masses. By "elites" I mean the well-off groups in the population such as party and government officials, civil servants, public-sector employees, formal employees of large SOEs, and other members of the upper or middle class (i.e., some business people, salaried professionals) who have disproportionately benefited from the Chinese political economy. This view of "elites" or elite groups is broader than the traditional views of "(political) elites" (e.g., party elders, Politburo members) in the literature on Chinese elite politics (Shih, Adolph, and Liu 2012; Shih 2004; Shirk 1993). The conceptualization of elites in this book focuses on socioeconomic status (e.g., income, social entitlements, occupation, employment sector) while the traditional conceptualization of elites in the elite politics literature is mostly based on political power. These two "elites" certainly overlap—without doubt the political elites (e.g., Politburo membership, party elders) receive abundant privileged economic and social benefits (i.e., exclusive access to special care, resources, and services). Nonetheless, not every member of the elites in this book is a party elder or Politburo member. Compared to the traditional view of "elites," the relatively inclusive conception of elites in this book brings in broader theoretical significance and implications because they include a larger proportion of the population[5] and constitute an indispensable group in the central leaders' calculation and deliberation for social welfare policy.

The other group of importance on the recipient side is the masses or the mass groups—the peasants, rural-to-urban migrants, informal workers, and the underclass. Despite being disadvantaged in economic and social benefit distributions, the mass groups account for the majority of the labor force or population and thus constitute another indispensable group for the Chinese leaders to consider in social welfare provision.

2.2.3. Strategy

The Chinese authoritarian regime, represented by the Center, uses stratified expansion strategy in social welfare provision to reward elite supporters of the regime and cultivate mass support; more important, the regime uses it to strike a balance between elites and masses to hedge against regime uncertainty and instability. The "stratified expansion strategy" of social welfare is preferred by the Chinese authoritarian regime in the reform era over the "play-off strategy" of mobilizing one group against the other in distribution; stratified expansion of social welfare better serves the top leadership's interest for inclusive development (e.g., Jiang Zemin's "three representatives"; Hu Jintao's "harmonious society" and "scientific development" ideologies) and also conforms to the economy model (i.e., market economy with Chinese characteristics) developed in China at the same time based on its existing and emerging social cleavages. The CCP has transformed itself from a revolutionary party to a ruling party for much of the post-Mao period (Dickson 2016). As such, no longer is the CCP determined to transform society, fundamentally reshaping it to fit its ideological visions as Mao Zedao did through the Great Leap Forward and the Cultural Revolution in his time. Instead, the CCP attempts to build up its legitimacy by incorporating social groups widely, including previously marginalized ones, by giving them social welfare benefits and improvements in their well-being (Zhao 2009; Zhu 2011).

The outcome of the stratified expansion of social welfare provision is that everyone gets something, but in different amounts. This distributive strategy has a lower cost than a comprehensive social welfare expansion and avoids forming a universalistic welfare state. However, as redistribution is contentious, there are also dysfunctional or unintended consequences of stratified expansion of social welfare. First, the gaps in social welfare benefits between different social groups or subnational regions are likely to enlarge as a result of the stratification, and this can be a new source of social grievances.[6] Second, given that the total amount of benefits provided is fixed (e.g., limited numbers of hospitals, medical professionals, and facilities), social groups, whether elites or masses, might be unhappy to see scarce benefits go increasingly to the other group. Yet, even as each group's benefits expand, as long as the resources supporting the expansion continue to grow, the dysfunctional consequences of the stratified expansion of social welfare are manageable. A more pressing problem for the Chinese regime is how to enforce the stratified expansion strategy of social welfare locally with decentralized multilevel governance and diverse local political economies.

To enforce its stratified expansion strategy, the Chinese central leaders, on the one hand, control the overall stratification pattern of social welfare provision to achieve an outcome that privileges the groups with political connections or influence over the other social groups; on the other hand, to local leaders, who have expertise in local governance, the central leaders delegate authority to expand the coverage and generosity of social welfare provision to accommodate diverse local and social needs.[7] However, this trade-off between control and delegation in social welfare expansion may be marked by the principal-agent problem between central and local leaders who often hold different priorities or preferences in specific policies. The central leaders (the principal) must take many measures such as frequent inspection tours to ensure the local leaders' (the agents') compliance and cooperation. The central-local tensions are further intensified when expansion of social welfare coverage and generosity by local leaders, who are driven by various local conditions and considerations, might shift the national stratification pattern away from the one the central leaders most favor.

China's local leaders possess centrally mandated authority and discretion to expand social welfare provision. The local leaders, for their part, aim to satisfy the Center in various work tasks to secure and advance their careers. However, there are circumstances in which local policy preferences diverge from those of the central leaders, and local leaders choose policies that deviate from the choice most preferred by the Center. After all, local leaders must work within the context of local constraints and resources to implement the Center's decrees. Moreover, as social instability is a veto point in China's official evaluation and promotion,[8] local leaders could provide welfare benefits in ways that can proactively address the bottom-up pressures—salient social needs and demand—to prevent social unrest in their jurisdictions. In this sense, implementing stratified expansion of social welfare and distributing expanded welfare benefits are contingent on the compliance of local leaders with the power and responsibility of social welfare provision. As a result, the dynamics of central-local interactions, such as control and evasion of control, stand at the core of the politics of China's social welfare expansion; there is considerable subnational variation in Chinese social welfare expansion.

My argument on the Chinese welfare politics has two important components. First, the central leaders take the initiative and have the most interest in expanding the social welfare provision while maintaining a fragmented and stratified social welfare distribution. The central leaders control the overall stratification of social welfare provision while delegating social welfare expansion to local leaders. Second, Chinese local leaders have centrally mandated authority and discretion in social welfare provision. Importantly, under a certain set of local political economy conditions, their policy choices in social welfare provision are not congruent with the central leaders' first choice. The next two sections turn to elaborating these two components of the argument.

2.3. The Center's Interests and Strategy for Social Welfare Provision

The top priority of Chinese central leaders is maintaining regime survival and stability. As threats to the regime can come from both elites and masses, choosing to distribute rents and goods only to one or the other is not an optimal strategy from the authoritarian leaders' perspective. Instead, authoritarian leaders try to efficiently balance the benefits between elites and masses to maximize their survival prospects.[9] The strategy that the Chinese leadership has adopted is to maintain a particularly privileged provision for the elites while preserving an essentially modest provision for the masses. To achieve this, however, the Center faces a choice between control and accommodation of social needs in the provision of these benefits. On one hand, the Center attempts to control who gets what, distributing more benefits to the social groups with political connections and influence for regime survival. On the other hand, the Center seeks to accommodate most other social groups to some extent, avoiding too much of a gap between the haves and the have-nots that could potentially foster public grievances and trigger social unrest. These questions arise: To whom does the Center aim to grant welfare privileges? Under what conditions does the Center choose to control social welfare provision, and under what conditions does it choose to accommodate social and local needs by delegating social welfare expansion to local leaders? How does the Center manage stratification and expansion of social welfare in the decentralized multilevel governance setting?

2.3.1. Privileging Elites in Social Welfare Provision

Of special importance for the survival of the Chinese authoritarian regime are party and government officials, civil servants, and public-sector and SOE formal employees—the so-called elites in this book. These groups are considered crucial for regime survival from the Center's perspective for three reasons. First, the state sector including SOEs is the main source of fiscal revenue, employment, and economic growth for the regime (Lardy 1998; Lau et al. 2000). Chinese leaders often remark that the development of SOEs is related to the political future of the regime. According to Xi Jinping, the party secretary of the CCP who took power in 2012, the party has the ultimate say over state companies: "Party leadership and building the role of the party are the root and soul for SOEs."[10] Through SOEs, the regime maintains a firm grip on the economy and on main revenue sources. It is estimated that urban SOEs contributed about 50% of Chinese industrial value-added/profits in 2005 (Huang 2008). Even in 2011, after two decades of economic transition from central planning to market, SOEs accounted for nearly 40% of China's industrial assets; about 40% of the state's total tax revenue still came from the state sector, which is much higher than the share from other sectors.

In addition to money, the regime needs "launching organizations"[11] such as the bureaucrats, legislature, police, courts, and judicial organs to assist in policymaking, policy implementation, and maintaining social stability. According to Chinese government statistics, in 2007 there were about 13.55 million civil servants (state officials) and 53.93 million state employees (including civil servants, legislators, judicature, teachers, doctors, salaried professionals, etc.). The Chinese regime relies on these groups (about 4% of the country's total population) to run the state and maintain its rule. The geographic concentration of these groups, such as government and party officials, bureaucrats, and public-sector and SOE formal employees in the capital or big cities, make collective action problems easier to solve (Wallace 2014). Another social group that the Center attempts to co-opt and privilege in social welfare provision is certain ethnic minority groups concentrated in the border and peripheral areas of the country (e.g., Tibet, Xinjiang). But the privileges conferred to ethnic minority groups are more implicit and usually made by the Center's special fiscal transfers to the ethnic minority regions rather than by general social legislation.

In sum, the Chinese central leaders attempt to placate the elites including party and government officials, civil servants, public sector and SOE formal employees by privileging them in social welfare provision. A large literature on patrimonial, rentier, and Leninist regimes also finds that non-democratic leaders often transfer more benefits to key elite constituencies because those distributions increase these constituencies' opportunity costs of defecting to a challenging coalition during political struggles against the leaders (Bates 1981; Boone 1990; Snyder 1992; Shih 2004). However, the Center's interest in privileging the elite groups does not mean that the other social groups do not receive social welfare benefits. The Chinese leadership knows the strategic wisdom of extending social welfare benefits to many other social groups once welfare privileges are granted to the elite groups.

2.3.2. Placating Masses in Social Welfare Provision

While the elites are privileged in social welfare provision, the Chinese regime does not ignore the masses in social welfare provision because a balanced social welfare system serves the regime's interests in maintaining political survival, social stability, and economic development.

Since Mao's era ended in 1976, the Chinese authoritarian regime has moved away from maintaining its legitimacy as deriving from the proletarian revolution and sees it now as resting on a fragile base of improving the economic well-being of the people. This "legitimacy fragility" makes the regime particularly sensitive and vulnerable to popular resistance and social unrest (Goldston and Tilly 2001; Hurst 2009; Cai 2006; Hurst and O'Brien 2002). Despite decades of continuous economic growth, social unrest, and public grievances over income inequalities, social inequity, and injustice have not disappeared but have instead expanded in China. Nationwide, the Chinese Ministry of Public Security recorded 8,700 so-called spontaneous incidents (such as street demonstration, protests, and riots) in 1993, rising to 11,000, 15,000 and 32,000 in 1995, 1997, and 1999, respectively (Pei 2003). In 2003, some 58,000 incidents were staged involving three million people, including farmers, workers and students (Ma 2004). The number of collective incidents in China increased to approximately 127,460 in 2008, 14.6 times the number in 1993 (Chung 2011). Against this backdrop, the Chinese regime's public security spending for maintaining social stability—dedicated to domestic forces such as armed police, courts, and judicial departments—has significantly increased and even exceeded its military spending (Wang 2014). Aside from coercion, the regime utilizes cooptation as another important strategy to placate society and prevent unrest. Social welfare expansion, extending various welfare benefits to broad social groups, serves as a crucial instrument for the cooptation strategy.

Another reason that the Center seeks to expand the social welfare provision to many other social groups is to hedge against the potential threats from elites. Autocratic leaders know that the launching organizations (e.g., bureaucrats and officials) strong enough to put them in power also have the resources to end their rule. One of the autocracy's political strategies to resolve this dilemma is to empower competing organizations or social groups to raise the collective action costs on the part of elites (Haber 2007). Under this political strategy, the distribution of social welfare is characterized as institutionally fragmented yet providing broad social coverage. That is, many political or economic entities are responsible for portions of the welfare system, but large groups in society enjoy at least some measure of social protection.[12] The principal feature of Chinese social welfare provision—stratified expansion—echoes this strategy as well. The Center established and maintains a fragmented social welfare system to achieve a "divide and rule" outcome, which, on one hand, consolidates various divisions among social groups to prevent alliances that could challenge the regime,[13] and on the other hand, ties the loyalties of various social groups to the Center. Both the work-unit-based welfare provision under Mao and the social welfare expansion since the late 1990s constitute similar attempts of cooptation and accommodation of social interests through institutional proliferation and fragmentation (Hurst 2011).

Last but not least, social welfare expansion also serves the Chinese central leadership's economic interests and plans. Since the 2008 global financial crisis, increasing domestic consumption has become a centerpiece of the Center's plan to stimulate economic growth that is a crucial source of the regime's legitimacy. The plan aims to shift China's economy away from its heavy dependence on exports and investment and toward a more sustainable reliance on domestic consumption. In the absence of a well-developed social security and insurance system, however, Chinese people tend to save more and spend less (Yang et al. 2011). From the Center's standpoint,[14] establishing a social safety net and expanding the social welfare provision to broad social groups also constitute a means of reducing disincentives to household consumption and bolstering domestic consumption. In other words, social welfare expansion contributes to the Center's efforts to restructure the economy and shift the economic drive from fixed asset investment and exports to domestic consumption.

2.3.3. The Center's Tools

By now, the reader may have gotten the impression that the Chinese central leadership intends to expand social welfare provision to many social groups once welfare privileges are granted to the politically important groups such as government and party officials, civil servants, and public-sector and SOE formal employees. To distribute benefits among many social groups in a way that maximizes political returns under changing and diverse local circumstances, however, the Center needs to delegate discretionary authority to local state agents in the provision of social welfare, because local officials have more information and local knowledge. The political economy literature suggests that decentralized provision of public goods brings positive output for various reasons. Lower levels of government are closer to their constituents and thus have more information about the preferences of local residents (Tiebout 1956). Local engagement increases the efficiency of public service delivery because local governments provide public goods in small units and can tailor them directly to local tastes (Oates 1972). The imperative of delegating social welfare provision to local governments seems more salient in a large country like China with vastly diverse local situations and needs.

The Chinese central leadership adopts a "control" tactic in maintaining the stratification of social welfare provision biased in favor of the elite groups and an "accommodation" (or delegation) tactic for expanding social welfare to other groups. Under resource constraints, the Center's priorities of pleasing elite groups and of expanding social welfare to many other groups inevitably compete with each other and sometimes, one trumps the other. But at most times it is the strategic balance and the feasible mix between these two that the Center hopes to achieve. A question naturally arises: How does the Chinese central leadership enforce its different tactics in social welfare provision across so many subnational regions and diverse social groups in its vast territory? The tools that the Center utilizes to achieve both control and accommodation in social welfare provision include fiscal transfers, social legislation, and personnel management.

The center-to-local fiscal transfer is the most direct and effective tool for the Center to use in controlling the provision of social welfare benefits. The central-to-local fiscal transfer system began in 1995 after the 1994 tax sharing reform,[15] through which the central government substantially enhanced its share in total tax revenue. The distribution of central-to-local fiscal transfers follows a clear geographic pattern: the amount of fiscal transfers sharply decreases from western regions to eastern ones. Specifically, the Center's fiscal transfers account for more than 70% of social health insurance financing in the peripheral ethnic autonomous regions in the northwest and less than 5% in the eastern coastal regions.

Two important facts indicate that the Center's fiscal transfers are determined mainly by political considerations—assuring that the privileged regions and groups receive more benefits than do others—rather than by a genuine concern for local social needs.[16] First, the northwestern ethnic minority regions with relatively small populations such as Tibet, Xinjiang, Qinghai, and Ningxia receive most of the Center's fiscal transfers (sometimes over 10 times the local-sourced fiscal revenue) (Guo 2008; Jeong 2014). This suggests that the central-to-local fiscal transfer is not a simple function of the size of the masses. Second, according to the results in existing empirical studies of the Center's fiscal transfer to localities (Shih et al. 2010; Zhan 2011; Wallace 2014), and as I will further discuss and empirically show in Chapter 4, the Center's fiscal transfers respond to the sizes of the local government payroll (salaries of local officials and bureaucrats, retired cadres, and decommissioned military officers) and the elite groups (such as public sector and SOE employees). These observations, when combined, point to the instrumentality of the Center's fiscal transfers in maintaining the stratification of social welfare provision.

Another tool that the Center employs to control social welfare provision is social legislation. Since the 1990s, through a series of legislation and regulations,[17] the Center has established a social welfare system that is characterized as fragmented and biased in favor of elites such as civil servants and public sector and SOE formal employees. According to the Social Insurance Law promulgated in 2010, social health insurance should be pooled at or above the county level. Within each of the pooling units (e.g., country or city), social health insurance is divided into at least three programs: one for urban employees, one for urban (non-working) residents, and one for rural residents. These different programs are stipulated to be operated, managed, and financed separately under the Center's supervision. Through the law, the Center declares that it will "establish" (*jianli*) and "perfect" (*wanshan*) the social insurance system that is very fragmented by design. In stark contrast to its detailed instructions on the stratification pattern of social health insurance, however, the Social Insurance Law does not stipulate the coverage and generosity specifically, except to vaguely state that they will be administered according to the Center's "rule" (*guiding*).

The ambiguity in legislation leaves the Center much room to define the local leaders' discretion in social welfare policymaking. In fact, the Center delegated plenty of discretionary authority to localities in specifying the coverage and generosity of social health insurance for the purpose of accommodating diverse local conditions in various administrative regulations[18] because administrative regulations are easier to modify and quicker to change than laws.

In addition to fiscal transfers and social legislation, the Center uses centralized and extensive personnel control to influence local social welfare provision. In the absence of competitive elections, the central leadership controls and monitors subordinate state agents through political centralization, characterized by the "party cadre responsibility system" that was introduced from the provincial level down in the mid-1980s governing job assignments, performance appraisals, promotions and demotions, and remuneration. Under this top-down personnel control system, local leaders are held accountable upward to the Center rather than downward to local people. To get promoted or even to maintain a career under the party cadre responsibility system, local leaders must meet a variety of policy targets set by the Center. Improving people's livelihood, including social welfare provision (*minsheng*), has become an increasingly important component of official evaluations.[19]

The centralized personnel system has important implications for policy enforcement in China. First, it significantly increases the cost of non-compliance on the part of local leaders and thus assists the Center in shaping the policy choices of hundreds and thousands of cities and counties. Local leaders who are interested in advancing their political careers in the system must internalize the Center's interest in local policymaking. It is important to note that the policy preferences of the Center and those of the local leaders do not always converge. A crucial factor that leads central leaders to hold different preferences from the local leaders is the Center's stronger interest in maintaining regime stability, because the national leaders represent the regime and are more responsible for its survival (Cai 2008). This difference in priorities between the central and local governments compels the Center to use its appointment control to obtain preferred outcomes (Huang 1996; Shen 2010). Some empirical research suggests that the Center establishes different policy targets or assigns different weights to the same policy targets in official evaluations in different regions in order to convey its differing priorities in these regions to the local leaders (Zuo 2014). Thus, the centralized official evaluation system helps align the interests of the central and local leaders. Moreover, the Center uses evaluation as a tool of ex-post control and monitoring of local leaders' performance and compliance, complementing the Center's delegation that grants considerable ex-ante discretion to local leaders in policymaking and implementation.[20]

Second, with general guidelines and delegated discretion from the Center, local leaders often make policy choices and experiments according to specific local conditions (Heberer and Trappel 2013). The diversity of policy measures that local leaders undertake according to the respective local situations is precisely what the Center seeks to stimulate in order to accommodate different local and social needs, especially in the domains such as social policy where the Center faces higher information costs. Ang (2016) calls this approach of fostering adaptive governance and development in China "directed improvisation" that consists of variation, selection, and niche creation processes. After the emergence of this diversity of local practice in experimenting or implementing the Center's policy, the Center uses "police patrol" (inspection tours) to assess policy outcomes, detect non-compliance, and punish opportunistic local leaders via the personnel system. Social policymaking in China is thus characterized by cycles of policy experimentation (Heilmann 2008).[21]

In summary, Chinese central leadership attempts to expand the provision of social welfare to maintain regime stability but it faces a choice between control and accommodation of social needs. The Center's strategy is to maintain a privileged provision for the elite groups such as party and government officials, civil servants, and public-sector and SOE formal employees while accommodating the basic needs of the other groups. To implement both control and accommodation in social welfare provision, the Center employs a variety of tools, namely, central-to-local fiscal transfers, social legislation, and centralized personnel management. This leads to questions concerning the local leaders. What is the incentive for local leaders to provide social welfare? How do they make policy choices that satisfy both the local situations and the Center's directives?

2.4. The Localities' Interests and Choices for Social Welfare Expansion

2.4.1. Local Motivations for Social Welfare Provision

Chinese local leaders are motivated to proactively design and provide social welfare in a manner that addresses the main social needs in their jurisdictions in order to maintain social stability and thus secure and advance their political careers. Chinese local leaders do not have many viable career alternatives outside of the political hierarchy, because comparable job opportunities rarely exist in the private sector. Hence, most local leaders care about their political careers and are eager to advance their careers in the established system (Li and Zhou 2005; Guo 2007; Shih et al. 2012).[22] Unlike the central leaders, local leaders might not consider regime stability their first priority. Nonetheless, local leaders are concerned about social unrest taking place in their jurisdictions, because social instability may jeopardize their political careers under the centralized evaluation and promotion system (O'Brien and Li 1999; Edin 2003a, 2003b). Hence, the career interests of local leaders are aligned with the Center's interests of maintaining regime survival and social stability.

In concert with local leaders' interest of maintaining social stability in their jurisdictions to secure and advance their political careers, economic growth and public goods provision are set as the principal responsibilities of local officials (Whiting 2004; Landry 2008; Ang 2016; Zuo 2015). Under resource constraints, these two tasks could sometimes constitute a trade-off for local leaders; further demonstrated in Chapter 5, given the different developmental stages of respective regions, local leaders might prioritize one goal over the other to different extents. Nonetheless, there is no local government in China that can ignore the Center's mandate of social welfare provision because doing so may cause social unrest which not only impairs local leaders' own political careers but also the Center's ultimate interest—regime survival and stability.

In social welfare provision specifically, local leaders need to meet the Center's dual mandate of expansion and stratification. Unlike the Center, local leaders stand on the frontline directly dealing with complex local situations and needs for social welfare. Administrative decentralization of social welfare policy further enhances the opportunities and discretionary power of local leaders to take into account local conditions or needs in policy implementation. Some existing studies find that many Chinese local officials not only provide and deliver social welfare benefits to the elite groups as the Center orders, but also attempt to accommodate local people in social welfare provision (Solinger and Jiang 2016). Even though Chinese local leaders are not seeking to maximize votes as their counterparts in democracies might, they nonetheless need to take the public's likely reactions, in addition to the Center's decrees, into account; otherwise, local leaders will risk, in the worst case, public grievances that can lead to social unrest, or in other cases, non-cooperation from the public in policy implementation. The Chinese local leaders are thus placed in a position that faces both top-down and bottom-up pressures in social welfare policymaking and implementation.

2.4.2. Local Constraints in Social Welfare Provision

In China, local conditions differ vastly, and these define the stake of each locality differently, therefore making local officials respond to the same central directive in differing manners (Chung 2000). In social welfare policymaking, local officials face political, fiscal, and social constraints that jointly shape their specific policy choices in social welfare provision. First, as elaborated in Section 2.3, local officials' policy choices are constrained by the Center's control via social legislation, fiscal transfer, and personnel control. As such, local policy implementation is inherently political in nature. In social welfare policy, the stratification pattern stipulated in the Social Insurance Law is considered a political principle for local leaders to follow in local social welfare policy. As part of the elite groups whose welfare privileges the Center attempts to protect and enhance during the welfare expansion, local leaders themselves benefit from the stratification pattern promoted by the Center and thus are incentivized to maintain it. Nonetheless, as implementors of the Center's welfare expansion policy under fiscal and administrative decentralization, local leaders bear most of the costs of maintaining the stratified social health insurance system in their jurisdictions, such as a heavy management and financial burden for the multiple separated health insurance programs, and public grievances toward the embedded inequality and inequity. In this sense, the Center's political control of stratification and mandate of social welfare expansion present a trade-off for local leaders in remaking and implementing the policy. How local leaders respond in policy initiatives and specifics, such as resisting, complying, or pioneering in maintaining social health insurance stratification, is related to the other constraints they confront in social welfare provision and their relations or interactions with the Center.

The second constraint that local officials confront in social welfare provision is fiscal stringency. The Chinese social insurance system, which is characterized as being highly decentralized yet predominantly government-run, makes local fiscal resources a particularly important factor in predicting local leaders' policy preferences. Since the centralization of revenue resulting from fiscal reform in the mid-1990s, the local governments' share of government budgetary revenue has continued to be less than 50% of the total, while its share in expenditure remained at roughly 70% of the total (Qian and Blomqvist 2014). On average, Chinese local governments bear about 70% of social health insurance financing for the non-working population, including peasants, elders, students, and children. For most localities, the Center's fiscal transfer for social welfare provision is far from enough, and many local governments face substantial budget deficits, so paying the medical bills in full and on time places a considerable burden on local budgets (Oi and Zhao 2007; Wong 2009). Moreover, according to the 2010 Social Insurance Law, local governments are responsible for any deficits of social insurance funds in their jurisdictions. This makes the funding situation, particularly the local government's fiscal situations, crucial in ensuring that the social insurance system functions properly.

Local government's fiscal resources condition the generosity of social health insurance they can provide. Given the Center's mandate of social welfare expansion, local governments with large fiscal revenues would increase the social health insurance generosity in their jurisdictions. It is noteworthy that Chinese local governments' fiscal revenues are not completely drawn or collected from local sources; as section 2.3 elucidates, the central-to-local fiscal transfer is an important source of revenue for local governments, especially for those in the periphery ethnic minority autonomous regions. Therefore, it is possible that both the coastal regions with advanced market economies and the periphery ethnic minority autonomous regions with less developed economies but abundant fiscal transfers from the central government can provide similarly generous benefits to their social health insurance beneficiaries.

The third constraint on local officials' policy choices regarding social health insurance is social risks.[23] Social policy often responds to demographic and labor market shifts (Peng and Wong 2008; Iversen 2001a; Esping-Andersen 1999; Rehm 2016) and the nature of social insurance typically involves pooling and sharing risks across different segments of a population or across different regions. The demographic or risk profile of localities can have significant impacts on the performance of social health insurance funds.[24] For example, regions with a younger population face significantly lower risks in health insurance than those with an aged population. Moreover, the lack of a nationwide risk pooling and redistribution mechanism in China's fragmented social insurance system makes regions with small or aging populations particularly vulnerable to exogenous shocks such as industrial accidents, disease outbreak, and labor market shifts.

Most important, decades of mass internal migration accompanying China's economic reform and openness have profoundly changed the risk profile of many Chinese regions. Migration is a key mechanism for risk pooling that leads to more homogeneous risk distribution and larger efforts of redistribution behind the social welfare development in advanced industrialized economies such as Germany, the European Union (EU), and the United States (Beramendi 2012; Rehm 2016). China's economic reform strategy in the 1980s, "letting some people (regions) get rich first" starting from the Special Economic Zones in the coastal areas, created a domestic labor market in which some inland provinces continuously "export" labor to the coastal provinces. Similarly, labor mobility works as a multiplier of social risks for these Chinese regions, creating stronger incentives for local officials to enlarge the risk pooling or coverage of social insurance.

In China, the influence of migration on regional preferences for risk pooling is similar for labor-inflowing and -outflowing regions. The rationale for social insurance expansion seems more intuitive in labor-outflow regions, where mass labor outflow exacerbates population aging and places burdensome payment pressures on local social health insurance funds.[25] As Chapter 5 details, local governments in the labor-outflowing regions must relentlessly enlarge social insurance coverage to counteract looming or existing deficits in local social insurance funds. The risk-magnifying mechanism applies to labor-inflow regions as well, because the regions receiving mass labor inflows are heavily reliant on labor-intensive manufacturing and service sectors. With the potentially high demand of medical service and the risk of potential mass labor outflows (returning to home regions), local officials in the labor-inflow regions prefer and attempt to obtain larger risk-pooling for social insurance to counteract the increased social risks brought in by migration.

2.4.3. Local Choices

Chinese local officials have both pressure and discretion to choose policy for social welfare expansion. The specific policy choices they make are jointly determined by the Center's control of the distributive pattern of social welfare provision, and local political economy that include (1) the central-local relation or interaction, and (2) local socioeconomic conditions, including the amounts of local fiscal resources and social risks in their jurisdictions. As the stratification pattern of social health insurance is set by the Center, local discretion mainly lies on the coverage and generosity of social health insurance. Specifically, local leaders have four different choices for social welfare expansion: (1) giving more people generous benefits (high generosity and coverage, or the "dual type"); (2) giving certain people more benefits (high generosity and low coverage, or the "privileging type"); (3) giving meager benefits to more people (low generosity and high coverage, or the "risk-pooling type"); and (4) giving only meager benefits to only certain people (low generosity and coverage, or the "status-quo type"). The specific choice local leaders make with respect to social health insurance expansion is contingent on local socioeconomic conditions given the Center's dual mandate of social welfare expansion and stratification. Table 2.1 summarizes the constellations of local political economy conditions and the corresponding local choices for social health insurance expansion.

Table 2.1. Local Conditions and Options for Social Health Insurance Expansion

| | | Fiscal Resources | |
		Poor	Rich
Social Risks	High	Risk-pooling type: large coverage and low generosity	Dual type: large coverage and high generosity
	Low	Status-quo type: small coverage and low generosity	Privileging type: small coverage and high generosity

Given that the Center's strategies in social welfare provision is to control the stratification pattern while accommodating diverse social needs or local circumstances through expanding generosity and coverage, different local political economy conditions generate different policy choices for social welfare expansion among Chinese subnational regions. In the regions where both social risks and fiscal revenues are low, local leaders have insufficient motivation and inadequate capacity to expand either coverage or generosity of social health insurance; they try to maintain a welfare provision for the elite groups such as government and party officials, civil servants, and public-sector and SOE formal employees to minimally meet the Center's expectation for expansion. As a result, the social health insurance in these regions remains the "status-quo type" featured as low coverage and low generosity.

By contrast, in the regions where social risks are high due to, for example, labor mobility, local leaders who are concerned about the increase of social risks and the adverse impact of migration on their ability to maintain social stability are motivated to expand the coverage of social health insurance as much as possible. Among the regions using social health insurance expansion reform to address increasing social risks, local leaders in the regions with abundant fiscal resources can afford to expand both coverage and generosity whereas their counterparts in the regions with meager fiscal resources tend to expand the coverage only. Thus, social health insurance in the former results in the "dual type" featuring high coverage and generosity, while social welfare in the latter results in the "risk-pooling type" characterized by high coverage but low generosity.

In the remaining regions, where the elite groups are historically concentrated, such as the capital city, provincial-level municipalities, and peripheral ethnic minority autonomous regions, given the Center's omnipresent control (e.g., restrictions on migration and earmarked fiscal transfers) and dominant priority of maintaining social stability there, local leaders care about stratification more than expansion of social welfare provision. Hence, they are likely to raise benefits for the elites while maintaining a minimum provision for the masses. The social health insurance in these regions results in the "privileging type" featured by high generosity yet low coverage.

2.5. Mapping Politics to Outcomes: Stratified Social Welfare Expansion in Authoritarian China

The outcomes of interest in this book are who gets what, when, and how from the social welfare expansion directed by the Chinese authoritarian regime in the first decade of the 2000s. Combining the Center's mandate of social welfare expansion and the localities' discretionary choices according to local political economy, the distribution of expanded social welfare benefits is significantly stratified, exhibiting striking variations across regions as well as social groups. For analytical simplicity, the empirical analysis in this book assumes that the Chinese political structure consists of only two levels, the central and the local levels, and that the logic underlying the interaction between central and local levels is probably applicable to the interactions between upper and lower levels within local governments. Therefore, the province—the highest local government in China, is used as the unit of analysis to examine the regional variation of Chinese social health insurance expansion.

Both coverage and generosity of social health insurance have been steadily expanded in China since 2004, but different social groups and provinces have benefited differently from this expansion. This stratified expansion of social welfare is attributed to both the Center's distributive strategy and the localities' diverse choices in response to both top-down and bottom-up pressures for social welfare provision. The expansion is manifested in the three dimensions of social health insurance: coverage, generosity, and stratification; these dimensions combined produce different models of social welfare expansion across provinces and social strata in China.

2.5.1. Coverage

The coverage of social health insurance, defined by the ratio of social health insurance beneficiaries to total population, is one of the most direct indicators of China's social welfare expansion. The Center has used this indicator in government documents, speeches, and local official evaluations to enforce the expansion. Hence, for the Chinese local leaders, enrolling more people into social health insurance programs in their jurisdictions is one of the main means of achieving the social welfare expansion target. The Center's statements about who should be included and when in social health insurance reveal its political priority and strategy for benefit distribution; the fact that who is actually included and when in social health insurance show the localities' resources and constraints for social welfare expansion on the ground. As Section 2.3 details, the Center gives priority to party and government officials, civil servants, and urban public sector and SOE formal employees in social welfare provision and wants to maintain these groups' welfare privileges while expanding basic benefits to the other groups. The outcome is a set of incremental and stratified changes of social health insurance coverage over time: the urban state sector including public-sector and SOE formal employees were first included in social health insurance; the coverage of social health insurance was gradually expanded to the non-state sector such as employees of foreign-owned firms and large private-owned firms, and in some localities even to migrant workers—the dominant workforce in median and small private-owned firms or businesses. After that came the creation of residency-based health insurance programs for peasants, labor market outsiders, and the urban poor.

Despite the centrally designed incremental process and trajectory of social health insurance expansion, the actual expansion of coverage has varied vastly at the local level. Regarding who to include (or not) in social health insurance, or social welfare provision in general, if the core concern for the Center is political legitimacy and social stability, the core concern for the local leaders is very different: risks added to or removed from the health insurance pool. The nature of social health insurance is to pool health risks and the associated costs (not only medical expenditure but also opportunity costs of employment, human capital, productivity, etc.) among social groups or regions. This leads to an expansive trend for social health insurance: the more healthy (young) people included, the better risk sharing is. Hence, non-political or structural factors such as demography, labor market, and migration often influence local leaders' decisions and choices for expanding health insurance coverage. All other things equal, the coverage expansion is more dramatic in the regions with high social risks, such as areas with high labor mobility and population aging or density.

In short, with the Center setting a stratified expansion strategy for providing social welfare and with this to be implemented by local leaders whose hands are tied by local socioeconomic situations, the coverage of Chinese social health insurance programs has increased over time yet varies significantly across social groups as well as provinces.

2.5.2. Generosity

The generosity of social health insurance, or the level of social health insurance benefits, defined by the per capita expenditure on social health insurance, is another important indicator of social welfare expansion in China. The coverage of social health insurance indicates the breadth of provision of affordable health care (how many people are covered); the generosity captures the depth thereof (what benefits these people receive). For individuals, once included in social health insurance, the key difference lies in the generosity of the program. Like many other government spending plans, the trend of social health insurance generosity is expansive in China—both demand and prices of health care increase over time as GDP grows and the population ages. But the focus and outcome of interest here are political in the sense that the money spent on one's health insurance benefits could have been spent on others' or on completely other uses. As such, the Center's commitment to expanding the generosity of social health insurance for certain or all social groups demonstrates its responsiveness to the needs of the targeted groups. The more generous their social health insurance is, the more privileged the groups are in resource allocation. Reflecting the Center's interest of privileging elites while maintaining a modest provision for the masses in social welfare provision, the generosity of Chinese social health insurance programs exhibits a clear hierarchy: at the top are government and party officials, bureaucrats, and state employees; in the middle are professionals, and formal employees of other urban sectors; and at the bottom are urban poor, peasants, and rural-to-urban migrants. Although the generosity has increased at both the top, the middle, and the bottom since 2004, the essential hierarchical structure remains intact, with top elites enjoying the most generous benefits and the bottom strata the least generous.

The generosity of health insurance within social strata varies notably across regions as well. For example, the same program (e.g., rural health insurance for peasants, urban health insurance for dependents such as elders, children, students, unemployed people) provides different types of health services and different levels of benefits in different provinces. It is the local leaders' discretionary power that determines what specific type and level of benefits local social health insurance programs provide. As the financing of residency-based social health insurance programs (e.g., URBMI, NRCMS) relies heavily on fiscal transfers and subsidies, especially from local governments,[26] the expansion of generosity of these programs is contingent on local fiscal conditions.

One may argue that the inter-regional difference in generosity of social health insurance can be a story of "local capture": the group that is able to influence local government's decisions by collective actions or rent-seeking activities receives more generous health benefits. This mechanism, though it may exist, is not powerful and has never been dominant in China considering the rigid hierarchy of health insurance generosity created by the Center and maintained institutionally via top-down personnel control and various centrally made laws and regulations about social health insurance.

In sum, the expansion of social health insurance generosity reveals the regime's responsiveness to the social need for health care. Even so, the hierarchy of health insurance benefits is maintained intentionally by the Center, which shows no intention to eliminate the regional disparity of health insurance generosity derived from different local fiscal conditions.

2.5.3. Stratification

Stratification, defined as the relative benefits of social health insurance a group receives or a province provides, captures the differences in health insurance coverage and generosity across groups and provinces. It is not a direct indicator but it is a prominent feature of Chinese social welfare expansion in the 2000s. To summarize the stratification pattern of Chinese social health insurance, (1) different groups get different benefits (coverage and/or generosity); (2) the same group in different provinces might get different benefits (coverage and/or generosity).

Compared to expansion, social welfare stratification is designed more implicitly and reveals more about the distributive politics of social welfare provision in China. Stratification of social welfare is not simply an unintended outcome of expansion of social health insurance coverage and generosity in the China's decentralized multilevel system; it is an intentional result of the Chinese authoritarian regime's distributive strategy of who gets what, when, and how. The authoritarian regime seeks primarily to maintain regime survival and stability; therefore, it differentiates health benefits among social groups and regions allowing it to divide and rule. To do so, the Center has created and maintained stratification of social welfare expansion (e.g., the elite groups are entitled to better health insurance programs than the masses) through legislation, fiscal transfers, and personnel control.

However, some local leaders might not strongly share the same preference for stratification as the Center does in the Chinese decentralized political economy. First, stratification means fragmentation and segmentation of social health insurance programs, and this dramatically increases the management costs and inefficiency of local social health insurance administration. Second, stratification breeds social inequality and grievances, increasing the chance of social unrest. Because of the decentralized design of health insurance administration in China, social grievances and unrest related to social health insurance mostly target the local rather than the central government. In other words, the local governments bear the direct costs and undesirable consequences of maintaining the stratification of social health insurance in their jurisdictions. Therefore, social health insurance expansion efforts made at the local level sometimes contradict or compromise, whether intentionally or unintentionally, the stratification of social welfare provision preferred by the Center. The power dynamics and preference divergence between central and local leaders often produce a nuanced variation of stratification in social health insurance across provinces.

In sum, stratification of social health insurance in China is politically constructed at the national level. At the subnational level, however, just like the implementation of social health insurance expansion in coverage and generosity, the magnitude of health insurance stratification is subject to local discretion and conditions. For example, migrant workers in the coastal provinces, though they received lower benefits than local state-sector or SOE formal employees, might

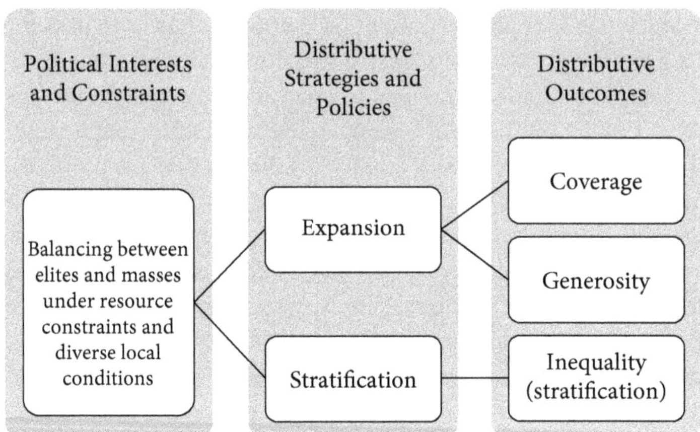

Figure 2.1 Theoretical Components of the Stratified Expansion of Social Welfare under Authoritarian Rule

still benefit more from the local health insurance expansion in the coastal provinces than their counterparts who stay in the inland provinces.

Figure 2.1 summarizes the three components of the theory explicated in this chapter about the stratified expansion of social welfare in China: political interests, distributive strategies/policies, and distributive outcomes. Before delving into the empirical analysis, Chapter 3 briefly reviews the history, institution, and economic background of social health insurance in China. After that, Chapters 4 and 5 investigate the distributive strategies and policies of the Chinese social welfare expansion, testing the first set of observable implications of the argument, which focus on the central and local leaders' distributive strategies and policies during China's social health insurance expansion. Then, Chapters 6 and 7 turn to the distributive outcomes including stratification, coverage, and generosity of China's social welfare expansion, testing the second set of observable implications of the argument, which focus on the actual distribution of expanded social health insurance benefits across provinces and social groups.

3

Overview of China's Social Health Insurance

The decades from 1998 to 2012 witnessed the establishment and expansion of a contributory social insurance system in China. Nonetheless, this system was not built from scratch but was founded on the socialist *danwei*-based welfare system operated in China during the 1950s–1970s. A review of Chinese social health insurance development under different generations of Chinese political leadership in the postwar periods shows a persistent hierarchy in the distribution of health care benefits in the Chinese society. Contrary to many expectations, the inequality in China's health care is a result not only of the present market economy but also the previous command economy; moreover, there was inequality not only when health insurance coverage was greatly expanded in the 2000s but also when coverage was narrow before 2003. When and how did the stratification of China's health care benefits come into being? What is the institutional infrastructure that has created and maintained the welfare hierarchy? In what economic context did unprecedented welfare expansion unfold in China? In this chapter, I answer these questions by reviewing the development of social health insurance in China since 1949 and by investigating the structural features of China's health insurance system and the broader economic context of its stratified expansion since the late 1990s.

The analytical purposes of this chapter are threefold. First, the chapter provides an overview of China's social welfare development, and health care provision in particular, for readers who are not familiar with this subject. It demonstrates that stratification and inequality of health care have been persistent and reinforced since the Chinese authoritarian regime came to power in 1949. This lays the groundwork for Chapter 4 that explains the Center's interest and strategy for maintaining the benefit hierarchy and stratification in social welfare expansion. Second, this chapter examines the power structure of health policymaking and the great transformations of the Chinese economy since the late 1970s, both of which have profoundly shaped the trajectory of social health insurance development and expansion in China. The macroeconomic evolution summarized in this chapter also contextualizes the political economy of China's stratified expansion of social health insurance presented in Chapters 2 and 6. Third, the overview of China's economic reform and openness provided in this chapter highlights the

Social Protection under Authoritarianism. Xian Huang, Oxford University Press (2020). © Oxford University Press.
DOI: 10.1093/oso/9780190073640.001.0001

diversification of regional economies in China. The regional economies are important in explaining Chinese local leaders' differential responses to health insurance expansion, further elaborated in Chapter 5.

This chapter is organized as follows: Section 3.1 reviews China's social welfare development, and health care provision in particular, since 1949. Section 3.2 investigates the institutional complexity of the health policy, showing key structural features of health policymaking in China: decentralization and fragmentation. Section 3.3 examines the economic context in which the expansion of Chinese social welfare provision, including health care, took place in the 2000s.

3.1. Pathways to Social Health Insurance in China

The pathway to social health insurance in contemporary China can be summarized in three phases. The first phase began in 1949 when the PRC was founded and ended in 1978 when economic reform and openness began. In this period, welfare benefits were organized and provided by work units (*danwei*) in cities or people's communes in rural areas. In cities, welfare benefits were fully financed through state budgets because of the nationalization of industry and finance after 1956; almost everyone, except high-level officials in the party, government, or military, got a similarly low level of benefits. Although the system claimed itself egalitarian to fulfill the country's ideological commitment to socialism, there was a severe urban-rural disparity in welfare benefits.

The second phase began in 1978, when economic reform and openness were initiated in China. In this period, the previous *danwei*-based welfare system was ineffective after the collapse of people's communes in rural areas and the bankruptcy of many SOEs in cities after 1994. As a result, millions of peasants and laid-off urban workers were left without social security or health insurance. In 1998 at the height of SOE reform in cities, the central leadership announced that they were establishing a contributory social health insurance for urban formal employees, in which employers and employees share the health insurance cost. Since then, the responsibility of social insurance administration has been shifted from employers to local governments, a significant departure from the previous *danwei*-based welfare system.

The third phase, from 1998 to 2011, witnessed the establishment and expansion of social health insurance for the population outside the urban formal workforce, such as peasants, urban poor, and dependents. However, the expansion of health insurance coverage was accompanied with deepening stratification of health benefits across social strata and subnational regions.

3.1.1. Phase I (1949–1978): The *Danwei*-Based Welfare System

For most of Mao's era (1949–1976), the Chinese health care system, including financing and to some extent delivery, were organized around work units (*danwei*).[1] Each *danwei* functioned as a self-sufficient "welfare society." The system was called a *danwei*-based welfare system or Iron Rice Bowl. As part of it, urban health care was introduced in 1951;[2] the rural part was initially piloted in selected provinces in 1955 and gradually extended nationally in the early 1960s. The health care provision consisted of three programs. The Cooperative Medical Scheme (CMS, *nongcun hezuo yiliao*) financed health care for members of the agricultural communes, or peasants; the Labor Insurance Scheme (LIS, *laobao*) and Government Insurance Scheme (GIS, *gongfei yiliao*) financed health care for SOE workers and state employees (including civil servants, teachers, medical personnel, university students, and others). These three health care programs differed remarkably in organization, financing, and generosity.

The GIS was the most generous among the three health care programs in this period. It was funded directly by government budgets according to annual per capita fixed allocations and was paid for by the level of government at which people were employed (Duckett 2011). GIS beneficiaries—mainly state employees—usually received treatment free at the point of delivery, paying only a nominal fee upon arrival at a clinic or hospital (Yin 1997). By contrast, the LIS was financed by enterprises whose expenditure on employees' medical treatment was factored into those enterprises' plans and the budgets of governments with whom the enterprises were affiliated within the planning system. Beneficiaries of LIS—mainly urban workers—had to pay small out-of-pocket expenditures for very small registration fees and perhaps some co-payments for certain medicines and for dependents who were not fully financed by employee schemes (Duckett 2011). Both GIS and LIS were financed through employers' budgets, and individual employees paid no premiums. Nonetheless, bureaucratic rank and size of the employing government department, university, or enterprise had an effect, and the plans had different benefits for individuals based on factors such as an employee's rank and contract (Dillon 2015). Those with access to the best curative services free at the point of delivery were most likely to be high-ranking government officials and workers in central government or state-owned enterprises; lower-ranking officials and workers in small urban government and collectives had less generous benefits. Similarly, permanent workers received better benefits than contract workers and migrant workers, while those who were punished for criticizing the party-state and labeled "rightists" between 1957 and the early 1960s were often denied any provision at all (Dixon 1981).

The least generous health care program at that time was CMS, the one for rural populations. It was founded on the institutions of collectivized agriculture set up in the mid-1950s: hierarchically structured subcounty communes and production brigades (often equivalent to townships). The organization of CMS was decentralized, and actual arrangements and provisions varied across the Chinese countryside (Duckett 2011). There were three main sources of funding for CMS: government budgetary investment, commune and production brigade funding, and members' contributions.[3] Although established by national policy decisions, it was not substantially financed or subsidized by either central or local state budgets. Therefore, protection seems to have been sporadic and limited, particularly in poor areas, by a shortage of finance. Because CMS was locally organized and financed across many thousands of communes in China there was huge variation in when schemes began and ended as well as in the nature and the extent of the protection they provided (Huang 2013). One of the most systematic studies found that the implementation of local CMS schemes between 1969 and 1975 fluctuated and was closely tied to growth in agricultural production (Lampton 1979).

Despite the egalitarian rhetoric prevalent in Mao's era, coverage and protection in the *danwei*-based welfare system was limited. Only permanent employees of government, large factories, and other big employers had access to good quality health care. Although the system was reformed many times during the Mao era, it never overcame its initial limitations (Dillon 2015). Coverage was extended to a significant share of the urban labor force but never reached all urban residents and reached much less the peasantry who constituted the vast majority of the Chinese population. In addition, several cleavages were embedded and persistent in the *danwei*-based social welfare system.

First was the urban-rural divide. In the 1950s, the CCP's Soviet-style development strategy focused on state-led industrialization, and this contributed to an urban bias in state investment that privileged workers over farmers. Urban residents benefited from more hospital beds and doctors per capita than their rural counterparts (World Bank 1983). According to an official report, in 1964, 90% of senior health workers and 73% of intermediate-level health workers were concentrated at or above the county level (Huang 2013). Other studies in the early 1980s showed that urban per capita expenditures on health were three times those of rural areas (Liu et al. 1995). Rural health spending constituted only 17% of total health funding (Hossain 1997) even though it was meant to provide risk protection for the 80% of the population living in rural areas. Second, even within a city, people were classified into cadres, workers, army, and intellectuals. These labels affected their access to education and employment as well as their social status (Leung and Xu 2015). A fundamental difference among urban residents existed between permanent employees in the state-owned and collective sectors. Workers in collectively owned enterprises earned on average only three quarters the income of workers in the state sector, and they enjoyed few welfare benefits to soften the impact of illness or old age (Dillon 2015). Third, even within state-owned enterprises there were differences between permanent and temporary workers, with the permanent workers enjoying more generous welfare benefits than the temporary ones.

3.1.2. Phase II (1978–1998): Transition from *Danwei*-Based Welfare System to Social Health Insurance

Economically, the *danwei*-based welfare system was doomed to malfunction as the market transition was initiated in the late 1970s and then gathered speed afterward. The agricultural communes collapsed in rural areas as China decollectivized its rural economy in 1979 and introduced the household responsibility system; this system assigned individual households rights to use a piece of land and allowed them to sell in the market the food they produced beyond their required quota.[4] Without that base for funding and organization, the CMS fell apart, leaving around 90% of all peasants uninsured and having to pay the full cost of any health care and drugs out of their own pockets (Qian and Blomqvist 2014).[5] In urban areas, the SOE reforms after the 1980s caused many enterprises to fall into bankruptcy or restructuring, and a large number of SOEs were closed down. Consequently, employment levels in SOEs fell sharply, and the workers who did keep their jobs often found their employers unable to honor their commitments to the LIS scheme (Gu 2001). Moreover, the *danwei*-based welfare system placed a heavy financial burden on work units (employers). Over decades, the non-contributory nature of the system resulted not only in the extremely inefficient operation of welfare provision but also in an unlimited growth of welfare demand. The older an enterprise was, and the more retired workers it had, the heavier was the welfare burden it had to bear. This resulted in a lack of level playing field for different enterprises, even for those in the same industrial sector and same location (World Bank 1997). The problem was exacerbated by increasing competition between the state- and private-sector enterprises. The poor financial situation of SOEs throughout the 1990s led to a crisis in the *danwei*-based welfare system and eventually its end.

As the total expenses of *danwei*-based welfare soared from the mid-1980s onward, the government was aware that a restructuring of the social welfare system would have to be an indispensable part of market-oriented economic reform. Reform of the *danwei*-based welfare system formally began in 1988. During the early stage of the reform from 1988 to 1994, health reform concentrated on reducing medical care expenses rather than on building a new insurance system (Gu 2001). One of the commonly imposed reform measures was that individual patients had to share 10% to 20% of outpatient fees and 5% to

10% of hospitalization fees, and expenditure for individual workers was capped at 5% of their annual wage or at the level of their monthly wage (Hong 1992). These measures were followed by "risk-pooling" experiments, in which groups of enterprises pooled funds to pay for treating their current or retired employees' serious illnesses (Duckett 2004). After the experiments with "co-payment" and "risk pooling" of health insurance in some cities from 1988 to 1994, compulsory social health insurance combined with individual premium contributions began to operate in about 60 Chinese cities in 1994 (Gu 2001).

Finally, the UEBMI was established by the central government in late 1998. According to this policy decision, all cities had to set up contribution-based basic health insurance schemes by the end of 1999. In these, employers were required to pay 6% to 8% of their total payroll into a local health insurance fund (HIF) and dedicate health insurance accounts (HIAs) held in the name of each employee. Employees were to pay 2% of their wages into their HIAs. In principal, HIAs pay for an employee's treatment costing up to 10% of the local average annual wage, after which the HIF pays. There was a limit on how much the HIF would pay for any single individual, set at four to six times the average annual wage (Duckett 2004).

3.1.3. Phase III (1999–2011): Expansion of Social Health Insurance

Compared to the former GIS and LIS, the UEBMI established in 1998 expanded coverage to non-state sectors and enterprises in the early 2000s, but its coverage was still limited for many reasons. First, enterprises in poor financial health were not able to pay the employer's portion of health insurance contributions. In particular, private firms and small businesses, whose employees were mostly young migrants, found it too costly to enroll them in urban employee health insurance. Second, members of certain societal groups, especially informal workers, peasants, and unemployed people, enjoyed no health security at all due to the institutional design of social health insurance that mainly targeted formal employees (but not their dependents). As a result, individuals' out-of-pocket payments as a share of total health expenditure grew from 20% to almost 60% between 1978 and 2002 (Zhang and Liu 2014). By 2003, the coverage rate of UEBMI was only 36%, and self-paying patients made up a large share of the health care market (Gu and Zhang 2006). Moreover, the urban-rural divide in the pre-reform health system was reinforced. During the 1980s, de-collectivization reform in the rural areas was considered successful. Peasants' income improved significantly and poverty rates were reduced dramatically. But the collective scheme of health care (CMS) was rapidly eroded, followed by a declining capacity of local governments to raise funds for public and social services. Nearly 80% of government health spending was going to urban health care, even though city dwellers represented only 42% of the country's population (Huang 2011). In 2000, the World Health Organization ranked China 144th out of 191 countries on overall performance of health care; in terms of health equity, China was 188th, almost at the bottom (Herd et al. 2010).

The SARS (severe acute respiratory syndrome) outbreak in 2003 shocked the Chinese central leaders, exposed the inadequacies of China's public health protection, and showed how the government's neglect had left the health care system unprepared to deal with its core responsibilities. In 2004, the vice minister of health, Zhu Qingsheng, said that 60% to 80% of farmers who were seriously ill died at home because they could not afford care (Huang 2011). According to a study by the State Council's Development Research Center (DRC) in 2005, the employment-based health insurance system and associated reforms turned China's health care into the exclusive privilege of the rich. More people were brought to poverty because of their high medical expenses.[6] Even though the economic performance of China in the 2000s remained impressive, the World Bank warned in 2006 that social issues, including inequality and environmental sustainability, seemed to have worsened (Leung and Xu 2015).

Since every citizen is a stakeholder in the health care system, fixing the problematic system is especially important for maintaining social stability in China. Unlike the pension system, in which a long time lag exists between contribution and consumption, social health insurance is more likely to have an instant and tangible impact on people's daily lives. An ineffective health care system had long been fueling social agitation in China. The Chinese government's neglect of health care in the 1990s also contributed directly to the rise of Falun Gong, a spiritual movement that includes a form of traditional Chinese exercises said to marshall supernatural forces to achieve good health, and the very movement that the government had sought to repress (Huang 2011). Since health care was inaccessible or too expensive for many citizens, millions turned to the spiritual movement for the health benefits that are believed to stem from its traditional Chinese exercises. By 1998, there were as many as 70 million Falun Gong members in China, and the regime fomented turmoil at home and long-lasting protests abroad by cracking down on Falun Gong in 1999 (Huang 2011). Public complaints and grievances about the country's health care system became the most severe social-political challenge the Chinese leaders had faced since the 1989 Tiananmen crackdown. More than 73% of China's hospitals reported violent conflicts between patients and health care workers in 2005 (Huang 2011). The then central party secretary, Hu Jintao, who took power in 2002, faced a society in which people were feeling increasingly insecure and worried about the rising cost of social services. A public opinion survey showed that corruption, health care, and food safety were the public's top concerns.[7] It is clear that the Chinese authoritarian government faced a formidable challenge to maintain social and political stability.[8]

A series of measures to address the soaring public grievances and complaints about health care were introduced from 2003 onward. The first was the NRCMS, introduced in late 2003 to replace the former CMS and aimed at providing health insurance to the rural population. By the end of 2010, in 22 out of 31 provinces, more than 90% of the rural population was covered by the NRCMS program thanks to huge government subsidies (see Figure 3.1). Under the NRCMS, peasants could receive partial reimbursement for their medical expenses in exchange for a small annual fee (about $1.50 in 2003). Second, a health insurance program known as URBMI, was kicked off in 2007 for the 420 million urban residents not covered by the UEBMI. In 2008, the government announced its intention to roll out the URBMI program in half of China's cities by the end of 2008 and to ultimately extend coverage to 100% of cities by 2010. By the end of 2010, more than half of urban residents in 12 provinces were covered by the URBMI program, again with considerable government subsidies (Figure 3.2). Target groups for the URBMI are children, the elderly, the disabled, and other non-working urban residents.

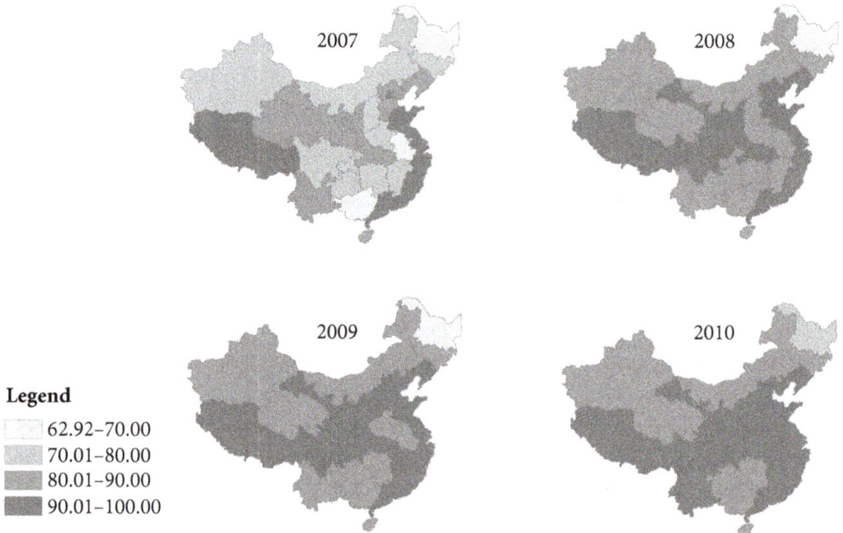

Figure 3.1 Coverage of the New Rural Cooperative Medical Scheme, 2007–2010 (% insured)

Data source: China Health Statistical Yearbooks.

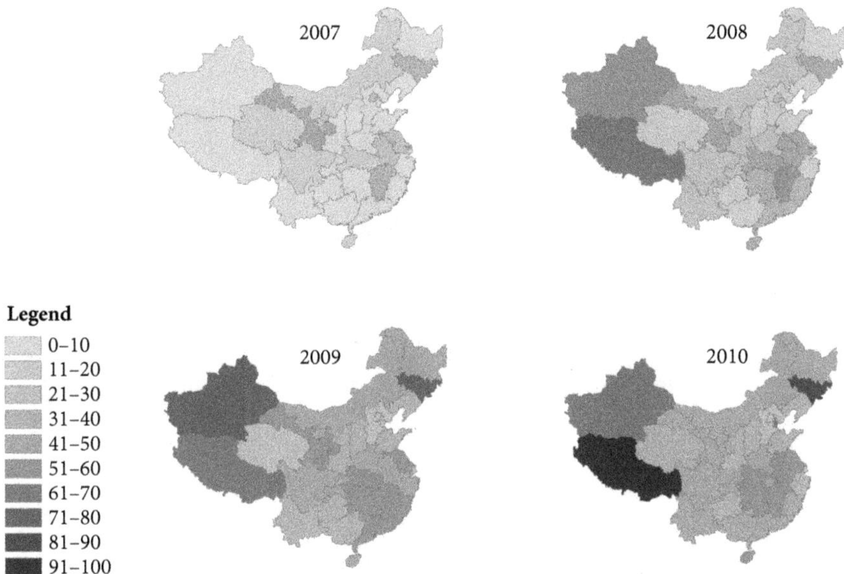

Figure 3.2 Coverage of Urban Residents Basic Medical Insurance, 2007–2010 (% insured)

Data source: China Human Resources and Social Security Yearbook.

Furthermore, in 2009, the Chinese government unveiled its most ambitious health reform plan to date and committed to spending an additional US$125 billion in the following three years, providing affordable and equitable basic health care for all. About 50% of the government's 2009 health reform funding was targeted for subsidization of enrollment in social health insurance.[9] Stimulated by the new influx of funding, the provincial average of UEBMI coverage increased from 68.02% to 95.88% in 2009, despite the presence of discernible regional variation (Figure 3.3). At the end of 2010, social health insurance coverage in 26 out of 31 Chinese provinces exceeded 80% (Figure 3.4). Since then, a social health insurance system with an aim of "universal" (*quanmin*)[10] coverage has been established. In 2013, out-of-pocket expenses as a share of total health expenditures declined to 33.9%, bringing China more in line with upper-middle-income countries, where out-of-pocket spending on health care averaged 31.0% (Dickson 2016).[11]

Accompanying the expansion of Chinese social health insurance coverage, however, has been an increasing stratification of health care benefits across social groups and subnational regions. The "universal" coverage of a social health insurance system has failed to address the huge gaps in access to health care between rural and urban residents, between public and private sectors, and between

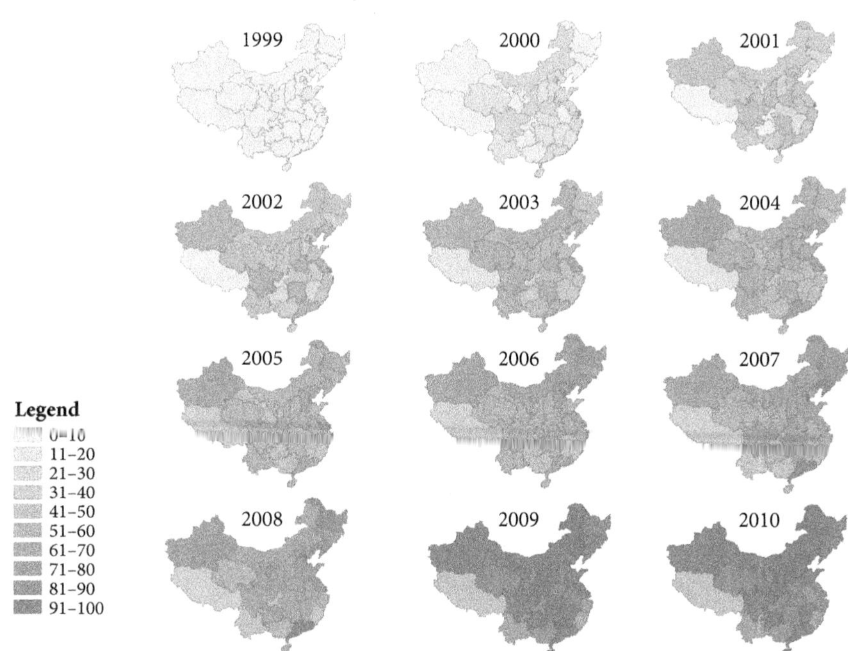

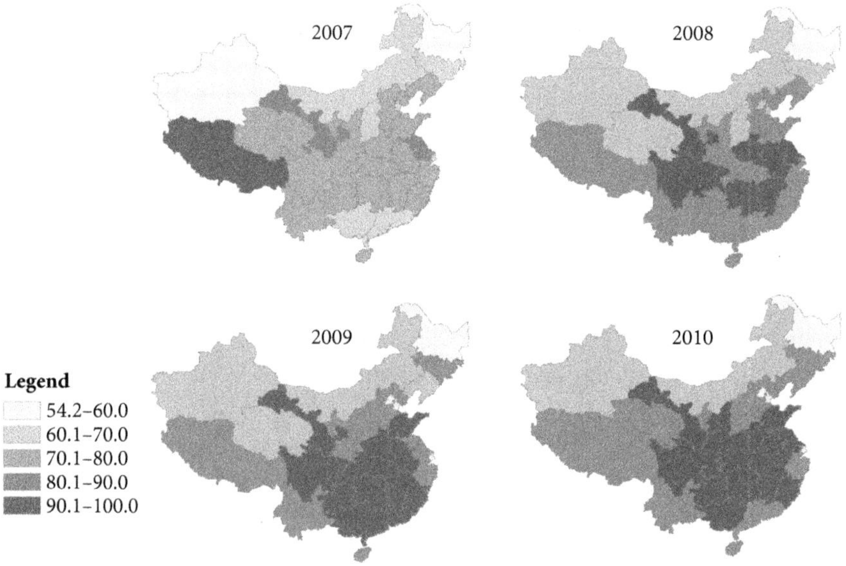

labor market insiders and outsiders. In 2006, China's former vice minister of health, Yin Dakui, revealed that 80% of China's health budget was spent on just 8.5 million government officials (Huang 2011). In 2010, the expenditure of the UEBMI program was 13 times the summed expenditures of the URBMI and NRCMS programs, meaning that the smallest group of social health insurance beneficiaries—urban formal employees—enjoyed an overwhelming share of the social health insurance benefits in China. A report by the Ministry of Human Resources and Social Insurance (MoHRSS) demonstrated that the UEBMI's inpatient reimbursement rate was notably higher than the URBMI's: the provincial average of inpatient reimbursement rates for UEBMI beneficiaries (mainly urban state-sector employees) is 67.68% of their medical expenditure and the rate for URBMI beneficiaries (mainly urban non-working people including the elderly, children, and students) is only 55.32%.[12] A similar pattern can be found for outpatient reimbursement. In 2010, the provincial average of outpatient reimbursement for UEBMI beneficiaries was 98.23 yuan per patient, one third higher than for URBMI beneficiaries. The level of benefits in the NRCMS program for rural residents, meanwhile, was even lower than the benefits offered through the URBMI program. According to a government formula based on per capita incomes, in 2010, a farmer might have been reimbursed for inpatient services only about one sixth as much as an urban formal employee in the state sector (Huang 2013). Furthermore, regional disparities in health care benefits are substantial. For example, the per capita expenditure for urban social health insurance in Beijing stands at 1,852 yuan/person (averaged from 2007 through 2010), more than four times the per capita expenditure in Jiangxi province.

As leaders became more concerned about the inequality in the expanded social health insurance and its political consequences, the policy to integrate health insurance across social groups and across subnational regions appeared on the government agenda and was frequently mentioned in government conferences. However, by 2010, little had been achieved in equalizing health care beyond policy deliberations and experiments. The Center's hesitation to reduce the elite groups' welfare privileges and the distributive conflicts among localities with respect to pooling the risks and redistributing benefits of social health insurance have been the fundamental obstacles to health insurance integration.

3.2. Power Structure of China's Health Policymaking

The tortuous development of China's social health insurance since the late 1990s has long-lasting features of decentralization and fragmentation in terms of policy authority and power. These two features might not necessarily result from the authoritarian nature of the Chinese regime, but they do echo the crucial institutional features of the "fragmented authoritarianism" model, which Kenneth G. Liberthal and Michael Oksenberg have characterized as policymaking in post-Mao China (Liberthal and Oksenberg 1988).[13] Under fragmented authoritarianism, policy outcomes are partly shaped by the incorporation of interests of the implementation agencies, such as bureaucratic agencies and subnational regions charged with enforcing the policy (Liberthal and Oksenberg, 1988; Mertha, 2009).

3.2.1. Decentralization

Although China is a unitary state in a legal sense, it is a country whose economy is managed in a highly decentralized manner, as the central government has delegated a great deal of authority over economic and social policies to provincial and lower levels of government. China's social health insurance system is vertically decentralized and horizontally fragmented. The highest executive organ in China is the State Council (or the central government) led by the premier and composed of close to 30 ministers plus heads of other administrative agencies. A vertical functional structure, which runs from the central government through several layers of local governments, creates strong competing systemic interests. There is a dissonance of goals between the principal (the central government, especially the top political leaders) who wishes to address public grievances and related social unrest by providing effective health care and services, and the agents (local officials) who wish to pursue their own interests (mainly career advancement) in the vertical functional structure. The central government (the Center) has broad political responsibilities and is more concerned with threats to the regime. The Center usually initiates new social policies and pilots the general direction of the policies for regime stability. The Center's desire to prevent social unrest was clearly behind the social welfare reforms in the 1980s and 1990s: priority was given to limiting the erosion of the pre-reform urban labor insurance as unrest is more fearful and visible in cities than in the countryside (Duckett 2003). Chapter 4 will further explore the Center's political and economic considerations for establishing and expanding social health insurance in the 2000s.

The work of specifying and implementing social and welfare reform policies, however, is handled by the local governments (provincial and subprovincial levels). The policy choices of local governments are not only linked to local leaders' self-interest but are also constrained and compelled by local socioeconomic and financial conditions. As a result, any opposition or bargaining from the local governments can compromise or protract policy implementation. Particularly with social health insurance, the central government has relied significantly on local governments to specify and develop policies, such as setting contribution rates (insurance premium), designing benefit packages, and defining eligibilities. This has allowed local interests and local leaders discretion to influence policymaking and implementation. Local leaders' preferences resemble those of central leaders in that they also seek to prevent social unrest and develop the economy, two key targets on which their performance is evaluated. But China's decentralized fiscal and administrative systems mean that in social policies, the local governments also must balance the need to preempt social unrest with the need to promote economic development. With evidence collected from fieldwork, Chapter 5 elaborates on the various local trade-offs and policy choices made in the expansion and stratification of social health insurance in the 2000s.

Despite the possibility that the decentralized system of social welfare provision has the institutional flexibility and agility to respond effectively to fluid and rapidly evolving policy challenges, it also has the potential to further obfuscate already blurred lines of responsibility and accountability, making it harder for citizens to obtain the services to which they are entitled, especially in China's relatively non-transparent authoritarian governance. Under China's decentralized public financing system, the Center shoulders about 30% of all public health funding and local governments are expected to finance the rest (Huang 2011). However, public health experts have found that many localities, in expanding social health insurance, were reluctant to specify how much of the cost they would subsidize and what measures they would take to achieve the targeted coverage rate that was uniformly set above 90% of local population.[14] In addition, the decentralized design of social health insurance leaves much room for strategic disobedience or manipulation by local leaders as illustrated in Chapter 5.

When China's urban health care scheme was first set up in the 1950s, it was handled by the official All-China Federation of Trade Unions, but after 1967, it was handed over to enterprises. The establishment of city- or county-based social health insurance in the late 1990s was essentially "centralization" of the pre-reform *danwei*-based system that operated during the 1960s through the 1980s. Since the reform in the 1980s, responsibilities of financing and risk pooling of social health insurance were substantially removed from enterprises and shifted to local governments, a measure aimed at alleviating the SOEs' burdens and improving risk sharing in health financing. Nonetheless, this change in social welfare provision also generated unintended outcomes of increasing the power of local agents. Local desire for accumulating pension funds was considered a key factor that facilitated China's rapid establishment and expansion of pensions in the early 2000s (Frazier 2010).[15] Local governments that might use a portion of social insurance funds as income to cover their administrative expenses have a particularly strong interest in keeping social insurance pooled at local levels, and this creates a formidable obstacle at the local level to further centralization of social welfare provision. China's social health insurance system has thus remained decentralized.

3.2.2. Fragmentation

Throughout China's history of social welfare development, no single ministry or bureaucracy has been entirely in charge of health policy. Most of the time, rural health insurance has been under the control of the Ministry of Health (MoH), while urban health insurance has fallen under the jurisdictions of the MoHRSS. Within the central government, at least four ministries (Human Resources and Social Security, Health, Finance, and Civil Affairs), one leadership group (Health and Medical Reform), and one commission (National Development and Reform Commission) are involved in health policymaking, either by jointly issuing official directives or by participating in health insurance research. The goals of Chinese ministries in health reform perfectly reflect widespread bureaucratic behavior: to increase bureaucratic power through larger budgets, more personnel slots, and greater regulatory power (Downs 1965; Hsiao 2007).

The MoH mostly represents the interest of the public hospitals, physicians, and other health workers. It plays a critical role in shaping health policy and managing and coordinating various health activities (Hsiao 2007; Huang 2013). It tends to defend health service providers' income, and in the early 1980s, it was behind measures permitting private practice and raising treatment fees.[16] Although the MoH continued to want to play a key role in social health insurance, in the 2000s its influence was reduced by the creation of the MoHRSS and it was further downsized to a vice-ministerial-level agency in 2013 named the Commission of Health and Family Planning.[17]

The former Ministry of Labor and Personnel, and then, from 1988 until 1998, the Ministry of Labor (renamed as MoHRSS after 2008) was responsible for pre-reform labor insurance (LIS). It tends to defend the interests of enterprises, especially SOEs (World Bank 1997). In the 1980s, it was involved in attempts to limit health spending by introducing employee co-payments and has also tended to emphasize the importance of redistribution and risk pooling (Yin 1997). But the MoHRSS has been absolved of any responsibility for the long-term non-working population, including dependents and urban poor. It is the Ministry of Civil Affairs that is now charged with poverty relief and medical assistance for the poor and the disabled.

The Ministry of Finance (MoF) is the bureaucratic agency responsible for balancing central government revenues and expenditures and is, therefore, involved in all policy areas (Liberthal and Oksenberg 1988). It is often portrayed as fiscally conservative and the "chief defender of the state" (Shirk 1993), seeking to minimize excessive budgetary commitments and avoid deficits. It has preferred to fund social insurance schemes for the working population over schemes paid from general taxation that would leave the state with greater responsibilities. The MoF is also likely to have backed a decentralized health insurance system because it would shift fiscal responsibilities to local governments (Duckett 2003). The National Development and Reform Commission, charged with economic planning and administering prices of important products including drugs and medical services, holds similarly conservative attitudes toward social insurance, that is, minimizing state investment and fiscal commitments to subsidizing potentially costly national schemes of social health insurance.

The different interests of these bureaucratic actors in health policy have led to bargaining, struggling, compromising, and consensus building among them. For example, health care provision has evolved incrementally from experiments with enterprise risk pooling and co-payments in the 1980s to comprehensive social health insurance for the employed in the early 1990s. This trajectory is the one that would be most acceptable to the key ministerial players: the early enterprise risk pooling and individual co-payments helped the MoHRSS solve the financial problems of some SOEs but would not have harmed hospital income or drawn on state finances and so would not have been opposed by the MoH and MoF (Duckett 2003).

Since the horizontal fragmentation of authority at the central level is carried down to each level of local governments, the interests of central ministries are replicated in their equivalent bureaus at the local levels (local equivalents). Municipal bureaus of MoHRSS, like their ministry, have an interest in seeing the social risk pooling for urban employees succeed (so that governments avoid direct financing and provision roles) because they are responsible for overseeing the management and usage of the pooled fund for urban employees. Similarly, municipal bureaus of MoH, following their ministerial superiors who have historically represented the interest of public hospitals, support health care provision all through public facilities. Local experiments with social health insurance policies thus became a way for individual ministries within the central government to promote their preferred reform direction and organizational interests by gathering support among their local equivalents. For example, the MoH, which initiated and administered CMS and the NRCMS later, and the MoHRSS, which was in charge of LIS and UEBMI and later URBMI, all claim credit for establishing and developing these programs under their respective supervision. Both MoH and MoHRSS have shown strong interest in taking over each other's supervised health insurance programs. Interestingly, they have implicitly resisted or explicitly refused to allow their respective social health insurance programs to be taken over by the other, while encouraging their local equivalents to merge the other's health insurance program into their own. They have often directed and sponsored local equivalents to actively initiate and implement policy experiments that facilitate their respective central ministry's capability to gain power or advantage during ministerial competition and struggle to manage the social health insurance funds at the central level.

However, it is important to note that in China, local interest and priority often trump the ministerial preferences in policy deliberation and implementation. As ministries nominally hold the same rank as provincial governments, their local branches or bureaus are subordinate to respective local governments. For example, both municipal bureaus of MoHRSS and MoH count on the municipal government for personnel, budgets, and facilities. As a result, it is the local governments—province, city, and county governments specifically—that have the final say in making and implementing local health policy, including decisions on the detail of social health insurance. Any policy experimentation in local health care or social health insurance cannot succeed or last without support from local political leaders whose policy preferences are shaped by both local interest and that of the center leaders.

Figure 3.5 displays the power structure of health policymaking in China. The decentralization and fragmentation of power or authority, with various policy preferences competing both vertically (between upper and lower levels of governments) and horizontally (among different lines of bureaus), have resulted in an incremental and protracted health reform process. Huge regional variation

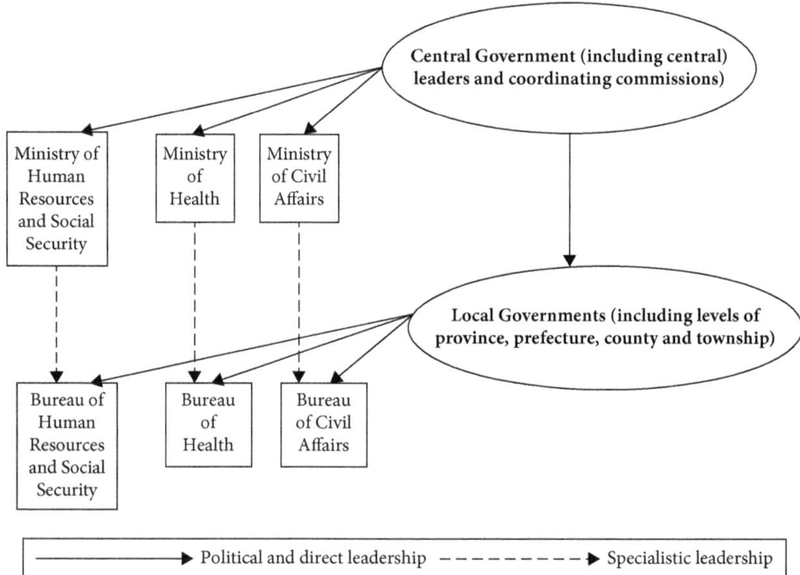

Figure 3.5 Structure of Health Policy Authority

and uneven implementation of social health insurance policies are bound to emerge under such policy authority structure.

3.3. Economic Context of China's Social Welfare Expansion

Social welfare policy is not made in a vacuum. Whether in democracies or autocracies, the profile of social welfare policies is closely related to the "production regime" (Soskice 1999; Haggard and Kaufman 2008; Wibbels and Ahlquist 2011).[18] China is not an exception in this regard. Although this book focuses on political actors and their interests and strategies in social welfare provision, the macroeconomic situations and the regional economies in which the political actors' interests and strategies play out are an important background for understanding the temporal and regional variations of social welfare provision. The Chinese production regime changes over time and across regions. This constitutes the economic context of China's social welfare expansion in the 2000s.

3.3.1. Economic Development and Structural Changes

Expanding social welfare benefits, no matter which group it targets, requires plenty of resources. Unlike the hierarchy or stratification of social welfare provision which is predetermined by the regime's authoritarian nature and constant in China over the past decades, expansion of social welfare provision is feasible only when the regime has resources available to support it. The timing of China's social welfare expansion is consistent with this economic rule. China's expansion of social welfare provision took place during the economic upturn in the first decade of the 2000s when its economy had been growing the fastest and smoothest since 1992 (Figure 3.6).[19] Thanks to the continuous economic growth, resources accumulated by the government for distribution increased significantly. During this economic upturn in the 2000s, government fiscal revenues increased steadily with the central government's budgetary revenue exceeding the local ones and remaining higher than the local revenues by 1% to 2% of GDP (Figure 3.7). Given the substantial GDP growth in the 2000s, the rising fiscal revenue as a share of GDP indicates greater increase of government revenue during the period. In terms of revenue sources (Figure 3.8), the importance of the business tax (e.g., company income tax, business tax) increased considerably while the importance of the consumption tax (e.g., value-added tax and consumption tax) declined slightly after 1994;[20] agricultural tax and tariffs accounted for less than 10% of government tax revenue in China throughout the 2000s.

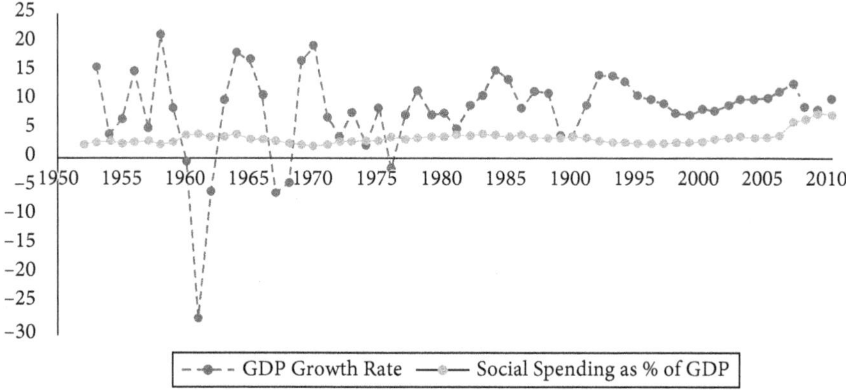

Figure 3.6 GDP Growth and Government Social Spending as Share of GDP in China (1950–2020)

Note: GDP was calculated at constant prices. Data from *China Statistical Yearbook*.

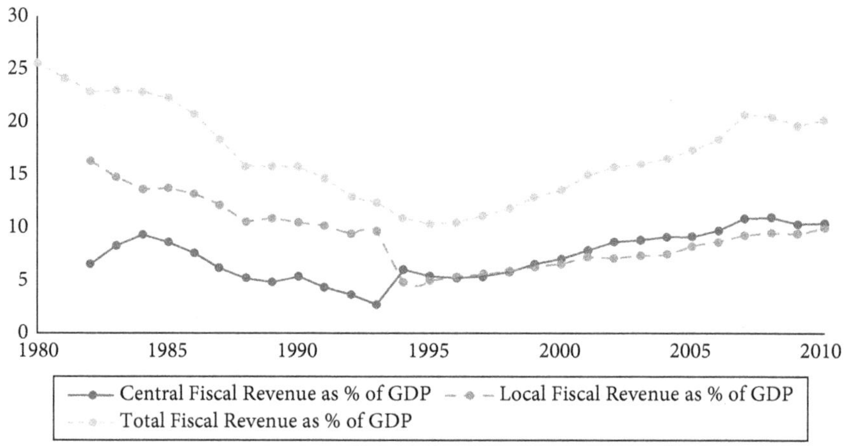

Figure 3.7 Total, Central, and Local Fiscal Revenues as Shares of GDP in China (1980–2010)

Note: GDP was calculated at current prices. Data from *China Statistical Yearbook*.

In the first decade of the 2000s, China overtook the United Kingdom, France, Germany, and Japan to claim second place in global economic ranking, trailing the United States.[21] During this period, China's economy was significantly boosted by exports and investment. Figure 3.9 depicts exports, investment, and household consumption, respectively, as a share of GDP from 1980 to 2010. China's entry into the World Trade Organization (WTO) in 2001 ushered in

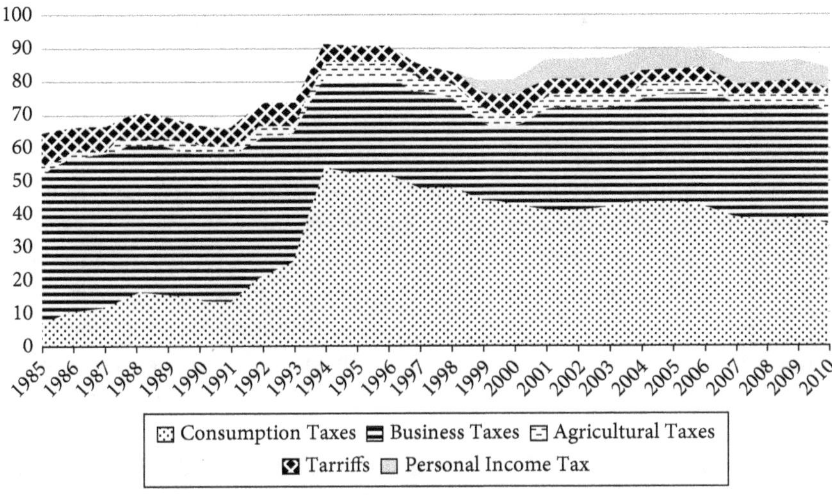

Figure 3.8 Composition of Tax Revenues in China (1985–2010)

Note: Consumption taxes include value added tax and consumption tax. Business taxes include company income tax and business tax. Data from *China Statistical Yearbook*.

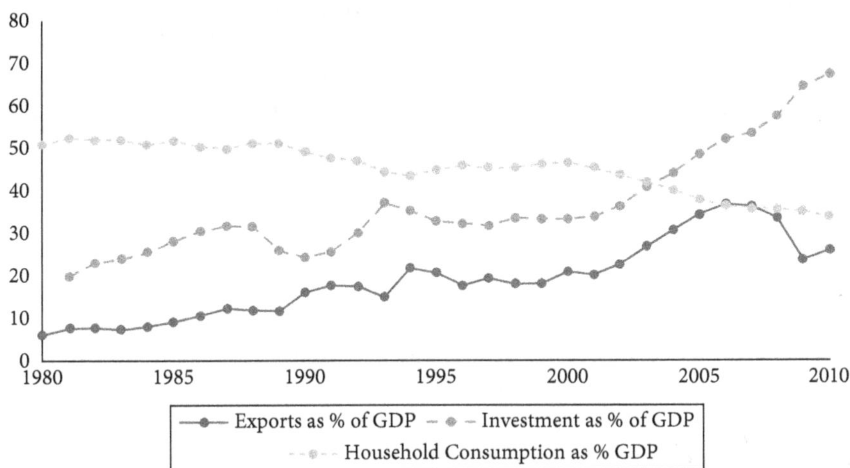

Figure 3.9 Exports, Investment, and Household Consumption as Shares of GDP in China (1980–2010)

Note: GDP was calculated at current prices. Data from *China Statistical Yearbook*.

an export boom, with exports averaging nearly 30% of its GDP from 2002 to 2010 despite a notable decrease during the 2008 global financial crisis. Besides exports, China's economic growth was relying heavily on investment that accounted for 50% of the GDP on average in the 2000s. The investment mainly came from domestic savings and was partially made by the governments of different levels. In contrast, the share of household consumption in GDP fell from 50% in 1979 to 35% in 2010. Overall, these macroeconomic data highlight several structural changes in the Chinese economy during the 2000s: (1) substantial economic openness; (2) increasing dependence on investment for GDP growth; (3) increasing importance of business (e.g., firms) in generating tax revenue.

Given the structural changes in the Chinese economy during the 2000s, the regime must pay more attention to social welfare issues for several economic reasons. First, economic openness that connects the domestic economy to the global market brings about higher volatility and risk of labor dislocation in the domestic market. For an authoritarian regime that is wary of labor militancy and social unrest, it is imperative to cope with this risk preemptively by providing basic social protection. Major social insurance provisions including pensions, health insurance, and unemployment insurance were initiated in China during the tide of SOE restructuring and layoffs in the late 1990s. The further opening up of Chinese markets to foreign investors and competitors in the early 2000s was accompanied by a dramatic expansion of social insurance coverage to private sector employees, informal workers, and migrant workers.

Second, heavy reliance on exports and investment for economic development makes the Chinese regime vulnerable to external shocks. This motivates it to strategically shift the driving forces of the economy and encourage domestic consumption and demand for sustainable growth. Establishing a decent social safety net, including a social insurance system, is one means of bolstering domestic consumption, insofar as the government can reduce disincentives to household consumption. The 2008 global financial crisis hit China hard and put the world economy into chronic recession. Since then, the Chinese regime has put domestic consumption at the center of its economic plan, strategically shifting the economy away from its heavy dependence on exports and investment, and toward a more sustainable reliance on domestic consumption. As then Premier Wen Jiabao said, "To boost domestic demand is a long-term strategic policy for China's economic growth and the way for us to tackle the financial crisis and stave off external risks."[22]

Third, China's exports have been concentrated on labor-intensive manufactured goods (including machinery and electronics), reflecting its abundant labor endowment. To maintain this comparative advantage in the international market and to upgrade industry in the domestic market, the government needs to invest in human capital, such as developing education and public health. To some extent the Chinese welfare regime in the post-reform era resembles the East Asian "productivist" welfare regime (Rudra 2007) that gives higher priority to human-capital-related programs such as basic education and health care than to protective programs such as unemployment benefits and living allowances. Figure 3.10

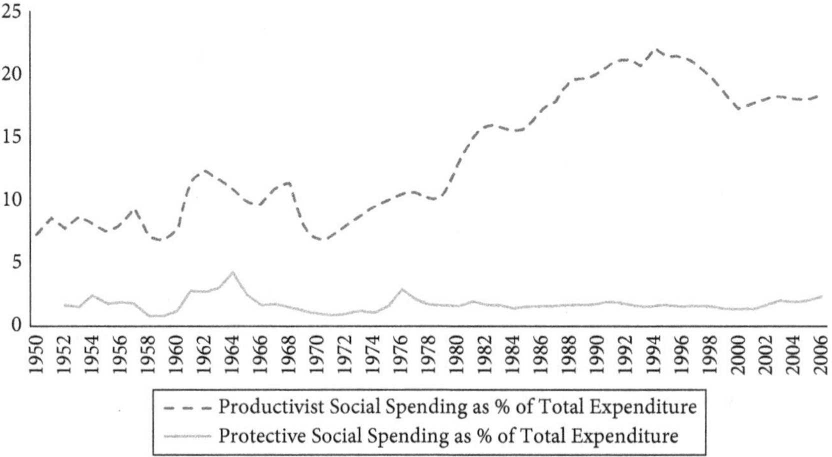

Figure 3.10 Productivist and Protective Spending as Shares of Government Expenditure in China (1950–2010)

Data source: China Compendium of Statistics (xin zhongguo liushi nian tongji ziliao huibian) by National Bureau of Statistics.

compares the shares of productivist spending (including education, science, and development, health spending) and protective spending (including pensions, social assistance, living allowances for injury, disability, or natural disaster) by the Chinese government from 1950 to 2006. It shows that the gap between these two types of spending significantly enlarged after 1978 with the productivist social spending far exceeding the protective one.

The structural changes in the domestic economy in the 2000s also constitute some constraints for the Chinese regime to expand social welfare provision. The country's heavy reliance on export and investment in economic development constrained its ability to increase the generosity of social welfare. Throughout the expansion, the regime attempted to provide basic, rather than comprehensive, social benefits to the labor forces without radically increasing labor costs. Until 2010, Chinese political leaders and ministerial officials relentlessly stressed that social insurance should be "low in generosity but broad in coverage."[23] Many Chinese private-owned enterprises complained that the burdens of social insurance contributions were too heavy and that they were not interested in joining social insurance programs (Gao and Rickne 2014, 2017; Giles et al. 2013; Nyland et al. 2006).[24] Accordingly, local governments that had obsessed about attracting investment sometimes compromised in expanding social insurance in private sectors (Solinger and Hu 2012; Frazier 2010; Gallagher and Dong 2011). During the 2008 Global Financial Crisis, the Center explicitly allowed enterprises to pay less social insurance contribution in order to keep employment.[25] Business's interest was evidently taken into account in both the legislation and policy implementation of social welfare expansion in China (Kornreich et al. 2012; Gallagher and Dong 2011; Gallagher et al. 2015).

In sum, the economic development and structural changes in China during the first decade of the 2000s both compelled and constrained the expansion of social welfare provision. On the one hand, social welfare expansion that can enhance social protection and increase domestic consumption and investment in human capital, became attractive to the Chinese regime partially for the purpose of economic development. In addition, the spectacular economic growth from 2001 to 2007 facilitated a dramatic expansion of social welfare provision by steadily increasing government revenue. On the other hand, the regime's dependence on exports, investment, and business tax for economic and revenue growth confined the social welfare expansion to providing minimum and basic benefits to the broad social groups, as the regime was wary of increasing both labor costs and resistance from the privileged groups including employers. Note that both the momentum and constraint of social welfare expansion vary across subnational regions that remarkably differ in levels of economic development, structure of the economy, and configuration of the labor market.

3.3.2. Diversification of Regional Economies

The third plenary session of the CCP's 11th Central Committee in 1978 marked the beginning of economic reform and openness in China. The decentralization of the economy and the devolution of authority and decision-making power to local governments are key characteristics of the Chinese reforms (Gallagher 2005). Understanding the regional economies in which the local governments' choices for social welfare expansion were made is as important as understanding the macroeconomic evolution and structural change.

As with other large countries, the Chinese economy experiences large regional differences. The sequencing of the Chinese reform process (i.e., foreign investment and trade liberalization first, private-sector development second, and significant SOE reform last) further reproduced and reinforced the regional disparities in China. Following Deng Xiaoping's directive of "allowing some people to get rich first," the Seventh Five-Year Plan (1986–1990) explicitly projected the country developing "three economic belts": the east for export-oriented industrialization, the inland for agriculture and energy, and the west for animal husbandry and natural resource extraction (Rithmire 2015; Fan 1997). The sequential staging of economic reform and openness continued into the early 2000s when regional disparities and income inequality stemming from decades of uneven development and reform policies began to attract political attention and some redistributive measures to counteract them (Rithmire 2015; Wallace 2014). The differentiation of regional economies during the economic reforms, specifically the distinct political economies of the Chinese coastal region (Beijing, Tianjian, Hebei, Shanghai, Jiangsu, Zhejiang, Fujian, Shandong, Guangdong, and Hainan), central/inland region (Shanxi, Anhui, Jiangxi, Henan, Hubei, and Hunan), northeastern region (Liaoning, Jilin, and Heilongjiang) and western region (Inner Mongolia, Guangxi, Chongqing, Sichuan, Guizhou, Yunnan, Tibet, Shaanxi, Gansu, Qinghai, Ningxia, and Xinjiang) is another key to understanding and explaining the regional variation of China's social welfare expansion in the 2000s.

The coastal region was given more resources and support for economic development in the 1980s and the1990s. Reform measures such as building Special Economic Zones (Shenzhen, Zhuhai, Shantou cities of Guangdong province, and Xiamen city of Fujian province) and Coastal Open Cities (Dalian, Qinhuangdao, Yantai, Qingdao, Ningbo, Wenzhou, Fuzhou, Guangzhou, Lianyugang, Nantong, Zhanjiang, Beihai, Tianjin, and Shanghai) deliberately conferred selected localities in the coastal region unprecedented preferential policies, such as tax holidays, reduced limits on bank loans, land use, currency exchange, and relaxed requirements for administrative approval of industrial parks, all in order to attract foreign investment and increase trade. For the Chinese regime, the foreign-invested sector functioned as a source of new competition for the state sector, as a laboratory for sensitive labor reforms, and as an ideological justification for deeper reform (Gallagher 2005). Initially confining foreign investment to the coastal cities obviated the need for what would have been protracted and painful negotiations over national policy (Rithmire 2015). The entrepreneurial local governments in the coastal region played a role like the East Asian developmental state (Ang 2016a, 2016b; Ong 2012) in cultivating a pro-business environment, providing public goods (e.g., infrastructure, contract enforcement), and facilitating research and development (R&D) in technology and science realms. Against this backdrop, the coastal region outperformed other Chinese regions in various aspects of economic development.

Table 3.1 presents the key economic indicators averaged throughout 2003–2010 for the Chinese regions: coastal, northeastern, central, and western regions, respectively. The level of economic development, indicated by GDP per capita, clearly falls from east to west in China: the coastal region was the richest while the western region is the poorest. Foreign trade per capita in the coastal region was 18 times larger than in the western region. In terms of agricultural development, the northeastern region had the highest output per capita thanks to its fertile land. The central and western regions lagged far behind the other regions in industrial and service sectors (their per capita secondary and tertiary industry outputs were less than half of those of the

Table 3.1 Economic Development in Different Chinese Regions (2003–2010)

	Coastal Region	Northeastern Region	Central Region	Western Region
GDP per capita	30,654.4	21,285.3	14,596.3	13,038.4
Foreign trade per capita	27,835.3	5,733.5	1,505.0	1,573.7
Primary industry output per capita	17,388.1	20,087.7	17,090.1	16,114.1
Secondary industry output per capita	123,292.3	86,733.1	57,770.9	48,479.5
Tertiary industry output per capita	102,447.9	63,198.5	41,434.0	39,515.6
Fiscal revenue per capita	21,930.8	13,601.1	7,893.2	8,882.0
Urban household disposable income	16,210.0	11,020.5	11,101.8	11,005.8
Rural household disposable income	5,726.5	4,283.4	3,744.1	2,988.1

Notes:

1. The coastal region includes 10 provinces: Beijing, Tianjian, Hebei, Shanghai, Jiangsu, Zhejiang, Fujian, Shandong, Guangdong, and Hainan. The northeastern region includes three provinces: Liaoning, Jilin, and Heilongjiang. The central region includes six provinces: Shanxi, Anhui, Jiangxi, Henan, Hubei, and Hunan. The western region includes 12 provinces: Inner Mongolia, Guangxi, Chongqing, Sichuan, Guizhou, Yunnan, Tibet, Shaanxi, Gansu, Qinghai, Ningxia, and Xinjiang.

2. The unit of foreign trade per capita is USD; the unit of the other items is RMB.

3. Data were averaged from 2003 to 2010.

Data source: China Statistical Yearbook of Regional Economy, 2004–2010.

coastal region). Accordingly, differences in local state capacity among these regions, measured by local government revenue per capita, were considerably large: the governments in the coastal region collected more than twice the revenue of their counterparts in the other regions. Although urban-rural disparity was large in all four regions, it was most serious in the western region and least serious in the northeastern region. Urban household disposable income in the coastal region was almost 1.5 times as much as the other regions, while the difference among the other three regions in urban household disposable income was much smaller.

Like China's export-oriented market economy, labor-intensive manufacturing sectors in particular took off in the coastal region during the 1980s and were significantly boosted by China's accession to the WTO in the early 2000s; demand for labor surged and generated unprecedented employment opportunities for the massive pool of peasant workers. The immense labor reserve was released from agriculture during de-collectivization in the late 1970s, when collective land use rights were redistributed to rural households. Starting from 1984, peasants were allowed to move into cities and towns for work and business without changing their rural status, on condition that they were responsible for arranging their own food grain, capital, and housing (Solinger 1991). The state's restrictions on rural-to-urban migration were further reduced throughout several experimental *hukou* reforms in the 1990s and 2000s (Wallace 2014). This exerted profound yet disparate impacts on the labor market across China's regions. Rural-to-urban migrant workers account for a considerable part of the overall labor force. The total stock of "rural migrant labor" was estimated to be about 155 million in 2010, over 10% of the Chinese population (Chan 2012). But distribution of migrant workers is extremely uneven across regions. The coastal region, especially the cities in Guangdong and Zhejiang provinces, and metropolises such as Shanghai and Beijing became labor inflowing areas while inland and western regions, especially the countryside in Anhui, Hunan, Hubei, and

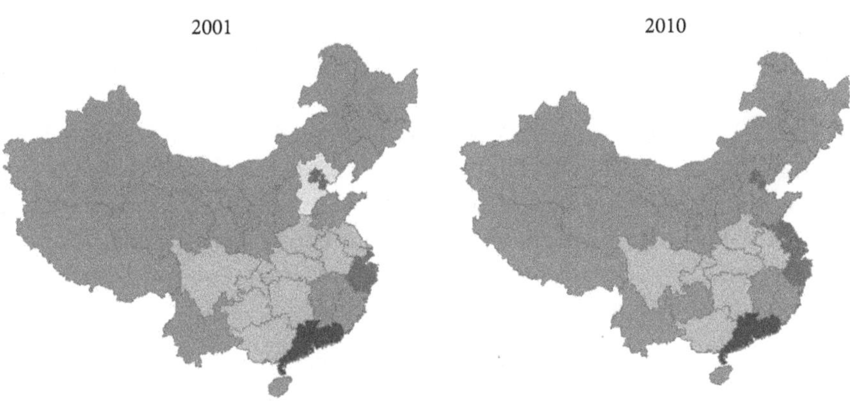

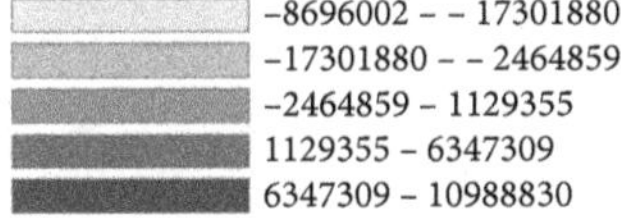

Figure 3.11 Internal Migration among Chinese Provinces (2001 and 2010)

Note: Negative value (the lightest color on the map) means net migrant outflowing provinces; positive value (the darkest color) means net migrant inflowing provinces.

Data source: Access China by the Economist Intelligence Unit.

For more information about this database, see https://www.eiu.com/handlers/PublicDownload. ashx?mode=m&fi=country-analysis/access_china.pdf.

Table 3.2 Urbanization in Different Chinese Regions (2006)

	Coastal Region	Northeastern Region	Central Region	Western Region
% of second and tertiary industry outputs in GDP	90.81	87.27	85.28	84.67
% of second and tertiary industry employment in total employment	62.4	54.2	44.8	38.4
% of non-agricultural *hukou*	48.15	47.41	27.13	26.63
% of urban residents in total population	59.88	55.15	38.96	36.74

Data source: China Statistical Yearbook.

Henan provinces, became labor outflowing areas (Figure 3.11). The local governments in labor-outflowing areas face greater pressures from population aging, labor shortage, and economic stagnation. The governments in labor-inflowing areas, in contrast, struggle with controlling labor cost and militancy, and dealing with labor market shocks due to the volatility of the international market.

Since the 1980s, urbanization has been facilitated and boosted by the massive influx of rural labor to cities in post-Mao China. Since the 1990s, a clear majority of China's workers are no longer in agriculture, and the country is thus no longer a predominantly agricultural economy (Naughton 2007). Urbanization is multidimensional and can manifest in many aspects such as economic output, employment, *hukou*, and population. No matter which dimension is used for comparison, the pace and magnitude of urbanization evidently differ across Chinese regions. Table 3.2 displays the shares of non-agricultural output, employment, *hukou*, and urban residents in 2006 across the four Chinese regions. It is obvious that these numbers, indicating the degree of urbanization, were consistently highest in the coastal region and lowest in the western region, with the northeastern and central regions falling in between. In all four regions, approximately 10% of the population was urban residents without non-agricultural *hukou*, meaning that a considerable portion of urban residents (e.g., migrant workers) are not entitled to urban social benefits. This implies that the actual urbanization rate in China is lower than the number on paper. Although the rural-to-urban labor inflow has greatly contributed to urbanization by bolstering the urban economy, only a small portion of the migrant workers obtained local non-agricultural *hukou* in coastal cities. By the end of the 2000s, local governments still had much discretion as to whether and how to include migrant workers into local social insurance (Gallagher et al. 2015).

Another critical change with profound impacts on China's labor market in the reform era is SOE reform and restructuring. Since the 1980s, SOEs and collective-owned firms have faced increasing competition from foreign and private firms, particularly in consumer-oriented industries, in addition to declining state subsidies and assistance. In September 1997, the Center decided to restructure SOEs into profitable firms, and a chief means to achieve this goal was laying off redundant workers to cut costs. The year of 1998 marked the beginning of the "three years of relieving difficulties" (*san nian tuo kun*), a round of SOE layoffs and ownership restructuring in the way of "grasping the large and letting go the small" (*zhua da fang xiao*). In 1999, the number of SOEs decreased by more than 40%; the share of SOE outputs in total industrial production was down from 80% in the late 1970s to 25%; the percentage of employed individuals in SOEs decreased from 68.4% in 1990 to less than 50% in 2001 (Lee 2007). Layoffs (*xia gang*) in various forms (e.g., early retirement, buying out) due to SOE reform and restructuring reached its height during the years of 1997 to 2000. At that time, about eight million SOE workers were newly laid off every year (Hurst 2009).

Like economic openness and internal migration, the SOE restructuring exerted differential impacts on the Chinese regions: it left the deepest mark on the "old industrial base" (*lao gongye jidi*) under the Soviet model of state-led industrialization in the northeastern region where the private and foreign sectors had been too small and underdeveloped to absorb redundant labor. Beginning in the 1980s, many SOEs in the northeastern region had difficulties balancing their books, fell into wage and pension arrears, and were forced to lay off workers (Hurst 2009).[26] The SOE reform and restructuring in the late 1990s publicly "opened up previously hidden unemployment, and further deepened workforce reductions" (Hurst 2009, 52). Unlike the rural-to-urban migrant workers flowing into the export centers in the coastal region, the SOE laid-off workers and early retirees are older and have specific skills that are not easily applicable to light or tertiary industries; they are usually local urban *hukou* holders and are less mobile across provinces. These formerly privileged industrial workers in the northeast urban areas did not passively accept the dismantling of the "social contract" or Iron Rice Bowl.[27] Studies of labor relations and politics in post-Mao China have documented several episodes of street marches, protests, petitions, and occasions of collective violence by SOE laid-off workers and retirees during reforms (Cai 2006; Hurst and O'Brien 2002; Hurst 2009; Lee 2007; Frazier 2004).

Local governments and enterprises often responded to SOE workers' protests with informal compensations such as a lump-sum severance payment, selected provision of welfare assistance, and re-employment opportunities. In the short-term, these negotiation-based or ad hoc compensations that usually stood outside the contributory social insurance system seemed more successful than formal compensations such as institutionalized minimum living allowance (*dibao*) or re-employment services (Hurst 2009). As local governments in the northeast region that were plagued by loss-making SOEs and labor dislocation often had difficulties paying compensations to SOE workers, the Center had to inject funds into the areas. In 1998, an extra 300 million yuan was allocated to the northeastern provinces as emergency funds because worker unrest reached a level to cause the Center's consternation about social instability (Lee 2007).

3.4. Conclusion

Social welfare expansion in China during the 2000s should be viewed in its historical, political, and economic contexts and studied as an integral part of the national and regional political economies of China. The social welfare expansion by the Chinese authoritarian regime, although broadening the access to basic health care via social health insurance, continues the lines of social stratification such as the urban-rural divide and the sectoral divides common in the previous *danwei*-based welfare system under the command economy. Moreover, responding to the great transformations of economy and society during decades of economic reform and openness in the 1980s and 1990s, the social welfare expansion that the Chinese regime embarked on in the late 1990s and the early 2000s "centralized" the social welfare provision from employers to the local governments but has maintained the decentralization and fragmentation of the provision at the local levels.

The economic rationale for the reform trajectory and process can be found in the macroeconomic evolution and diverse regional economies of the country. First, economic openness and the desire to stimulate domestic consumption for sustainable economic growth motivated the Chinese regime to establish social insurance and expand social protection. Nonetheless, heavy reliance on investment and business for GDP growth and revenue generation did not encourage the regime to commit to a generous welfare state. Second, the diversity of regional economies, including the structure of the local economy, migration, urbanization, and the labor market, reinforced by decades of economic reform and openness in post-Mao China, make it an imperative for the Center to allow local discretion in social welfare expansion, a clue to understanding the variety of local responses to social welfare expansion. It is under these structural and economic conditions that my exploration of the interests and strategies of major political actors (i.e., the central and the local leaders) in Chinese social welfare provision unfolds in chapters 4 and 5.

4

The Center's Distributive Strategy and Fund Allocation

Like leaders in other autocratic countries, the Chinese central leaders need to strike a balance between elites and masses in benefit distribution in order to maintain regime survival and stability. Since threats to the survival and stability of autocracies can come from either front—elites or masses—choosing to distribute rents and goods only to the elites or only to the masses is not an optimal strategy from the autocratic leaders' perspective. When autocratic leaders concentrate too many benefits on elites, they become vulnerable not only to threats from within the empowered elites but also to unrest from the discontented masses. Yet when autocratic leaders reduce the privileges of elites and empower masses through universalizing benefits, they risk betraying the very elites on whom they rely to ensure political survival. Thus, autocratic leaders must distribute benefits or allocate resources between elites and masses in a strategic manner to maximize the prospects of regime survival and stability; the risk of unbalancing between elites and masses characterizes the distributive politics in autocracies.

In light of the above argument, Chapter 2 provides a theoretical account of why and how the Chinese authoritarian leaders adopted a stratified expansion strategy in social welfare provision—perpetuating a particularly privileged provision for elites while developing an essentially modest provision for the masses— to manage the trade-off in benefit distribution between elites and masses. This chapter specifies the formation and development of the Chinese regime's stratified expansion strategy in social welfare provision by drawing qualitative evidence from the central leaders' speeches to ministerial and local officials, central work conference memos, and media reports. These materials demonstrate the intertwining of expansion and stratification in Chinese central leaders' social welfare decisions and policies between 1998 and 2011. Specifically, the Center established a social health insurance program for urban formal employees in response to the massive lay-offs and early retirements during the SOE reform in the late 1990s. It further strategically expanded social health insurance to other economic sectors and social groups after 2003 for both political and economic considerations. Throughout the expansion, the Center intentionally and relentlessly protected the elite groups' benefits using fiscal transfers so that the stratification of health benefits among social groups was maintained.

Social Protection under Authoritarianism. Xian Huang, Oxford University Press (2020). © Oxford University Press.
DOI: 10.1093/oso/9780190073640.001.0001

Through a quantitative analysis of the Center's fiscal transfers to provinces between 1999 and 2009, this chapter further demonstrates that the Center allocates more funds to the provinces with larger elite groups. Both the distributive strategy and fund allocation of the Chinese regime reflect its intrinsic interest in social welfare distribution: privileging the elites while providing the masses with basic and minimum benefits.

This chapter is organized as follows: Section 4.1 draws on government documents, leaders' speeches, and government conference memos to uncover the Center's economic and political considerations for establishing a contributory social health insurance for the urban formal employees between 1998 and 2002. Section 4.2 continues to draw on the primary materials to reconstruct the Center's interests for expansion and stratification of social health insurance between 2003 and 2011. Section 4.3 uses a provincial-level data set about the central-to-local fiscal transfers to specifically examine the relationship between the elite groups in a province and the Center's fiscal transfers to the province, validating the political explanation of social health insurance stratification. Section 4.4 summarizes the findings and concludes the chapter.

4.1. Establishing Social Health Insurance for Urban Formal Employees (1998–2002)

More than a genuine response to social movements, social health insurance was initiated in China as an auxiliary measure for economic reform and openness, especially for the SOE restructuring in the late 1990s and accession to WTO in 2002. In 1998, the Center issued a directive for establishing social health insurance (UEBMI) for urban formal employees—mainly SOE workers—when it launched a new round of SOE reform, called "take off difficulty [for SOEs] within three years (1999–2002)" (*san nian tuo kun*). At the next year's central economic work conference, Jiang Zemin, party secretary at that time, stated that "establishing a sound social security system is an important aspect of creating a socialist market economy and a necessary condition for successfully reforming SOEs and restructuring the economy. We need to develop the social security system, with the focus on unemployment and old age and health care; gradually expand its coverage; and increase the level of social security."[1] The leaders' economic-reform motivation not only accounted for the timing of establishing social health insurance in China, but also set the tone for the early stage of social welfare reform in post-Mao China, giving rise to three features of the social health insurance policies between 1998 and 2002: prioritizing efficiency to equity, targeting the urban SOE workers, and carrying out the reform in an incremental and gradual manner like China's other economic reform measures.

In the late 1990s, the central government initiated social health insurance to alleviate the financial burden on SOEs, shifting the responsibilities of managing and financing health care provision from SOEs to the government, mainly the local governments. As then Premier Zhu Rongji, a well-known tough reformer, specified to central and local bureaucrats of social welfare affairs: "Firms and institutes only need to fulfill the obligation to pay social insurance premiums. They no longer bear the responsibility of managing social insurance payments and memberships. . . . Retirees and the unemployed should detach themselves from their enterprises or institutes. Community committees (*shequ zuzhi*) will be in charge of managing the social insurance memberships and distributing benefits."[2] Meanwhile, the contribution and benefit levels of the newly established and socially pooled health insurance were set at minimum, sparing both government and enterprises a commitment to a generous welfare state. In 1997, Premier Zhu Rongji made a speech titled "Social Health Insurance Should Be Low in Level but Broad in Coverage,"[3] which vividly revealed the Center's strategic view on social protection. As this speech was widely cited and echoed in the following years in government directives and documents about health insurance, "being low in level but broad in coverage (*di shui ping gaung fu gai*)" characterized Chinese social health insurance policies in the late 1990s and early 2000s.

Considering the financial resource shortage of both government and SOEs, and increasing economic openness in the late 1990s, a broad yet minimum social health insurance seemed economically reasonable. But when we read the central leaders more carefully, the political facet of establishing a social health insurance system in urban China during the late 1990s and early 2000s becomes clear. Why did the initial social health insurance programs target SOE workers rather than the other groups? How did the regime appease the vested interests or elite groups by protecting their welfare privileges when transforming the *danwei*-based welfare system into a socially pooled and contributory health insurance system?

As SOEs and urban reforms deepened in China during the mid-1990s, social unrest and collective incidents organized by laid-off workers and retirees rocketed (Cai 2002; Hurst and O'Brien 2002; Frazier 2004). The central leaders believed that "social welfare and wage issues were the most common and direct cause of workers' protests and demonstration."[4] The imperative of maintaining social stability in the late 1990s and early 2000s was further strengthened by two upcoming historical events with profound impacts on the political economy of China: accession to the World Trade Organization in 2001 and leadership succession at the 16th Party Congress in 2002. Remarks to provincial leaders by then vice president Hu Jintao, who was designated by the party elders as the successor of Jiang Zemin who stepped down in 2002, reflected the deep anxiety and concern about social instability within the Chinese central leadership at that time: "This year is critical for our party and nation in history as we will hold the 16th Party Congress in the second half of the year. Maintaining social stability during this time is particularly crucial. . . . Especially, since early this year, the number of collective incidents among localities has significantly increased. Among them, the collective actions by SOE employees are particularly prominent and deserve more special attention. . . . Participants of those incidents were mostly former employees, laid-off workers, retirees, and current employees whose wages and health benefits were in arrears."[5]

As such, a bundle of preemptive measures was undertaken for maintaining social stability in the early 2000s. First, local leaders—especially the "first in command" (*di yi ba shou*), party secretaries—were held accountable for the disastrous collective incidents taking place in their jurisdictions. In a speech to provincial leaders in 2002, Hu Jintao said, "When collective incidents that impair social stability break out, local leaders especially the party secretaries should investigate, command and handle the problem in person. We have learned from past experiences that it is crucial that the leaders involve themselves in persuading the dissatisfied and resolve the discontent at its early stage. Those who miss the opportunity of resolving the problem and cause disastrous outcomes due to arrogance, ignorance, and squabbling will be held accountable and be punished seriously."[6]

Second, social insurance programs including old age and health insurance were rapidly put into effect in 1998. According to then vice minister of Labor and Social Security, Wang Dongjin, 940 million people were enrolled in basic social health insurance by the end of 2002, and 65% of them were SOE employees, including retirees. Selecting and protecting these groups was strategic and politically favorable as "appeasing these groups helps appease the entire industrial workforce at the battlefield of SOE reform and restructuring. This also sets an example for those employees who haven't joined social insurance yet."[7]

Third, fiscal transfers to provide subsistence to laid-off workers and retirees of SOEs were notably increased. The Center raised its budgetary transfers to basic pension and minimum living allowance from 48.5 billion yuan to 51.2 billion yuan in 2002 and specifically ordered the local governments "to actively modify fiscal spending structure, enhance social security funding even at the cost of other expenditures."[8]

Fourth, when setting the local agenda for SOE bankruptcy and restructuring, the Center prescribed local governments to consider workers' potential reactions. For example, on April 9, 2002, in response to the looming social unrest and increasing pressure to maintain social stability, provincial leaders were gathered to Beijing for a central work conference on social stability issues. Premier Zhu Rongji, discussing the lessons learned from two large-scale and long-lasting collective incidents organized by SOE laid-off workers in Daqing and Liaoyang cities on the rust belt in China's Northeast, instructed local leaders to "further formalize and strictly follow the protocol of dismissing redundancy. Do not enter the bankruptcy process unless the funding and measures to settle the lay-offs and their social insurance are ready. Do not rush into bankruptcy if the enterprise has a large staff and has difficulty settling with those who have been laid off."[9]

While such preemptive measures were taken to appease labor militancy, policies to enhance the welfare benefits of party cadres, government officials, and civil servants continued. When preaching "social health insurance should be low at level and broad at coverage," then premier Zhu Rongji also stressed that "the basic medical insurance payment standard should be the same for enterprises, [but] for government and public-sector staff, the Ministry of Finance should provide more money to cover necessary medical costs that go beyond basic medical insurance. We cannot reduce the amount paid by the state for their health care and should gradually increase it. They will feel alienated if social health insurance doesn't show some favors for them, and in fact that would also be *unfair* [italic by the author]."[10] In addition to indicating the preferential treatment for these elites, this quote also shows that the money for their health care benefits was drawn directly from the fiscal coffers in addition to regular social insurance funds that usually paid for basic benefits only.

In sum, the establishment and development of social health insurance in China during the late 1990s and early 2000s was a product of the central leaders' economic and political considerations and strategies at that moment. The initial social health insurance programs targeted the urban formal employees, mainly SOE current workers, laid-off workers, and retirees, providing them with minimum protection during the turmoil of SOE bankruptcy and restructuring and more important, preempting and reducing social unrest. As expanding the benefits to the marginalized social groups such as SOE laid-off workers and early retirees might upset the elite groups, such as government and public sector employees who had been enjoying welfare privileges for decades, the Chinese central leaders were trying to balance the interests of different groups by compensating the vested interests with extra benefits financed directly from state budgets in addition to social health insurance funds. However, such balancing became more delicate and complicated as external economic and internal socioeconomic circumstances were demanding further expansion of social health insurance for the masses after 2002.

4.2. Stratified Expansion of Social Health Insurance (2003–2011)

4.2.1. Expansion of Social Health Insurance

The outbreak of the SARS epidemic in 2003 was a head-on blow for the Chinese government. When SARS struck, medical services were minimal in most of rural

China; in urban areas where the newly established social health insurance was "low in benefits" and strictly formal-employment-based, medical services were inaccessible to many of the poor and precariously employed as well as to rural-to-urban migrant workers. The epidemic caused 329 deaths and infected 5,237 people with SARS within six months before the Chinese regime realized and admitted how insufficient public health care was in China despite the country's remarkable GDP growth for two decades. At the central work conference to learn the lessons from fighting SARS, then president Hu Jintao, who took office during the SARS epidemic, stated that "through fighting against SARS, we have realized, more deeply than ever before, that China's economic and social development, urban and rural development are not coordinated; the development of public health has greatly lagged behind, and the health care system is flawed."[11] This speech was the prelude to the rapid expansion of social health insurance in China from 2003 to 2011.

The expansion began with the establishment of a health insurance program for the rural population, NRCMS, in 2003 and peaked at the "enlarging coverage of health insurance" (*yiliao baoxian kuo mian*) campaign promoted by a new round of health reform in 2009. The results of expansion can be seen in terms of population coverage and generosity. During this period, rural residents, urban non-state-sector employees,[12] rural-to-urban migrant workers, and urban non-working residents were incrementally incorporated into social health insurance, though usually put in separate health insurance programs. Fiscal transfers and subsidies for social health insurance significantly increased, especially for urban non-working residents and the rural population.[13] According to government reports, social health insurance, including UEBMI, URBMI, and NRCMS, covered over 90% of the Chinese population by the end of 2010.[14] As in the first phase (1998–2002), the social health insurance expansion that characterized China's health care policies between 2003 and 2011 can be attributed to the government's economic and political strategies at that moment.

Despite the effect of SARS in 2003, China's GDP grew by 9.5% that year. In the following four years, the annual growth rates of GDP and government budgetary revenue stayed above 10% and 20%, respectively. In 2007, the end of the Hu Jintao-Wen Jiabao administration's first term, China hit its highest GDP growth rate (11.4%) since 1995 and became the world's third largest economy and trading nation. During the heyday of Chinese economy between 2003 and 2007, the CCP central leadership set out new economic goals: industrial upgrading, increasing self-dependent innovation, expanding domestic consumption, and supporting regional coordinated development. Meanwhile, the Hu Jintao administration developed a new governing goal of "building a harmonious socialist society" (*goujian shehui zhuyi hexie shehui*), that aimed to spread the economic and social benefits to broader social groups. At the second plenum of the 16th National

Congress of the CCP in 2005, then party secretary Hu Jintao explained the Chinese economic situations and key issues to all members of the CCP Central Committee. Only on two occasions during the speech did Hu Jintao mention developing and expanding social welfare (including education, pension, health insurance, etc.): when talking about expanding domestic consumption to cultivate momentum for economic growth, and when talking about adjusting income distribution to secure long-term economic development and social stability. Accordingly, social welfare expansion was considered an important means to achieve these economic and political ends. As Hu stated, "Developing social welfare and social security to improve people's well-being is not only a necessary requirement for social harmony and stability, but also an important force for expanding domestic consumption and driving economic growth."[15]

The nexus of economy and social welfare expansion in China further manifested in government policies during the 2008 global financial crisis. Since the 2008 crisis, Chinese central leadership has recognized the imperatives of expanding and relying on domestic consumption for economic development. Hu Jintao said to his provincial subordinates in 2010: "Despite the many measures taken to expand domestic consumption demand and stimulate economic growth, the growth rate of GDP decreased to 6.1% this year. It indicates that the risk, due to uncertainty and the volatility of the global market, would be even higher if our economy continued to rely on the overseas market."[16] Earlier at the CCP central economic work conference in 2008, Hu Jintao had remarked, "Especially in the face of the global financial crisis, speeding up the improvement of social security and social insurance systems is conducive to amplifying domestic demand and promoting economic development, to protecting people's livelihood and to promoting social harmony and stability."[17] He specifically directed that "public finance should increase investment in social security and social insurance systems, improve social protection, expand coverage of basic old-age insurance and health insurance for urban workers and social basic health insurance for urban non-working residents, and elevate the pooling level of basic social health insurance."[18]

Social welfare expansion and reform further gained more attention and priority on the government's agenda since 2008, not only for expanding domestic consumption but also for maintaining social stability. At the end of 2008, Hu Jintao predicted that "with the current economic development difficulties, the conflicts and mass incidents among the people may increase. If not handled swiftly and appropriately, they will have adverse impacts on social stability." He concluded that "the more difficulty there is in the economy, the more attention we must pay to people's livelihoods."[19] In light of these directives by the central leaders, expansion of social health insurance coverage and generosity was added into the government's official evaluation.[20] To reduce domestic unemployment and social unrest due to the 2008 global financial crisis, the Chinese government injected 4 trillion yuan into infrastructure construction, low-cost housing, and health and education provisions (Bulman 2010). Local labor bureaus relentlessly persuaded enterprises to keep redundant workers. According to then vice minister of MoHRSS, Hu Xiaoyi, 23 out of 31 provinces lowered enterprises' social insurance premium payments in 2008.[21]

However, a deeper and hidden political motivation for the Center to expand social insurance benefits to the broader social groups in the period of 2003–2011 was to maintain and protect the welfare benefits and privileges of the elite groups (i.e., party and government officials, civil servants, and state and SOE formal employees). In 2004, social health insurance for urban formal employees, UEBMI, covered over 118.47 million people including 86.63 million state-sector employees and 31.84 million state-sector retirees.[22] Based on the MoHRSS's investigation in 25 provinces in the fall of 2004, 20 of China's 31 provinces, including 142 prefectural units, were running deficits in social health insurance funds.[23] According to the vice minister of MoHRSS at that time, the trend that social health insurance runs into deficits was prevalent.[24] Driven by the tremendous pressure to pay off the medical bills for urban state-sector employees and retirees, in 2004 MoHRSS put forth a plan to expand UEBMI coverage to non-state-sector employees such as employees of foreign-owned enterprises, joint ventures, and private firms; it further expanded the UEBMI coverage to rural-to-urban migrant workers (peasant workers) in 2006. As a result, from 2006 to 2008, the coverage of UEBMI increased by 45%; and 60% of the newly enrolled were migrant workers whose average age was below 30 in the mid-2000s.[25] Thanks to the inclusion of millions of young workers from non-state sectors and the rural-to-urban migrant workers into the risk pool of UEBMI, social health insurance funds became more sustainable: the ratio of incumbent employees to retirees increased from 2.66:1 in 2006 to 2.99:1 in 2008.[26] Then vice minister of MoHRSS in 2009, Hu Xiaoyi, proudly proclaimed in a ministerial annual meeting that "in retrospect, our decision in 2006 to expand social health insurance to the peasant workers is absolutely right. Inclusion of those peasant workers [into UEBMI] in the past three years has contributed to the stable functioning of the [UEBMI] funds, in addition to enhancing the peasant workers' well-being."[27]

The expansion of social health insurance coverage between 2003 and 2011 has greatly improved the risk pooling of social health insurance, but it could also intensify the distributive tension in health care between elites and masses. In a populous developing country like China, health care resources and services are always limited. In this circumstance, the more access the masses have to the limited resources, such as tertiary hospitals and medical services provided in large and capital cities, the fewer health care conveniences and benefits the elite groups can enjoy. Moreover, extending health insurance benefits to the previously marginalized groups such as peasants and migrant workers makes social health insurance less of a privilege for the elite groups. These repercussions can pose a challenge to the balance of interests between elites and masses and do harm to the stability of the Chinese authoritarian regime. Therefore, the expansion of social health insurance from 2003 to 2011 was balanced with intentionally maintaining the health care privileges of elite groups, which inevitably resulted in significant stratification of health care benefits.

4.2.2. Stratification of Social Health Insurance

Creation of the Social Insurance Law and the reform (or lack of reform) of government officials' health care between 2003 and 2011 further manifested the central leaders' inclination to maintain the stratification of social health insurance benefits. In October 2010, then President Hu Jintao promulgated the Social Insurance Law affecting old-age insurance, health insurance, and unemployment insurance. The timing and content of this law shows the CCP central leadership's support for a stratified expansion of social insurance. The Social Insurance Law, on one hand, consolidates the dramatic expansion of social insurance since 2003, including expanding social health insurance to peasants and urban non-working residents. On the other hand, it institutionalizes the coexistence and segmentation of three social health insurance programs in China: UEBMI, URBMI, and NRCMS. The law stipulates that citizens, according to their socioeconomic status (e.g., employment, *hukou*, etc.), must join the particular social health insurance program for which they are eligible. Moreover, the Social Insurance Law clearly distinguishes Chinese social insurance from conventional social-rights-based or universalistic welfare. The law states, "The social insurance system adheres to the principles of wide coverage, basic protection, multi-level and sustainability; the generosity of social insurance shall correspond to the country's level of economic and social development."[28]

The Social Insurance Law is ambiguous about government employees' (including government and party officials, and civil servants) health insurance program. Both the 1998 UEBMI regulation and the 2011 Social Insurance Law can be interpreted as implying that party and government officials and civil servants should join the social health insurance program for urban employees, that is, UEBMI. In practice, this requires a fundamental reform of the health care provision for officials: either completely abolishing the former GIS, which is fully financed by government budgets and essentially free for the recipients and their dependents, or transforming the GIS into a contributory social health insurance program in which party and government officials and civil servants start to pay premiums and out-of-pocket expenses for health care as do the other groups in social health insurance. In a stark contrast to the rapid expansion of social health insurance between 2003 and 2011, the reform of government officials' free health care has been slow and partial. By the end of 2011, one quarter of 31 provinces (including the capital city Beijing) still kept the GIS outside of the social health insurance system to which users contributed.[29] Reform plans for the free health care for central-level government and party officials, involving the vested interests of approximately 100,000 officials, were unclear at the time of writing.

The lagging or lack of reform of government employees' free health care means that a considerable portion of the elite groups including central-government employees, have no caps, deductibles, coinsurance, or out-of-pocket payments for health expenses. With no limits on medical expenses, the cost of government employees' health care was soaring during 2003–2011. For example, in the Pinggu district of Beijing, the budgetary expenditure of government employees' health care increased annually by 20%. In 2008, Pinggu's budgetary expenditure for government employees' health care was 32 million yuan and the actual expense was 43 million yuan—literally "out of control" as described by the vice director of the MoHRSS district bureau in Pinggu.[30] In Guangdong province, as another example, in 2004 the per capita actual expense for government employees' health care was 7,000 yuan higher than the per capita budgetary expenditure on average.[31] In 2011, the Guangdong government spent 150 million yuan on government employees' health care and 130 million yuan on the urban non-working population's health insurance; but the number of government employees was only 2.3% of the urban non-working population![32]

In sum, the study of central leaders' internal speeches, work conference memos, and media reports uncovers the CCP's economic and political considerations behind the stratified expansion of social health insurance between 2003 and 2011. Throughout this period, the masses (peasants, urban non-state-sector employees and non-working residents) were incrementally incorporated into the social health insurance system with enhanced benefits in order to support the economic reform and restructuring that require a broad social safety net and increasing domestic consumption. The expansion was also made to prevent social unrest and maintain social stability during various public health, economic and social crises the Hu-Wen administration encountered in the first decade of the 2000s. The central leaders and technocrats carefully engineered the expansion so that it did not confront the vested interests of elite groups (e.g., government and party officials, civil servants). Instead, by incorporating non-state-sector employees and young migrant workers into the social health insurance system, the expansion significantly improved the risk pooling of existing health insurance programs for urban state-sector employees and retirees. Moreover, the free health care of certain elite groups (government officials and civil servants) was mostly kept intact throughout the expansion period between 2003 and 2011.

Unlike the expansion of social health insurance to the broad social groups, the Chinese central leaders rarely talk about the GIS reform in public. Nonetheless, secondary materials (e.g., media reports and investigations) indicate that a huge amount of state money was spent on health care for party and government officials, civil servants, and public-sector employees throughout 1998–2011.[33] A careful reading of central leaders' speeches also shows that this money mainly came from government budgets and was transferred regularly from the central to the local governments. Given the scarcity of firsthand materials about the elite groups' privileged health care benefits, I turned to the central-to-local fiscal transfers that are crucial to supporting the elite groups' health care benefits and welfare privileges during the expansion period to further demonstrate the CCP central leaders' support for the stratified expansion of social welfare provision.

4.3. Central-to-Local Fiscal Transfers in China

The study of the CCP central leaders' calculation and support for a stratified expansion of social welfare provisions in China since the late 1990s suggests a correlation between its fiscal transfers to the local governments and the stratified expansion of social welfare provisions. From 2003 to 2011, the Center was explicitly using fiscal transfers to support the social welfare expansion. For example, in 2008 the Center allocated 43.2 billion yuan as an earmarked transfer to localities for paying SOE laid-off workers' or retirees' health insurance premiums, expanding the coverage of social health insurance to these particular groups.[34] For another example, in 2011, the Center made a commitment to subsidizing non-working people's (including peasants') social health insurance premiums by an earmarked transfer to some provinces as high as 200 yuan/person.[35] Besides these payments (or "earmarked transfers" as elaborated later in this section) explicitly made for social welfare expansion to the masses, the Center also allocated fiscal transfers implicitly to protect and maintain the elite groups' benefits or privileges.

4.3.1. Composition and Trends of Central-to-Local Fiscal Transfers in China

Fiscal transfer is an important and effective tool with which the Center can influence local spending. Under China's fiscal system, in which the majority of local tax revenues have been centralized since the mid-1990s, most local governments cannot make ends meet if they must rely solely on locally sourced revenues.[36] Figure 4.1 shows the gap between locally sourced fiscal revenue and expenditure as a share of locally sourced fiscal revenue, for each Chinese province.[37] It indicates that with the exception of several rich provinces in the coastal region (e.g., Beijing, Jiangsu, Guangdong), without the Center's fiscal transfers, the majority of Chinese provinces would have run fiscal deficits between 1998 and 2010. The central-to-local fiscal transfers are an indispensable part of local fiscal revenues, enhancing the local governments' capacity to spend by putting extra money in their hands. For some localities, especially those in China's western region (e.g., Tibet, Qinghai, Gansu, Ningxia, Xinjaing), the Center's fiscal transfers accounted for the largest portion of local total fiscal revenues (Figure 4.2). Hence, the central-to-local fiscal transfers are crucial for understanding the fiscal conditions (constraints or resources) that local leaders face in distributing public services and welfare benefits among the social groups in their jurisdictions.

More important, central-to-local fiscal transfers can shape the distribution of local spending by changing local fiscal autonomy and constraint. In general,

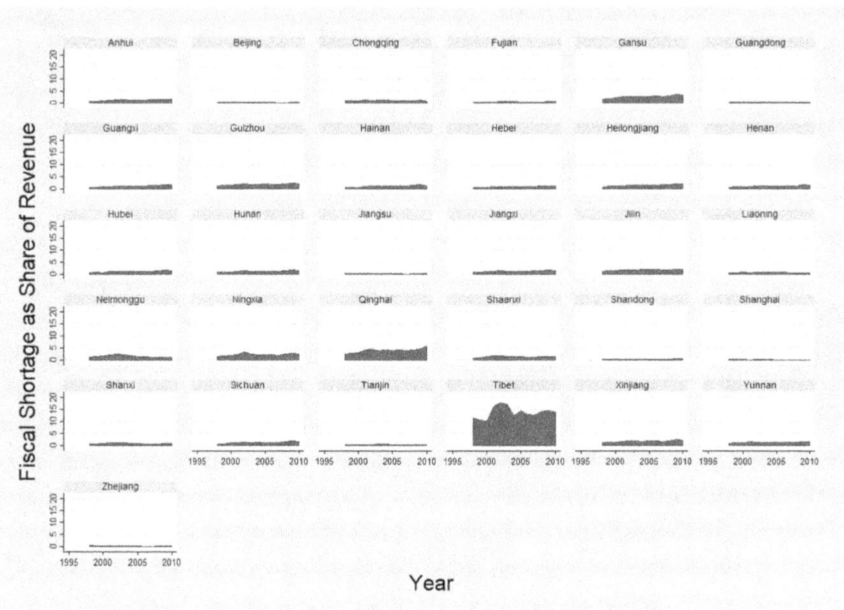

Figure 4.1 Fiscal Shortage by Province (1998–2010)

Note: Fiscal shortage is measured by the difference between local-sourced revenue and expenditure as a percentage of local-sourced revenue. The data do not account for local extra-budgetary revenue.

Data source: Local Fiscal Statistics (di fang cai zheng tong ji zi liao).

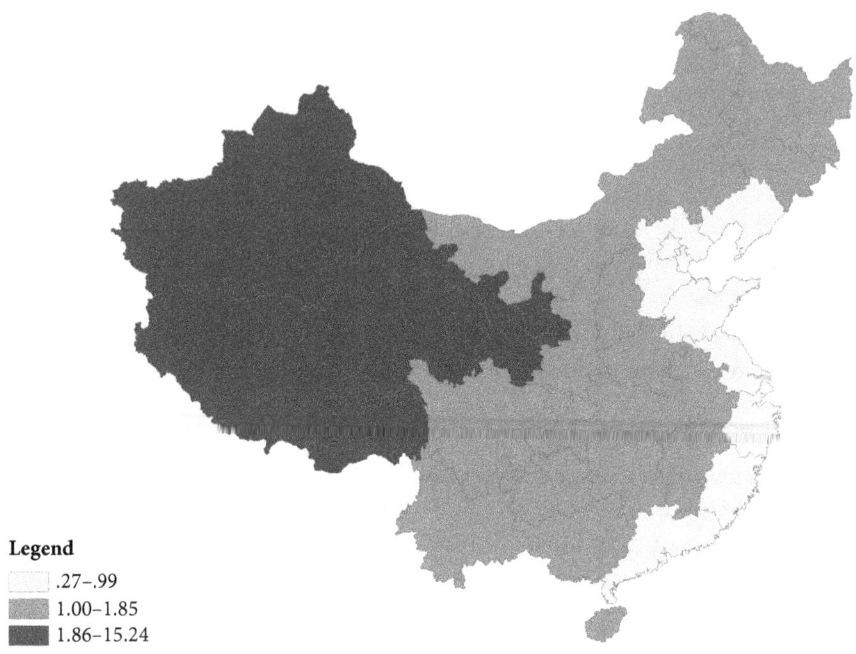

Figure 4.2 Central-to-Local Fiscal Transfers as Ratios of Local Government Revenue (1999–2008)

Data source: Local Fiscal Statistics (*di fang cai zheng tong ji zi liao*).

the Center makes three types of transfers to the local governments annually: tax rebates, general purpose grants (also called "equalization transfers"), and special purpose grants (also called "earmarked transfers"). The former two are made according to set formulas that take into account local tax revenues and expenditures. In particular, the equalization transfer claims to reduce inter-regional disparity by favoring ethnic minority regions and border areas. The ex-ante formulas reduce the Center's discretion in allocating these funds while the local governments have discretion in how to spend them. In contrast, the earmarked transfer, without ex-ante formulas, is much more unpredictable for local governments and its local use is specified, but the Center has much discretion in allocation. It is worth noting that most earmarked transfers require matching funds from local governments. Since rich provinces are more capable of providing the matching funds, all else being equal, they are more likely to obtain the Center's earmarked transfers than their poor counterparts. Table 4.1 summarizes the key features of the three types of fiscal transfers made by the Chinese central government.

Table 4.1 Comparison of Three Types of Central-to-Local Fiscal Transfers

Attributes	Tax Rebate	Equalization Transfer	Earmarked Transfer
Formula-based	Yes	Yes	No
Key factors included in the formula[a]	Amounts and growth rates of value added tax and excise taxes in each province	Local shared and own taxes, local expenditure, ethnic minority regions, or border areas	
Center's discretion	Low	Low	High
Localities' discretion	High	Medium[b]	Low
Require matching funds by the province	No	No	Yes

[a] The factors included in the fiscal transfers can be found in *The System of Equalization Transfers in China*, Zhihua Zhang and Jorge Martinez-Vazquez, Andrew Young School of Policy Studies, Working Paper 03-12, July 2003.

[b] Some grants, such as grants for increasing the standard wages of civil servants, which have a special well-defined purpose for use, are included in the category of "general purpose grants (equalization transfers)" because these grants are allocated on the basis of equalization principle criteria (Zhang and Martinez-Vazquez 2003). Hence, local governments' discretion in using the general-purpose grants gets compromised in reality.

To study the trends, composition, and determinants of the center-to-local fiscal transfers, I compiled a province-level dataset from 1999 to 2010 based on government publications: *Local Fiscal Statistics* (*di fang cai zheng tong ji zi liao*).[38] In these publications, the data for earmarked transfer are not available at the provincial level for most years between 1999 and 2010; and the data for equalization transfers at the provincial level are incomplete (some equalization transfer items are not included before 2008); however, all tax rebates as well as total transfers at the provincial levels are fully documented. Accordingly, my dataset has four categories of central-to-local fiscal transfers at the provincial level: tax rebates, equalization transfers, other transfers (mainly including earmarked transfers and some unspecified equalization transfers), and total transfers (sum of the previous three categories).[39]

According to the data, from 1998 to 2009, the central-to-local total transfer per capita has increased ninefold, with equalization and earmarked (approximately) transfers increasing the most (Figure 4.3). Moreover, the per capita total transfers increased from eastern to western areas, with Tibet receiving the most (Figure 4.4). Both these temporal and spatial trends in fiscal transfers are

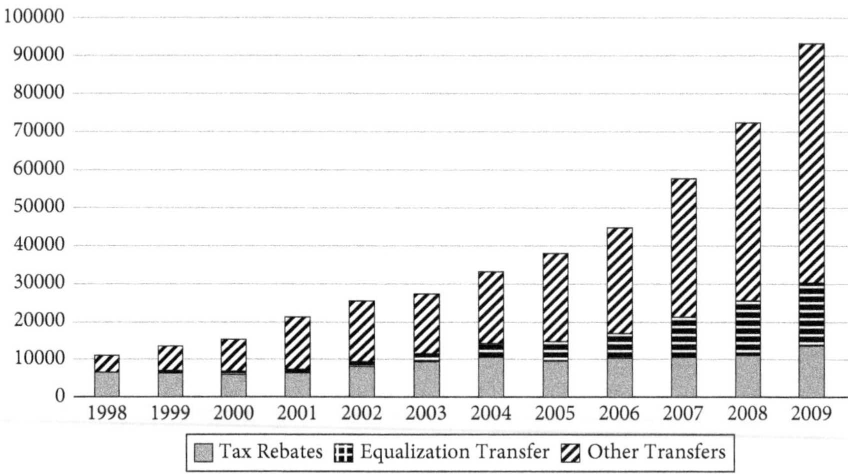

Figure 4.3 Composition of Central-to-Local Fiscal Transfers by Year (1998–2009)

Data source: Local Fiscal Statistics (*di fang cai zheng tong ji zi liao*).

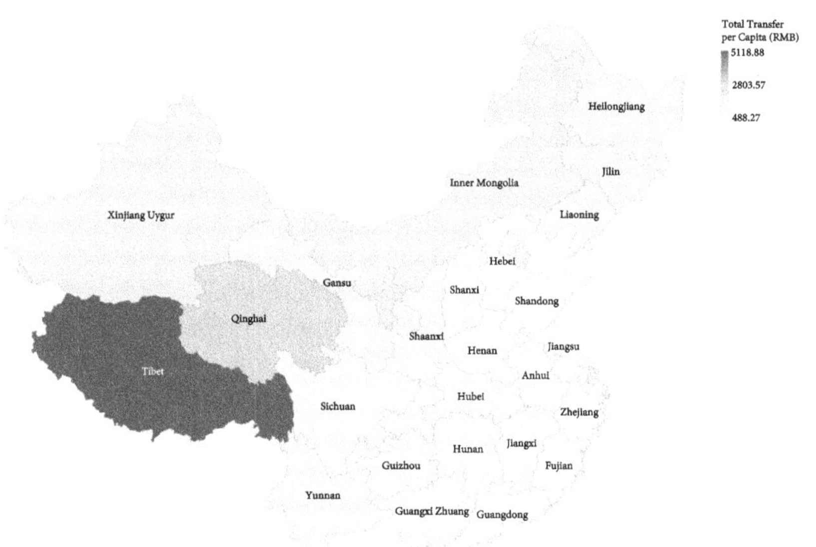

Figure 4.4 Central-to-Local Fiscal Transfer per Capita by Province (1998–2009 Average)

Data source: Local Fiscal Statistics (*di fang cai zheng tong ji zi liao*).

consistent with the findings in other studies of China's government finance (Lou and Wang 2008).

More pertinent to the study here is the inter-regional variation in the Center's fiscal transfers to local governments (specifically, provincial-level governments). Figure 4.5 presents the composition of total central-to-local transfers across provinces. In the period of 1998–2009, except for the richest provinces (the metropolises and the southeast coastal provinces) that collected the most taxes and hence received higher tax rebates, tax rebate accounted for approximately 20% of total transfers for an average province in China. In contrast, equalization transfers accounted for about 10% of total transfers for an average Chinese

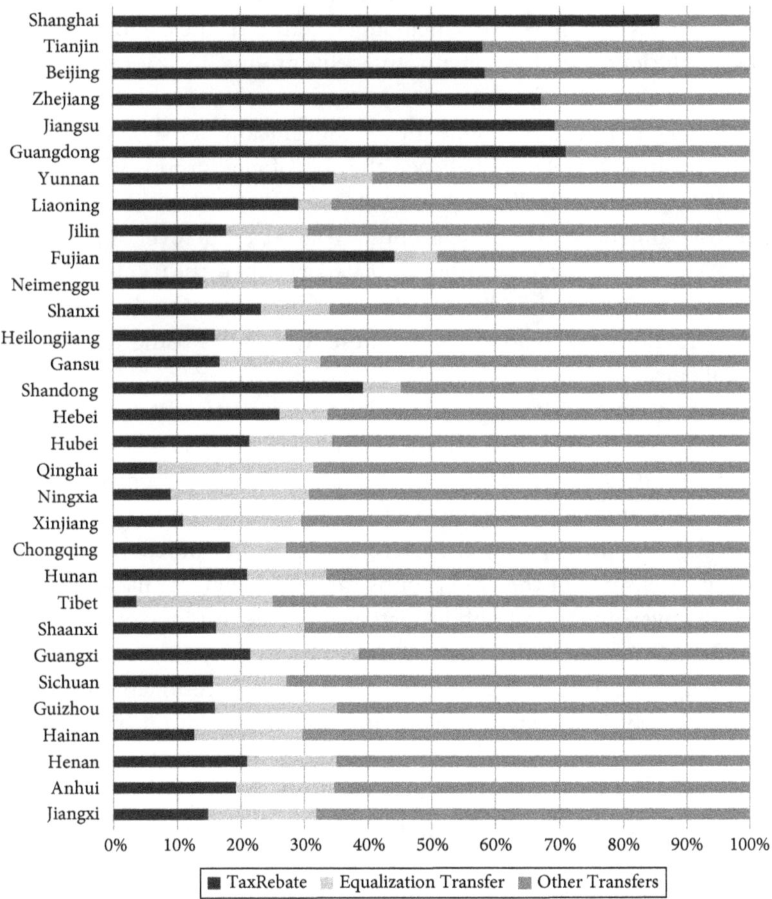

Figure 4.5 Composition of Central-to-Local Fiscal Transfers by Province (1998–2009 Average)

Data source: Local Fiscal Statistics (*di fang cai zheng tong ji zi liao*).

province, with northwestern provinces receiving much more and those in China's southeast receiving much less; for most provinces, other transfers (mainly earmarked transfers) constituted the majority of fiscal transfers that local governments received from the Center.

4.3.2. Determinants of Central-to-Local Fiscal Transfers in China

The study of Chinese central leadership's strategy for social welfare provision in Sections 4.1 and 4.2 points us to the political rationale for the Center's allocation of fiscal transfers to local governments. In order to maintain the elite groups' generous welfare benefits including health care, the Center directs more transfers to the localities that contain larger elite groups. The more discretion the Center has in allocating fiscal transfers, the stronger the correlation is between fiscal transfers and the size of elite groups. Specifically, we should see a significant and positive correlation between the size of elite groups whose interests and benefits the central leadership attempts to protect and the Center's transfers to local governments where these groups are largest; moreover, this correlation should be stronger in the "other transfer" category, where the Center enjoys more discretion in allocation than in other kinds of fiscal transfers (e.g., tax rebates, equalization transfers). Below I tested these hypotheses using the provincial-level fiscal data.

The dataset covers 31 Chinese mainland provincial units (including four provincial municipalities, five ethnic autonomous regions, and 22 provinces) from 1998 to 2009. Dependent variables are the three categories of central-to-local fiscal transfers per capita: tax rebates, equalization transfer, and other transfers for each province from 1998 to 2009. The key independent variables are various measures of the elite groups for each province: fiscal dependents (including government and public-sector employees and retirees whose salaries and benefits are included in government budgets), state-sector employees (including government, public-sector, and SOE employees), and urban *hukou* holders, respectively, as a share of a province's total population. These measures are not exclusive to each other. For example, fiscal dependents must include all civil servants who are also counted as state-sector employees and highly likely to be urban *hukou* holders. Among the three measures, urban *hukou* holders are the most inclusive measure of the elites while fiscal dependents are the strictest measure. In the following analysis, I include these measures of elites one by one in the model for each dependent variable. All these measures of elite groups were expected to be positively correlated with at least one of the three dependent variables.

Two alternative explanations of the center-to-local fiscal transfers were also tested. First, the central government's fiscal transfers might respond to local fiscal and welfare needs. In order to test this needs-based hypothesis, I included three independent variables measuring local needs for fiscal transfers from the central government: the fiscal shortage measured by the difference between local-sourced fiscal revenue and expenditure as a share of local-sourced fiscal revenue; the elderly dependent rate by the ratio of elders to the working population; the ethnic minority population (as they usually have lower incomes than the Han population) as a share of the total population. Second, the central government's fiscal transfers might respond to local economic situations, such as the level, performance, and structure of the local economy. To test this economy-based hypothesis, I included three economic independent variables: local GDP per capita (logged value), annual GDP growth rate, and ratio of agricultural output to total outputs. Consumption indexes for each province were included to control for the factor of inflation that might affect the amount of center-to-local fiscal transfers. Table 4.2 summarizes the descriptive statistics of all variables.

Table 4.2 Descriptive Statistics of Variables in Fiscal Transfer Analysis

	Count	Minimum	Mean	Max	Standard Deviation
Equal transfer per capita	372	0.00	160.39	3618.62	368.02
Other transfer per capita	372	18.61	758.11	10612.64	988.75
Tax rebate per capita	372	71.72	295.25	2122.85	311.40
Fiscal dependents (%)	372	2.34	3.85	6.55	.95
State-sector employees (%)	403	3.05	6.19	23.96	2.70
Urban *hukou* holders (%)	403	13.36	31.85	72.99	12.66
Ethnic minority (%)	401	0.23	15.28	98.62	21.72
Elders (%)	403	5.09	11.52	21.88	2.60
Fiscal shortage (%)	403	4.91	48.66	94.70	19.71
Agriculture (%)	403	0.66	15.05	37.91	7.54
GDP growth (%)	403	5.10	11.46	23.83	2.48
Log GDP per capita	403	7.77	9.42	11.24	0.74
Inflation rate	402	96.40	101.62	110.10	2.45

Data source: fiscal transfers and dependents data are from *Local Fiscal Statistics* (*di fang cai zheng tong ji zi liao*); data on urban-*hukou* holders are from *China Population Statistics Yearbook*; ethnic minority data are from 2000 and 2010 population census data as well as 1995 and 2005 1% population census data; all other data are compiled from *China Statistical Yearbook* (1999–2010).

According to China's Budget Law, government budgets including fiscal transfers should be made in line with the previous year's. Hence there is high possibility of serial correlation in the fiscal transfer data, meaning that the level of one year's fiscal transfer affects the level of future years. Using first differencing variables or including a lagged dependent variable is a common modeling strategy in analysis of fiscal data. When the serial correlation is severe, however, the first differencing model is more efficient than the lagged dependent variable model (Harvey 1980). Hence, I chose first differencing over including the lag dependent variables in the regression modeling. I first-differenced all the variables and adopted the cross-section-time-series (CSTS) regression model specified below in which the estimated coefficients β should be interpreted as "the change in $y_{i,t}$ explained by change in $x_{i,t}$." $y_{i,t}$ is the per capita equalization transfer, tax rebate, or other transfer for province i in year t; and $x_{i,t}$ is the vector of independent variables for province i in year t, where $i = 1, 2, \ldots 31$ and $t =1998, \ldots 2009$.

$$\Delta y_{i,t} = \beta \Delta x_{i,t} + \varepsilon_{i,t}$$

Table 4.3 presents the CSTS analysis results for the three dependent variables in order: tax rebate, equalization, and other transfers. The findings can be generally summarized as follows. First, the political hypothesis that the central government makes more transfers to the provinces with larger elite groups is supported by results on all three dependent variables. Second, the central government's non-tax-rebate transfers, such as equalization and earmarked transfers, do respond to local fiscal needs: all things being equal, the larger a fiscal shortage a province has, the more equalization and earmarked transfers a province receives. Third, the central government's fiscal transfers also seem to favor the province with a larger agricultural sector (measured by outputs). Despite discernible differences across the three categories of fiscal transfers, the political hypothesis about the center-to-local transfers is clearly corroborated by the provincial level data; the needs-based hypothesis is valid only in certain kinds of fiscal transfers (equalization and earmarked transfers); and the economy-based hypotheses is partially validated (only the size of agricultural sectors is significantly associated with fiscal transfers of all kinds).

Specifically, Columns 1–3 in Table 4.3 show that the increase in the Center's tax rebate to a province is positively associated with the growth of the province's fiscal dependents or urban *hukou* holders; this correlation is statistically significant at a 99% confidence level. This is consistent with the political hypothesis. In contrast, there is no evidence that the increase in the Center's tax rebate to a province can be attributed to the increase of fiscal or welfare needs in the province. In

Table 4.3 Determinants of Center-to-Local Fiscal Transfers

	Tax Rebate			Equalization Transfer			Other Transfer		
	1	2	3	4	5	6	7	8	9
Fiscal dependents	52.910[**]			15.430[*]			78.230		
	(18.010)			(7.145)			(70.030)		
State		9.294			30.520[*]			100.800[***]	
		(7.682)			(14.180)			(28.060)	
Urban *hukou* holders			5.529[**]			−2.152			−9.244
			(1.839)			(6.618)			(5.207)
Ethnic Minority	−11.120[***]	−10.250[***]	−10.200[***]	−1.601	−2.995	−11.610	19.210	15.340	22.940
	(3.001)	(3.038)	(2.868)	(7.308)	(6.447)	(31.200)	(47.270)	(46.580)	(47.730)
Elder Dependents	5.356	4.473	3.980	−0.870	−1.883	−15.490	13.060	9.513	13.390
	(4.570)	(4.540)	(4.447)	(1.427)	(1.643)	(12.930)	(14.910)	(13.500)	(14.600)
Fiscal Shortage	−0.169	−0.205	−0.152	2.587[**]	2.481[**]	10.150[***]	6.536[***]	6.056[***]	6.548[***]
	(0.311)	(0.315)	(0.293)	(0.798)	(0.761)	(2.904)	(1.778)	(1.735)	(1.792)
Agriculture	7.131[**]	6.737[**]	6.603[**]	12.880[*]	11.690[*]	66.240[**]	34.870[**]	31.520[**]	35.630[**]
	(2.292)	(2.181)	(2.253)	(5.191)	(4.719)	(21.010)	(12.640)	(11.880)	(12.700)
GDP Growth	4.563	5.188	4.396	−12.220[**]	−11.110[**]	−8.145	−16.820	−12.810	−15.470
	(2.418)	(2.679)	(2.619)	(4.496)	(4.253)	(12.210)	(10.310)	(11.170)	(10.790)

Continued

Table 4.3 *Continued*

	Tax Rebate			Equalization Transfer			Other Transfer		
	1	2	3	4	5	6	7	8	9
GDP per capita	123.000[*]	99.850[*]	115.000[*]	394.900[***]	344.800[***]	1227.700[***]	590.900[***]	418.800[***]	562.000[***]
	(52.020)	(48.860)	(53.970)	(78.020)	(60.570)	(208.3)	(129.100)	(110.600)	(136.800)
Inflation	−4.872[**]	−5.406[***]	−5.545[***]	2.714	2.969	−22.630[***]	−19.630[***]	−19.210[***]	−20.530[***]
	(1.564)	(1.327)	(1.380)	(1.475)	(1.573)	(4.949)	(4.427)	(4.476)	(4.7610)
Constant	15.220	25.520	14.950	−113.000[***]	−92.33[***]	−315.800[**]	−187.500[*]	−110.000	−174.000[*]
	(15.410)	(18.380)	(13.970)	(31.810)	(25.37)	(119.2)	(81.570)	(73.120)	(73.770)
R^2	0.124	0.124	0.103	0.300	0.303	0.297	0.220	0.224	0.218
N	338	338	338	338	338	369	338	338	338

Standard errors in parentheses; [*] $p < 0.05$, [**] $p < 0.01$, [***] $p < 0.001$.

fact, an increase in tax rebate is found negatively associated with an increase of ethnic minorities in the province's population, which is against the needs-based hypothesis that the central government makes more fiscal transfers to the provinces with larger fiscal shortages or larger elderly or minority populations. But this is not a surprise as tax rebates are to reward and motivate local efforts of tax collection by returning a portion of the taxes collected to the local governments. As for the results on the economic independent variables, they indicate that the increase in the tax rebates can be partially explained by the growth of the agricultural sector (measured by outputs), level of economic development, and lower inflation in the province.

The results regarding equalization transfer (Columns 4–6 in Table 4.3) further support the political hypothesis. The increase in equalization transfer to a province is found positively associated with the growth of fiscal dependents or state-sector employees in the province's population. Unlike tax rebates, equalization transfers can be explained by the fiscal shortage in a province: an increase in equalization transfers to a province is significantly associated with an enlarged fiscal shortage in the province, which partially corroborates the "equalization" purpose of such transfers. Provinces with larger agricultural outputs or slower GDP growth are more likely to receive a higher equalization transfer from the central government; however, provinces with higher GDP per capita are also more likely to receive the equalization transfer. Hence, the Center's equalization transfer seems not to be purely following the "equalization" or redistribution rationale in allocation as rich provinces (higher GDP per capita) tend to receive more equalization transfers than poor ones.

The hypothetical political rationale of the Center's fiscal transfer is further corroborated in the results on other transfers (Columns 7–9 in Table 4.3). It finds that the increase in other transfers made by the Center to the province is significantly associated with the larger number of state-sector employees in a province. Expansion of fiscal needs also partially explains the increase in other transfers the province receives. Other transfers, including various earmarked transfers, seem to favor provinces with a higher GDP per capita, as rich provinces are better able to provide the matching funds required to receive earmarked transfers. Like tax rebates, other transfers are significantly associated with larger agricultural outputs or lower inflation in a province.

So far, we have seen that each of the measures of elites is significantly and positively associated with at least one category of the Center's fiscal transfers to provinces. Since the Center has a different degree of discretion in allocating fiscal transfers across the three categories, it is expected that in "other transfers," the category of fiscal transfers where the Center has the most discretion in allocation among provinces, the correlation between size of elite group and per capita transfer should be the strongest and largest. To test this, I standardized the coefficients of elite groups and grouped them by the category of fiscal transfers, so that we can compare the magnitude and significance of these coefficients across the different fiscal transfers (Table 4.4). The comparison shows that all coefficients of the elite groups (e.g., fiscal dependents, state-sector employees, and urban *hukou* holders) reach the largest magnitude when "other transfers" is the dependent variable. But only the coefficient of state-sector employees when "other transfers" is the dependent variables reaches the highest significance across the three dependent variables. The coefficients of the other two measures of elites—fiscal dependents and urban *hukou* holders—get their highest significance when the dependent variable is "tax rebate," the category of fiscal transfer where the Center has the least discretion due to ex ante set formulas. Hence, there is only partial support for the hypothesis that the correlation between elite groups and the Center's fiscal transfer is strongest or largest when the Center has more discretion in allocating the transfer funds, depending on which measure of the elites is in use.

Although the political explanation of the Center's fiscal transfers to localities is supported by most results from the CSTS analysis using the provincial-level fiscal data, some limitations of the data are worth noting as well as the caveats for drawing implications out of these results. Most important, the fiscal transfers are not exclusively for the purpose of health care benefits. In fact, subsidies for health care or health insurance, whether for the elite groups or for the general masses such as peasants, are only a small fraction of the Center's fiscal transfers to local governments. But the fiscal transfer data are still preferable for this study due to a couple of considerations. First, to my knowledge, the data on the Center's transfers specifically for health insurance and health care are either unavailable or unclear for analysis. Second, it is the fiscal transfer payments in general, rather than the specific transfers for health care purposes, that profoundly shape the local governments' fiscal resources that are considered crucial for local policy choice for health insurance expansion and stratification. A caveat for interpreting

Table 4.4 Standardized Coefficients of Elite Groups in the Different Models

	Tax Rebate	Equalization Transfer	Other Transfers
Fiscal Dependents	.161**	.134*	3.180
State-Sector Employees	.009	.083*	1.291**
Urban *hukou* holders	.014**	−.016	−.118

Note: the three dependent variables (tax rebate, equalization transfer, and other transfers) are in the same scale (per capita, unit: yuan); the coefficients are collected from Table 4.3 and standardized by ratio of the standard deviation for that particular independent variable and the standard deviation for the particular dependent variable.

the above analysis results using the general fiscal data is that the correlations between elite groups and the Center's fund allocation might be underestimated because of multiple purposes of the fiscal transfers.

The other limitation of the fiscal transfer data is that although they are compiled from the same source, it might not be appropriate to pool and compare them across years. The categorization of fiscal transfer varies over time: even under the same title (e.g., tax rebate, equalization transfer), the content of a specific kind or category of transfer can change substantially in some years. Hence, the three categories of fiscal transfers employed in the above analysis are approximate only. The caveat derived from this limitation is that the comparison of coefficients of interest across the three fiscal-transfer categories is suggestive only and it is questionable that the Center has more discretion in the category of "other transfers" (which includes some equalization transfers and most earmarked transfers) than in the other categories such as "equalization transfer."

Despite these limitations in measurement, data, and analysis, there are two validated points from this quantitative study. First, the Center's fiscal transfers can substantially influence the fiscal resources of local governments, especially those with meager local-sourced fiscal revenues. Second, the Center's fiscal transfers are made, at least partially, out of political considerations, namely, to maintain the elite groups' welfare privileges and benefits including health care. In Chapter 6, I treat local fiscal resources, including local-sourced fiscal revenues and the fiscal transfers received from the central government, as a key to examine how they shape local policy choices in the generosity and coverage of social health insurance during the stratified expansion of social health insurance in China from 1999 to 2010.

4.4. Conclusion

Given the resource constraints, and constantly changing international and domestic situations in the late 1990s and 2000s, the Chinese central leaders desired and devised a stratified yet expansive social welfare system to maintain social stability and facilitate economic restructuring. This system was not built overnight but had gone through an incremental and multi-stage process from 1998 to 2011. The deliberations and calculations reflected in the central leaders' speeches show that at first, the Center intended to target the urban state-sector employees in social welfare expansion including social health insurance to preempt social unrest due to SOE reforms and mass lay-offs; a few years later, the Center extended the expansion to non-state-sector employees including migrant workers to increase risk pooling in the existing social insurance programs; meanwhile, the Center incorporated other populations such as informal workers, peasants, and dependents into the social insurance system to facilitate further economic restructuring and maintain social stability.

The stratification of social welfare benefits throughout the expansion period is implicit and often obscured by the dramatic expansion of social insurance coverage. Various internal speeches and communication made by central leaders and ministerial technocrats revealed their hidden concerns and measures undertaken to maintain the elite groups' welfare privileges and benefits during the social welfare expansion. Careful reads of the primary materials suggest that in China's decentralized fiscal system, the Center's fiscal transfers to local governments act as an important means for maintaining the welfare privileges of elite groups (e.g., government and party officials, civil servants, state-sector employees). This chapter later examined the central-to-local fiscal transfers from 1999 to 2009 to discover their patterns and determinants. The finding was that the larger the elite groups in a province, the more fiscal transfers the province received from the Center. This empirical evidence supports the preceding argument presented in Chapter 2 about the Center's interest and support for the stratified expansion of social welfare provision.

Chapter 5 turns to the local leaders, whom the Center must rely on to implement the stratified expansion of social welfare provision in the subnational context. What are local leaders' interests and trade-offs in social welfare provision? How do they respond to the Center's mandate of stratified expansion of social welfare provision in diverse local circumstances with complex social needs? The chapter addresses these questions empirically.

5

Local Motivation and Distributive Choices

Chapter 4 explained the Center's interest and its stratified expansion strategy for social welfare provision. While the Center maintained political control of stratification as it mandated expansion in social welfare provision, it turned to local leaders to implement this policy. The focus of this chapter shifts from the Center to the local leaders. I examined how the Center's strategy was implemented and modified by local leaders within shared national parameters and across a variety of local settings facing vastly different opportunities and constraints. The combination of political centralization and fiscal decentralization impels Chinese local leaders to specify major policies in local circumstances, while balancing the Center's various mandates and directives with local resources and constraints. As such, Chinese local leaders are pressed by two, sometimes competing, forces in policymaking and implementation: top-down political pressure from the Center for policy compliance, and bottom-up motivations or constraints derived from local conditions for policy deviation. Many questions arise about Chinese local leaders. What are their motivations for social welfare development? How do they trade off and respond to the top-down and bottom-up forces in remaking and implementing social policy such as expansion of social health insurance? Why do local policy responses differ across regions?

I argue that, like the central leadership, Chinese local officials pursue social welfare development in their jurisdictions largely to maintain social stability. But, unlike the Center, the local governments directly bear most of the cost of implementing social welfare expansion in local circumstances. Accordingly, local leaders, by taking advantage of their discretionary power, often adapt, or even distort, the Center's stratified expansion strategy of social welfare provision according to local economic and fiscal conditions as well as social needs. For most localities, especially those in the western and northeastern regions of China with relatively low labor mobility and/or fiscal revenues, the Center's standard for expansion of social health insurance is so high that local leaders struggle to find sufficient local resources and solutions to meet the targets; for some localities in the coastal and central regions with high labor mobility and/or fiscal abundance, expanding social health insurance is possible because of local conditions and social needs; however, even these local leaders struggle to ensure that expanding social health insurance does not decrease the stratification of health care benefits devised by the Center for political considerations—that is,

Social Protection under Authoritarianism. Xian Huang, Oxford University Press (2020). © Oxford University Press.
DOI: 10.1093/oso/9780190073640.001.0001

to be sure that the elite continue to receive the most benefits. The reasons for the regional differences in local responses and performances in social health insurance expansion are not only the regional disparities of socioeconomic conditions and resources but also the fundamental conflict or contradiction in the Chinese authoritarian regime's distributive strategy of providing an expansive provision of basic benefits to the masses while maintaining the welfare hierarchy or privilege for the elites. This conflict or contradiction is more manifest at the local level than at the central level because the resource constraints (e.g., fiscal, administrative, and economic) are more salient and the social reactions are more immediately felt at the local level.

To support this argument, I utilized the information and evidence gained from my fieldwork, especially in-depth interviews with 68 government officials, many of them at the provincial and prefectural (city) levels, in 16 Chinese provinces between 2009 and 2013. I used a number of direct quotations from my interviews in the analytical narratives of this chapter. I undertook several measures to minimize the bias in my usage and interpretation of the quotes. First, I provided the context of the interview conversations as well as basic background information on my interviewees as much as possible. Second, I used only those quotes in which the underlying points could be cross-validated in my interviews with others or in other materials gathered from reliable sources (e.g., secondary literature, government publications, and media reports). Third, I organized and excerpted my interview notes by themes, issues, key words, or topical models to avoid "cherry-picking" particular interviews or interviewees to support my argument. Through the qualitative materials, I attempted to build a nuanced understanding of the local distributive calculation and choices in the stratified expansion of health insurance in China during the first decade of the 2000s. The distributive outcomes of those local choices in health insurance expansion are systemically examined in Chapters 6 and 7.

This chapter is organized as follows: Section 5.1 discusses the motivations of Chinese local governments to expand social welfare. Faced with the need to promote both economic development and social stability, Chinese local leaders turned to a variety of strategies for health insurance expansion in the first decade of the 2000s: some localities resisted and feigned compliance for the Center's directives of health insurance expansion while others initiated and actively experimented with expansive policies. Section 5.2 illustrates these local strategies and policy choices with materials drawn from my fieldwork and interviews. Section 5.3 discusses the central-local interactions in maintaining the stratification of social health insurance during the expansion with a focus on the divergence of interests between the Center and the localities and the reasons for local policy deviation. Section 5.4 summarizes and concludes this chapter.

5.1. Local Motivation for Social Welfare Development

Since 1978, the Chinese central leadership's priority has shifted from revolution or class struggle to economic development. In the following decades, the Center, for the purpose of promoting economic development, empowered and incentivized local leaders by adjusting the bureaucratic and fiscal systems to be compatible with local leaders' self-interest in economic development. First, economic development was highlighted and set as a hard target in the official evaluation of local leaders (O'Brien and Li 1999; Edin 2003a, 2003b; Whiting 2004). Local leaders who attempt to stay in office or be promoted must satisfy the upper levels (and eventually the Center) in driving and achieving economic development in their jurisdictions. Second, as local governments are allowed to retain gains from local economic development by sharing taxes with the central government and collecting their own revenues, economic development, by generating business and rent-seeking opportunities, can enhance local leaders' income and personal wealth (Ang 2016; Oi 1992) in addition to their career prospects. Not only are portions of local leaders' salaries and bonuses linked to local economic performance, but various grey and fringe benefits of local leaders are also contingent on local economic development. In other words, local leaders are made stakeholders in the local economy by China's political system. Consequently, Chinese local leaders exert tremendous effort to promote economic growth in their jurisdictions in anticipation of their personal political and economic advancement. Scholars have found that Chinese local officials are acting as corporate entrepreneurs in promoting and devising local economic development (Ang 2016; Oi 1992).

Economic development is not the only work that Chinese local leaders are held responsible for in their jurisdictions. As well as performance on economic development (e.g., growth of fiscal revenue, GDP, and investment), they are also evaluated by the upper levels on social development including improving people's livelihood (e.g., employment, social safety net, social insurance, education, housing, etc.), protecting the ecological environment, and so on (Liu and Tao 2007; Zuo 2015). Based on content analysis of (provincial level) official evaluation rules that cover one third of Chinese municipal leaders, Zuo (2015) found that the weights assigned to social development targets have even exceeded the weights to economic development in the official evaluation of many localities. Hence, economic and social development are two main targets in both the Center's official evaluation and the local leaders' goals.

In theory, economic development and social development are complementary, but in the real world, with constraints of personnel, finance, and resources, these two goals often require a trade-off for Chinese local leaders. Given the relatively low level of economic development and the imperative of economic transition and reform in China during the first two decades after 1978, it is not surprising that Chinese local leaders usually put more weight on economic development than on social development in their thinking and work efforts. After all, social development, especially improving people's livelihood, requires abundant government spending and thus must be based on ample local fiscal revenues and advancement of economic development. As a Chinese local official tried to explain to me during an interview, "When economic development conflicts with social development, the former trumps the latter because people need to eat and have subsistence first [before aspiring to development]."[1] This "productivist" view of social development is commonly found among the 68 Chinese government officials I interviewed between 2009 and 2013 at all levels from the central to the township and 16 different provinces from coastal to western regions. Concerns about increasing labor costs, burden on enterprises, and adverse impact of social insurance contributions on employment especially during an economic crisis or downturn are quite common among Chinese officials.[2]

Exceptions exist, however, in the coastal region where a few local officials expressed a weaker version of the "productivist" view of social development. A Dongguan officer's comment about the relationship between economic and social development really stands out in my fieldwork. He said, "Ten years ago [late 1990s and early 2000s], we [Dongguan government] more considered enterprises' interest, hoping to relieve their [social insurance contribution] burden. In recent years, local enterprises have developed—those still underdeveloped should be out of the game now. [At this time], our policy is more driven by considerations of social welfare and social stability. But this doesn't mean that economic development can resolve social welfare problems automatically [without the government's efforts]." A labor supervisory officer in Kunshan city near Shanghai pointed out more bluntly, "We prefer to protect labor interest given that capital's basic rights and interest are not hurt. After all, labor incidents such as protests and strikes are political issues." These comments point to the deeper consideration and especially the political motivation Chinese local leaders have for social policy making: maintaining social stability, which sometimes might have been obscured by the aforementioned "productivist" views of social development.

Economic development is a necessary but not sufficient condition for China's social welfare expansion. As the quantitative analysis of distributive outcome of Chinese social health insurance shows in Chapter 6, the level of economic development (commonly indicated by GDP per capita) cannot fully explain the regional variation of social health insurance expansion in China. In fact, less developed regions do not necessarily provide less social welfare than the developed regions. For example, certain periphery provinces in the western region with a relatively underdeveloped economy provide generous social benefits comparable to the ones in Beijing, the country's capital city. After all, the Chinese regime's emphasis on economic and social developments serves its ultimate political interest in maintaining the legitimacy and stability of its authoritarian rule (Dickson 2016; Zhao 2009). This ultimate interest is signaled to the local leaders in the centralized bureaucratic system in which social stability is a target with veto power in a local leader's official evaluation (Edin 2003a, 2003b; O'Brien and Li 1999) and maintaining social stability is stressed relentlessly in various leaders' speeches and government documents as shown in Chapter 4.

Knowing the necessity of maintaining social stability and the considerable points or weights assigned to social development in official evaluations, Chinese local leaders who want to stay in office or be promoted can't ignore social policy. Social welfare provision and expansion, for the sake of maintaining social stability, are sometimes made by local leaders independent of the consideration of economic development. A local officer in Dalian city of Liaoning province close to Japan gave me an example in which the health insurance expansion was implemented potentially at the cost of local business and economic growth: "After the enterprises' social insurance contribution was raised in the industrial-development-park district [*gongye kaifa qu*], the burden on enterprises increased a lot. Due to the recession of the Japanese economy and enterprises in recent years [the years following the 2008 global financial crisis], now it is more difficult for us to attract investment. Despite this, we insisted on raising enterprises' social insurance contribution because we must meet the Center's social insurance expansion target."[3] A similar example was found in Kunshan city of Jiangsu province in China's coastal region where social insurance expansion conflicted with the local business and economic interests during the economic downturn in 2008–2009, but local government chose to follow the Center's expansion directive anyway.[4]

To sum up, Chinese local leaders are obligated to promote both economic development and social development in their jurisdictions. Under resource constraints, these two goals often constitute a trade-off for local leaders; in different developmental stages and regions, local leaders might prioritize one goal over the other to different extents. Nonetheless, there is no local government in China that dares to ignore the Center's mandate for social welfare development because doing so may cause social unrest which not only impairs local leaders' political careers but also the Center's ultimate interest— survival and stability of the regime. Local leaders make at least some effort, and in some cases shown in the following sections, certain leaders exceed the Center's expectation in social welfare expansion. It is based on this premise that we continue to examine how the Chinese local leaders responded, actively or passively, to the Center's stratified expansion strategy of social welfare provision between 1999 and 2010, and why these responses differed across regions and across time.

5.2. Local Responses to Health Insurance Expansion

In 2009, the Chinese central leadership unveiled its most ambitious health reform plan in history and committed to expanding social health insurance to provide affordable and equitable basic health care to all.[5] But the implementation of this health reform is remarkably uneven at the local level. The different policy choices at the local level regarding coverage and generosity of social health insurance have disparate impacts on the overall distribution of social health insurance benefits, some of which may diverge from the Center's primary interest. Specifically, some local leaders preferring not to change the pooling level or coverage of social health insurance due to local fiscal stringency or low social risks are reluctant to cooperate with the Center in social health insurance expansion. By contrast, some other local leaders eagerly expand the coverage of social health insurance to counteract the high social risk in their jurisdictions; their efforts might change the stratification pattern and deviate from or even contradict the Center's preference for a stratified social welfare system in favor of the elite groups. Thus, the interactions between central and local leaders, including efforts of control and evasion of control in social welfare provision, stand at the core of the politics of Chinese social welfare expansion. The central-local interaction in social welfare expansion not only exemplifies the contradiction embedded in the Chinese authoritarian regime's design of social welfare provision (e.g., achieving expansion with stratification) but also shows the complex relationship between the Center and local governments with, sometimes, divergent policy preferences, priorities, and goals. In the rest of this section, I elucidate the local resistance to and noncompliance with the Center's directive for social health insurance expansion then turn to the opposite dynamics also found locally: local pioneering initiative and experimentation in expanding social health insurance.

5.2.1. Resistance and Noncompliance

In the first decade of the 2000s, especially since the 2009 health reform, the Center has used several quantified targets for social health insurance expansion—which were included in local official evaluations—such as coverage rate, reimbursement rate, and share of surplus in social health insurance funds.[6] These targets were usually set at specific numbers and applied to all localities. Hence for local leaders, expansion of social health insurance means a uniformly higher coverage rate, higher reimbursement rate, and moderate fund surplus in social health insurance. As a local officer commented, "For the purpose of maintaining social stability, the reimbursement rate of social health insurance has been continually raised [by the Center]. Moreover, the reimbursement rate is considered a hard target and applies to all localities. Many local governments can't meet this target at all. Even those that can afford to meet the target now are doubting that the health insurance funds can sustain [a further increase]"; this local official concluded that "the upper-level government is short-sighted, only caring about political achievement."[7]

Given the vast regional differences in resources and constraints in Chinese localities to meet the Center's health insurance policy targets, many local tactics and practices emerged to make the numbers look good in the indicators for social health insurance expansion. As Chapter 3 has shown, the northeastern and western provinces have relatively low labor mobility and fiscal revenues. The local leaders there have insufficient motivation and capacity to substantially expand coverage of social health insurance. As a result, the most common response in these provinces to the Center's mandate of social health insurance expansion is implicit resistance or feigned compliance. In one provincial-level officer's own words, "Some of our local governments cannot even pay their staff's salaries on time, let alone expand social health insurance [to the people]."[8]

To meet the Center's social health insurance expansion target, local officials in some western and northeastern provinces tolerated or even encouraged duplicate enrollments in social health insurance. Under China's current *hukou* system, millions of rural-to-urban migrants, including peasant workers and rural-born students who work or study in cities for years, still keep rural *hukou* status. In terms of *hukou* status, they are entitled to rural social health insurance benefits through the NRCMS run by the local governments in their hometowns; yet, in terms of employment location and residence, many of them are qualified for urban social health insurance benefits such as the UEBMI or the URBMI depending on the local discretionary rule or policy in the cities where they live. Local officials in the western and northeastern provinces compete to put migrants—the "floating population"—on their social health insurance enrollment rosters, even though they do not receive health services locally. By doing so, they not only easily satisfy the upper levels' demand to increase the size of social health insurance enrollment in their jurisdictions, but they can also ask for more fiscal subsidies from the upper-level government since the amount of fiscal subsidy is usually linked to enrollment size.[9] The more fragmented the local social health insurance system is, the easier it is to make and hide duplicate enrollments. Therefore, duplicate enrollment is quite common in provinces in the northeastern and western regions where multiple social health insurance programs co-exist without much integration; in this way, these local governments can receive greater subsidies for social health insurance from the Center. According to a social insurance officer of Guangxi province in China's southwest, before 2010 the amount of social health insurance duplicate enrollments in Guangxi was estimated to be as high as 30% of local health insurance beneficiaries, compared to

10% nationwide.[10] In 2011 and 2012, the Center frequently sent inspection teams to the western and northeastern regions, examining social health insurance enrollment documents and auditing insurance funds to verify the enrollments of local social health insurance.[11]

It is also common among western and northeastern provinces to make enrollment to the urban and rural resident health insurance (i.e., URBMI, NRCMS) mandatory and based on households instead of individuals. For instance, even though some peasant workers have been enrolled in urban employee health insurance (UEBMI) in their resident cities in coastal provinces, they were made to contribute to the NRCMS of their hometowns with their other family members. An interview with a local officer in Guangxi province revealed that "the expansion of URBMI coverage is mainly dependent on enrolling school students (including those rural-born) to health insurance. In principal, both URBMI and NRCMS enrollments are voluntary. However, local governments usually make them mandatory via administrative means to meet the Center's targets for the local leader's official evaluation and to make political achievements."[12] The cost of compulsorily enrolling rural households including the rural-to-urban migrant workers into rural health insurance (NRCMS) is usually shared among various levels of local governments (e.g., township, county, and city governments) and even township or village-owned enterprises, in addition to the Center's subsidies based on a head count of health insurance participants.[13]

In the central and coastal provinces where labor mobility is relatively high, local motivations are compatible with the Center's mandate for expanding health insurance coverage. In these regions, however, the difficulty of social health insurance expansion usually lies on the generosity dimension. Local leaders, whether in the coastal or central regions, are concerned about rising labor costs or fiscal sustainability in the face of the Center's mandate for continual increase in health insurance generosity. In my interviews with local officers, I often heard their complaints about the "irrationality" of the Center in ordering continual increases of health insurance generosity. These complaints echo two key points I have made about the Center's interest and strategy for social welfare provision elaborated in Chapter 4: first, the Center's decisions on social health expansion are made mainly out of political considerations; second, successful implementation of the expansion is contingent, to a considerable extent, on fiscal subsidization.

When talking about the challenges and problems of local social health insurance, a local officer of Jiangsu province in the coastal region made a point that is similar to my first point: "Social insurance benefits do not match social insurance contributions. The level of benefits is continually elevated by the Center without a corresponding increase in health insurance contribution. The Center raised the benefit level without actuarial calculation."[14] In a similar context, a Zhejiang local office's comment uncovered a common concern about the sustainability of health insurance expansion under local economic and fiscal constraints: "As the reimbursement level has been raised, the pressure to further increase the benefit level is always there. In a recent speech, Premier Li Keqiang announced that the reimbursement rate of social health insurance should be above 70%. It is hard to meet this target in practice. Given the already high fiscal subsidies to social health insurance, further increase of health insurance benefits must increase health insurance contributions [from individuals and enterprises]. I doubt we [local governments] want to do that."[15]

The Center ordered the reimbursement rate of urban residents' health insurance (i.e., URBMI) to increase to 70% of individuals' total medical expenditure by 2011. To meet the Center's target of increasing health insurance generosity, localities came up with many tactics for calculating the reimbursement rate to report in the official evaluation. During my interviews between 2011 and 2012, I learned at least three local tactics to boost the reimbursement rate of social health insurance to satisfy the Center. The first is to exclude the most expensive hospitals, where many services and medicines consumed are not fully covered by regular social health insurance, in calculating the total medical expenditure—the denominator for reimbursement rate.[16] In 2010, the share of inpatient expenses at tertiary hospitals (the highest grade of hospitals in China) in total inpatient expense was 59.7% for urban employees.[17] Localities that exclude this important portion of medical expense from calculation will overestimate the actual reimbursement rate of local health insurance.

The second tactic is to exclude certain popular medical services, such as outpatient service, in calculating the total medical expenditure. In Kunshan city of Jiangsu province, the local health insurance policy for outpatient reimbursement is very generous compared to many other Chinese cities. In 2010, Kunshan's annual average of outpatient reimbursement was 3,000 yuan/person (about 500 USD/person) and it had no reimbursement cap. Despite this, local leaders did not include outpatient services in calculating the reimbursement rate of social health insurance for the official evaluation because it is impossible to reach the Center's targeted reimbursement rate when "the range of outpatient expenditure is broad and the level is high."[18] In 2010, outpatient services accounted for 38.2% of total health insurance expenditure for urban employees.[19] Without considering outpatient expenses, the reimbursement rate is also likely to skew upward.

The third tactic for boosting the reimbursement rate of health insurance is to lower the surplus in social health insurance funds. In order to encourage localities to raise the benefits of social health insurance, the Center set a red line on the surplus of social health insurance funds in its 2009 health reform plan: "Social health insurance funds should balance expenditure and revenue, keeping a moderate surplus. . . . [L]ocalities with a high surplus should raise the generosity of health insurance and lower the surplus within a reasonable range. In principal, the surplus in rural health insurance funds should not exceed 15% of the annual funds or 25% of the total accumulated funds."[20] Since then, monitoring and regulating surplus of local health insurance funds has been one of the key measures the Center has taken to induce localities to increase the benefits of social health insurance. Figure 5.1 demonstrates the change in surplus for UEBMI and URBMI funds, respectively, from 2008 to 2010 by province. For a better comparison across provinces and years, the surplus is presented as the number of months that the respective health insurance funds can sustain without contributions.[21] On average, the UEBMI surplus could sustain 19.6 months in 2008 and

Figure 5.1 Social Health Insurance Funds Surplus in 2008 and 2010 by Province

Notes:

1. Surplus is presented by the number of months that the health insurance funds can sustain without contributions.

2. Surplus data from *China Labor Statistical Yearbook*.

3. UEBMI = Urban Employee Basic Medical Insurance; URBMI = Urban Resident Basic Medical Insurance.

17.8 months in 2010; likewise, the URBMI surplus could sustain 24.1 months in 2008 and 13.8 months in 2010. The decrease of surplus in the urban health insurance funds implies that the Center's control and monitoring of fund surplus were effective, at least to some extent. Further comparing these two figures finds that the decrease in fund surplus is larger in URBMI, the health insurance for urban (non-working) residents, than in UEBMI, the health insurance for urban formal employees. Moreover, almost all provinces had reduced URBMI surplus from 2008 to 2010 while only half of provinces had reduced UEBMI surplus during this period.

In my interviews, some local officers told of the trade-offs they constantly faced between maintaining a sufficient surplus in the social health insurance funds and raising the reimbursement rate to the Center's standard.[22] Sometimes local governments had to sacrifice the surplus in the social health insurance funds to reach the Center's targeted reimbursement rate so as to satisfy the annual official evaluation. In Lidu township of Jiangxi province in the central region, the local practice to meet the Center's target of increasing health insurance generosity was simply to give everyone a lump sum of cash withdrawn from the rural health insurance funds. The Lidu township officers, struggling with the balance between a health insurance surplus and a reimbursement rate increase to satisfy the upper-level government, came up with a trick: they took out a certain amount of money from the rural health insurance funds within the Center's limit on rural health insurance surplus, then divided the money by the number of rural households, and gave each household its proportional amount of money. In 2010, every household in Lidu received 15 yuan in cash (less than 3 USD) from the township government for "NRCMS outpatient reimbursement." However, to justify this "reimbursement" expense, township officers made up the reimbursement documents—creating medical bills and receipts, photocopying NRCMS participants' ID and *hukou* pages, and inputting relevant information into the online bookkeeping system. As a local officer commented, "The cost of administering this 'reimbursement' expense is much higher than the 15 yuan/household cash benefit."[23] The Lidu case might be extreme; in many other localities, a high reimbursement rate was usually achieved simply by using, even running out, surplus in social health insurance funds.[24]

5.2.2. Pioneering Initiatives and Experimentation

Contrary to the local resistance to health insurance expansion in regions like the northeast and the west of China, local initiatives for expanding the coverage of social health insurance in some other Chinese regions are often ahead of the Center's plan and directives. One commonality of the regions with substantial

or advanced social health insurance expansion is that they encounter high social risks, resulting from population aging, mass migration, or labor market
shifts, which motivate local leaders to dramatically expand social health insurance coverage despite a possible decrease in the stratification of health insurance.
Social health insurance expansion per se is encouraged by the Center. However,
expanding social health insurance in a manner that attenuates stratification
undermines the Center's interest, as it generally results in diluting benefits to
the elite groups. Two examples of local social health insurance reform illustrate
the central-local interest divergence in the practice of health insurance expansion: (1) pooling together all the health insurance programs within a local unit
(e.g., county, city, or province); and (2) pooling some urban health insurance
(e.g., URBMI) with rural health insurance programs (NRCMS).

One of the most radical initiatives in social health insurance expansion can be
found in Dongguan city of Guangdong province, a small and young city located
in the Pearl River Delta Area in the coastal region—one of the wealthiest areas
in China. By 2008, Dongguan had 6.9 million residents; among them, 75% were
migrants without local *hukou*. Dongguan is the first prefectural-level city in the
country to abolish divisions of social groups (e.g., urban vs. rural, indigents vs.
migrants, labor market insiders vs. outsiders, state vs. private sector divisions,
etc.) in social health insurance enrollment. Beneficiaries, no matter their income, *hukou*, or employment status (sector, employer size, informality, etc.) all
receive the same package of social health insurance benefits. Such radical reform
measures not only significantly expanded the coverage of social health insurance
in Dongguan but also removed its institutional fragmentation and stratification. Meanwhile, the generosity of social health insurance increased as coverage
expanded. Since 2008, the Dongguan government has subsidized migrant and
peasant workers to join urban social health insurance programs.

The Center has wavered in its responses to Dongguan's radical health insurance reform. On one hand, the Center did not wholeheartedly endorse such reform measures, as "universalism" is never the Center's preferred model for social
welfare provision. According to a Dongguan local official, the city was implicitly "punished" by the Center in many ways because of its radical health reform,
such as losing in the national competition for the title of "the Cleanest/Healthiest
City" (*quanguo weisheng chengshi*).[25] Since the Social Insurance Law took effect
in 2011, Dongguan leaders have encountered increasing pressures to moderate
or even reverse some of the previous reform measures because the Center's preferred stratification pattern of social health insurance has been written into law.
By the summer of 2011, one compromise that the Dongguan local leaders made
in health insurance reform was to introduce supplementary health insurance
benefits for civil servants on top of the local universal health insurance, in order
to maintain a higher level of health care benefit for this privileged group.

Aside from exerting top-down pressure on Dongguan leaders to slow down their radical reform experiments, however, there is not much the Center has done to reverse the health reform in Dongguan. The radical yet pragmatic heath reform measures are welcomed by Dongguan residents, most of whom are young migrants from other provinces, and no social unrest resulted from the change as of 2011. More important, all reform initiatives are financed through local coffers; as one official said, "We receive nothing from the Center for social health insurance benefits."[26]

A similar and even more radical expansion of health insurance took place in Shenmu county of Shaanxi province—a coal-production area in China's northwest. In March 2009, the Shenmu government announced a new health insurance program called "universal free health care" (*quanmin mianfei yiliao*), in which local people could get almost free health care by joining local social health insurance.[27] Like the Dongguan health insurance program, the Shenmu health reform put ordinary residents, peasants, and government officials into the same health insurance pool so all received the same benefits. Shenmu's health reform intended not only to expand health care benefits to everyone with Shenmu *hukou* but also to break the boundaries between urban and rural residents and between bureaucrats and ordinary citizens in welfare provisions. In the context of China's stratified and fragmented social health insurance, such a progressive reform measure was rare and controversial, attracting much publicity and discussion among Chinese academia and media since then.[28] In less than two years since the Shenmu health reform was launched, Mr. Guo Baocheng, the county party secretary who devised and actively promoted the "universal free health care" model in public was demoted and transferred to another place.[29] Shenmu's progressive social welfare reform has decayed since this personnel change made by the Center.

The Dongguan and Shenmu examples represent a scenario in which local pioneering incentives for inclusive expansion of social health insurance directly contradict the Center's strategic interest in maintaining a welfare hierarchy and stratification. Unlike the Dongguan and the Shenmu governments, which can afford to expand both coverage and generosity of social health insurance, local governments in many other Chinese regions with high social risks due to mass migration prefer to expand social health insurance coverage without raising the generosity. An instinctive response of most local leaders who seek to expand social health insurance coverage is to go after the "outsiders," enrolling peasants, rural migrants, and informal or private-sector employees who were previously excluded from the social insurance system. Health insurance expansion is generally encouraged by the Center, but how to expand coverage without changing the Center's preferred stratification pattern of social welfare provision is controversial even within the central leadership itself. In the central provinces such as Sichuan and Hunan provinces, a moderate yet effective local initiative to expand coverage is to pool together the health insurance programs for urban non-working residents (e.g., URBMI) and rural residents (NRCMS).[30] According to the central government's estimates, by 2011 this reform measure had been undertaken by one tenth of Chinese cities, most of them located in regions with high labor mobility such as Guangdong, Hunan, and Sichuan provinces.[31]

The Center has at least two concerns about expanding social welfare provision by merging the urban and rural health insurance programs. First, doing so may hurt the vested interests of some bureaus. Before 2016, the social health insurance program for the rural population (NRCMS) was supervised by the MoH,[32] while health insurance for the urban population (e.g., UEBMI and URBMI) had been supervised by the MoHRSS. Each of these two ministries took credit for administering the respective programs and had tremendous interest in keeping and expanding them.[33] Tensions between these ministries/bureaus arose regarding who should oversee the urban-rural integration of health insurance and who should administer social health insurance after the integration. The ambiguity of the central leadership's decisions on whether and how to merge these health insurance programs[34] led to a variety of local practices in social health insurance integration. Among the 30 prefectural-level cities and 150 counties that had pooled these two health insurance programs (URBMI and NRCMS) together by 2011, some localities put the newly integrated program under the supervision of MoH, some put it under the MoHRSS, and others switched back and forth; a few tentatively put the program under the supervision of a third agency.[35]

The second concern, and the fundamental one for the central leadership, is that expanding social health insurance coverage by merging separate health insurance programs may change the stratified social welfare provision model that is most preferred for political considerations. Of special importance for the survival of the Chinese authoritarian regime is giving different groups different benefits in social welfare provision to weaken their will and capacity for horizontal mobilization that could be a threat to regime stability. Thus, the Center has to trade off the economic gains (e.g., better risk pooling and redistribution) against the political risk (e.g., fewer welfare privileges for the elite groups) of integrating urban and rural social health insurance.[36] As a result, a compromise measure for local leaders who try to expand social health insurance coverage by pooling together different social health insurance programs without inviting the Center's intervention is to differentiate benefit packages for different social groups in the newly integrated health insurance. For example, in Chengdu city of Sichuan province, where the integration of rural and urban social health insurance programs is openly endorsed by the Center, the benefit differentials between rural and urban (non-working) residents are maintained in the new rural-urban integrated health insurance program called Urban and Rural Resident Basic

Medical Insurance (URRBMI). The URRBMI program has three schemes with distinct contribution and benefit rates. Even though rural people can choose the scheme with the highest benefit level, they must pay higher premiums that account for a greater percentage of their disposable income in order to qualify for the enhanced benefits. These pay-out differences in the stratified health insurance end up reinforcing urban-rural divide: urban residents continue to choose the health insurance scheme with the highest benefit and contribution rates while rural residents typically elect the one with the lowest rates.[37]

5.3. Local Responses to Health Insurance Stratification

A considerable part of the politics of social welfare expansion in China lies in the central-local struggles over the implementation of the expansive yet stratified health insurance policy. The root of the central-local tensions in social welfare provision is the Center's competing goals behind social welfare provision. On one hand, the Center attempts to control who gets what, distributing more benefits to the groups that are politically connected or important from the Center's perspective; on the other, the Center seeks to delegate decisions over social welfare provision to local leaders to accommodate many other social groups and the diversity of local situations. The Center's competing and contradictory goals both constrain and compel local leaders, generating various policy choices at local levels, some of which diverge from or even contradict the Center's most desired direction. Given the Center's extensive personnel control and exclusive legislative power, however, many of the central-local struggles or disagreements result in compromise on the part of the local governments, though some of them end in deadlocks of social health insurance reform.

5.3.1. Divergence of Interests

According to the 2011 Social Insurance Law, local governments are responsible for deficits in local social insurance funds. That is, when social health insurance funds run deficits, the local government[38] must take out money from their fiscal coffers to fill the gap. Because of this, local officials have contradictory interests for maintaining the stratification of social health insurance. On one hand, local leaders themselves are part of the vested interest groups enjoying various health insurance privileges, such as not having to pay health insurance contributions after they retire, and having individual health expense (saving) accounts[39] that drain away, on average, 28.4% of employers' (including the government) health insurance contributions for individual use,[40] in addition to receiving a supplementary health insurance or health care subsidy. In this sense, maintaining the stratification is obviously in local leaders' self-interest.

On the other hand, local governments pay a considerable price for maintaining health insurance stratification. First, health insurance privileges such as individual health expense accounts have evidently increased the risk of running deficits in health insurance funds. For example, in Gansu province in western China, 50% of contributions to UEBMI were put aside for individual health expense accounts, so only the remaining 50% of contributions were used for inpatient reimbursement, which accounts for 70% of UEBMI spending. As a Gansu officer explained, "That's why the social health insurance funds are running deficits: we use 50% of health insurance contributions to cover 70% of health insurance expenses."[41] Nationwide in 2010, the growth rate of the funds in individual health expense accounts was 19.5% while it was only 13.2% in health insurance pooling funds; the accumulation rate of the funds in individual health expense accounts was 21.5%, greatly exceeding the accumulation rate in health insurance pooling funds, which was only 11.9%.[42] In some localities, the money lying in individual health expense accounts takes up 60% of total health insurance funds.[43] It is eventually the localities, rather than the Center, that must find ways to make up the shortfall in health insurance pooling funds for reimbursing the general public's qualified medical expenses.

Second, social unrest and complaints about health insurance inequality and fund deficits might harm local leaders in their annual performance evaluation and even their promotion. Although it is not common that a local leader gets punished or demoted by the Center solely because of health insurance policy,[44] the stratification and fragmentation of health insurance has contributed to several important social issues, such as the urban-rural divide and social inequality and stratification, all of which breed social instability. A local officer remarked during my interview, "Decades of working experience [in the social welfare bureau] made me see clearly that the general public (*lao bai xing*) are dissatisfied and feel insecure because of the striking inequality in social benefits. The feeling of unfairness in their minds can easily escalate into social conflict when they see other people getting better benefits."[45]

Third, the stratification and fragmentation of health insurance has caused a surge in administrative costs and at the same time a loss of efficiency. The various social health insurance programs follow different procedures and have distinct rules of funding, reimbursement, and administration. Moreover, information and resources are usually not shared across programs. As a result, health insurance programs are often operated and managed by separate and duplicate agencies under the local government. Many grassroots-level staff of the social health insurance agencies (e.g., accountants, information technology (IT) support, administrators) are contractors, whose salaries and benefits are paid completely from local coffers (including local health insurance funds); only the directors and deputy directors of these agencies are at the civil-servant rank and paid from the central government's budgetary expenditure.[46] Hence, local governments bear most of the administration cost of managing the stratified and fragmented social health insurance.

In summary, local leaders are part of the vested interests that share the Center's preference for maintaining the stratification of social health insurance; nonetheless, local leaders also directly bear the cost of maintaining the stratification. Hence, the more local governments care about fiscal balance, administration efficiency, or social stability, the less they are willing to maintain the stratification of social health insurance despite the fact that their personal interest in health insurance might be compromised to some extent. In China's centralized bureaucratic system, the stakes for complying with the Center are high for local leaders. Nonetheless, it is not uncommon to see cases of local noncompliance or deviation from the Center's directives for maintaining the health care privileges of retirees, urban formal workers, and state employees. The rest of this section, drawing evidence from my fieldwork between 2009 and 2011, reveals the divergence of interests between the Center and local governments in maintaining the stratification of social health insurance: the Center wants to protect the privileged groups by maintaining the segmentation and stratification of social health insurance, while the local governments, directly encountering fiscal and social pressures in their jurisdictions, attempt to mitigate the stratification to some extent by making piecemeal and incremental reforms in health insurance regarding the privileged groups such as retirees, urban formal workers, and state employees.

5.3.2. Protecting Retirees

To reduce resistance during the transition from the previous socialist *danwei*-based welfare system to a social insurance system, the Center's 1998 UEBMI regulation did not require urban retirees to pay social health insurance premiums.[47] This was also to protect the vested interest of urban formal workers who were guaranteed a full pension and lifetime employment by the regime in the socialist era. When population aging sped up and the ratio of retirees to workforce surged in China during the 2000s, this privilege of retirees became controversial and subject to change. Especially at the local levels where shortfalls in health insurance pooling funds were looming, local officials sometimes hesitated to defend retirees' health insurance privileges. In Liaoning province in China's northeast where SOE workers comprise the majority of the workforce, 7 out of 14 prefectural cities were running deficits in health insurance funds as of 2011. As for the reasons for this, a local officer put it frankly: "The dependency rate is too high; retirees don't pay in health insurance but receive monthly payments from the pooling fund (*tong chou ji jin*) of social health insurance."[48] The local predicament, particularly salient in the old industrial base of the Chinese northeastern region, is that the high number of retirees leads to a heavy burden on social health insurance and they strongly resist abolishing the preferential treatments for retirees in health insurance contribution. In the localities with a mass inflow of young labor, however, support for retirees' health insurance privileges is under siege even though the Center reaffirmed its support for retirees' no-premium-payment privilege in the Social Insurance Law that took effect in 2011.

In the Pearl River Delta of Guangdong Province where millions of young migrant workers are employed in the export-oriented manufacturing sectors, local governments used to require retirees to pay health insurance premiums in order to keep their health insurance benefits after retirement. This local practice was pressured to change after 2010 when the Center reaffirmed retirees' no-premium-payment privilege in health insurance through the Social Insurance Law. In July 2011, Dongguan government announced a new policy regarding retirees' health insurance contribution, adding a prerequisite number of years of contribution (premium payment) for retirees to enjoy the no-premium privilege.[49] Similarly, the local government of Zhongshan, another small and open city in the Pearl Delta area of China's southeast, modified its policy regarding retirees' health insurance premiums, changing its requirement for retirees' health insurance contribution from monthly payments for lifetime to a lump sum payment.[50] Note that the 2011 Social Insurance Law doesn't specify an uniform prerequisite (e.g., years of premium payments before retirement) for the retirees' no-premium benefit, which creates a loophole for discretion by local leaders.[51]

5.3.3. Protecting Urban Formal Workers

In the Center's health insurance directives and the 2011 Social Insurance Law, the division between employment-based health insurance (e.g., UEBMI) and residence-based health insurance (e.g., URBMI and NRCMS) is stark. Nonetheless, at local levels, the boundary between these two is often blurred deliberately. The examples of health insurance expansion and integration in Dongguan city and Shenmu county discussed in Section 5.2 are extreme cases in which local governments explicitly and institutionally broke the boundaries in social health insurance for formal employees and for other groups. In other cases, the breach of the boundary for formal workers' health insurance is implicit and subtle. For example, some local governments allow and even encourage non-employees to join the urban employees' health insurance program in order to obtain the best health care from the system. This usually takes place in the coastal region where the household income of average residents is high and local health insurance has a high surplus thanks to a mass inflow of young labor.

In the coastal region, *hukou* and employment status are not rigid determinants of individuals' health insurance benefits. In Kunshan city near Shanghai, for example, over 10,000 local non-employees join UEBMI every year by paying both the individual's and the employer's portions of health insurance premiums. Moreover, migrant workers who are likely to work under temporary or short-term contracts pay the same amount of UEBMI premiums and get the same level of reimbursement benefits as local employees because "migrant workers are a dispensable part of local economic development" in Kunshan.[52] Although the Kunshan government didn't explicitly change the institutional boundary between the different health insurance programs as the Dongguan and Shenmu governments did, it did effectively mitigate the inequality between formal and informal employees in health insurance entitlements through slack implementation of the Center's directives of segmenting and stratifying social health insurance enrollment.

5.3.4. Protecting State Employees

In the socialist *danwei*-based welfare system, Chinese state employees (*ji guan shi ye dan wei ren yuan*) including civil servants and public-institute employees (e.g., employees of public hospitals, schools, media, etc.) were put under the GIS program for health care. Under this scheme, state employees did not pay insurance premiums or co-insurance, yet they received full reimbursement for medical expenses. Hence, the GIS was commonly considered "free health care" (*gong fei yi liao*) in China. As the *danwei*-based welfare system was transformed into a contributory social insurance system in the late 1990s, the mismatch of the GIS with the social health insurance system became apparent. Discontentment with the GIS has increased among both state and non-state employees. On one hand, non-state employees resent the inequity of health benefits, especially the health privileges (e.g., no premium, full reimbursement, access to prestigious hospitals) their counterparts in government agencies or public institutes were given; on the other hand, state employees were dissatisfied with the various limits or inconvenience of GIS compared to the UEBMI, such as limited hospital choices and small risk-pooling. Local officials of the social welfare bureau also complained about the looming fiscal pressures and deficits in GIS funds and the administrative burden of running GIS as a separate health care scheme for a relatively small portion of the population.[53] Thus, the trend toward reform, especially merging the GIS into the social health insurance for urban formal employees (i.e.,

UEBMI), became popular at the local level, though it was mostly confined to the GIS for the less privileged among the elite groups: employees of public institutes (*shi ye dan wei*) and prefectural or lower level government agencies. By 2012, 7 out of 31 Chinese provincial units still kept the GIS scheme separate from social health insurance.[54]

During the dramatic expansion of social health insurance among the mass groups (e.g., peasants, urban poor, etc.) in the 2000s, the Center attempted to appease state employees who had vested interests in the GIS. The Center preserved the welfare privileges of state employees in the 1998 UEBMI regulation by stating that "civil servants (*guo jia gong wu yuan*) are entitled to subsidies for health care in addition to the basic social health insurance benefits."[55] In line with the Center's protective stance regarding state employees' health care privileges, three quarters of provincial units that have undertaken the GIS reform eventually initiated and developed a supplementary health insurance or "double reimbursement" scheme (*er ci baoxiao*) for civil servants in order to maintain these groups' health care privileges after the GIS reform.[56] The supplementary health care benefits for civil servants are financed through either government budgets or drawing funds from the UEBMI pool. In 2010, the per capita budgetary subsidy for retired government officials' health care was 16.5 times greater than the one for peasants and urban non-working residents.[57] The reimbursement rate of basic and supplementary social health insurance for civil servants was estimated to exceed 95% of their medical expenses (95% of their expenses for outpatient service and 97% of their expenses for inpatient service),[58] compared to barely 70% of medical expenses for urban enterprise employees and just 50% of medical expenses for urban non-working residents. Meanwhile, the high-ranking (e.g., provincial and above) government officials' health privileges, such as free health care services and special hospital access and rooms, were kept intact; all central-level civil servants remained in the GIS and outside the social health insurance system by the end of 2012.[59]

Due to the scarcity of data, it is impossible to systematically examine whether and how inclusion of state employees into the social health insurance system has affected risk pooling and the administrative efficiency of Chinese social health insurance. At the least, their inclusion increases the population coverage of social health insurance and thus enlarges the risk pooling of social health insurance, which is generally believed to be conducive to better risk sharing and income redistribution. Figure 5.2 demonstrates the share of state employees in UEBMI as a portion of total beneficiaries by province in 2010. In that year, at least six provinces (Beijing, Shandong, Guangdong, Jiangxi, Jiangsu, Hubei) still kept GIS for their civil servants outside the social health insurance system. In the central and western provinces with relatively underdeveloped economies (e.g., Guizhou, Guangxi, Gansu, Henan, and Qinghai), state employees accounted for

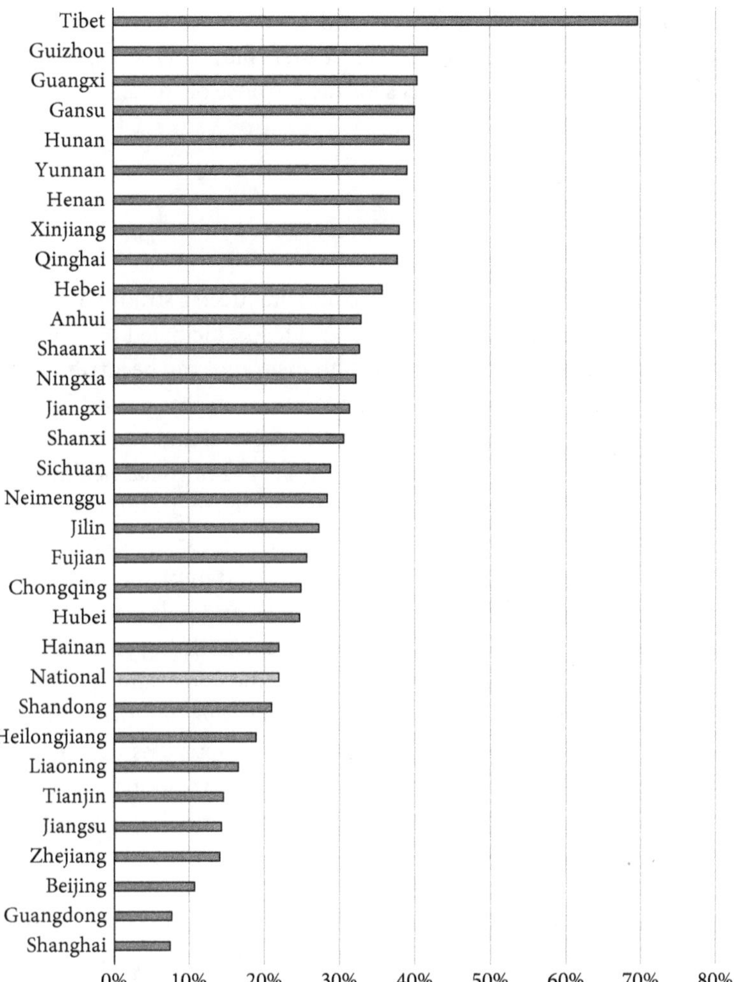

Figure 5.2 Share of State Employees in Urban Employee Basic Medical Insurance, Enrollment by Province (2010)

Note: Data from internal report about the operation of Urban Employee Basic Medical Insurance and Urban Resident Basic Medical Insurance in 2010, Urban Basic Social Health Insurance Report, Ministry of Human Resources and Social Insurance, 2010.

about 40% of UEBMI participants. In these provinces, abolishing the GIS may significantly improve the risk pooling by considerably increasing the funding and participants of social health insurance. This also gives us a hint as to why in the economically advanced provinces such as Beijing, Shandong, Jiangsu, and Guangdong, local governments were reluctant or slow to embark on GIS reform. In these rich and large regions that are likely to have more alternative sources for social health insurance expansion and funding, such as non-state-sector employees and migrant workers, the local leaders may feel less urgency to touch the vested interests of state employees for the purpose of social health insurance expansion.

5.4. Conclusion

The Chinese authoritarian regime devised and practiced a stratified expansion of social health insurance between 1998 and 2011. As elucidated in Chapter 4, the stratified expansion strategy for social health insurance can be attributed to both the Center's economic and political considerations in that period, and eventually to its ultimate interest of maintaining the survival and stability of authoritarian rule. Most important, the stratified expansion of social health insurance was implemented by local leaders who were motivated to promote economic and social development in their jurisdictions for their own career advancement. Like the Center, the local governments' interpretation and implementation of health insurance expansion are shaped by both economic and political considerations, such as advancing economic development and maintaining social stability, although they face vastly different local conditions and constraints to do so.

Drawn from the insights and qualitative materials gained from my intensive fieldwork in China between 2009 and 2013, this chapter has not only demonstrated the regional variation in local policy choices and responses to the Center's directive of stratified expansion of social health insurance but has also provided nuances and examples of the local calculations and tactics in implementing the expansion. In the localities with relatively low social risks and/or fiscal revenue such as the western and the northeastern provinces, local leaders who considered it less imperative or fiscally difficult to expand the coverage and/or generosity of social health insurance came up with many tactics to resist social health insurance expansion or to be deceptive about it; in the localities with high social risks and/or abundant fiscal revenue such as the eastern coastal provinces, local leaders innovatively and proactively reformed local social health insurance to expand coverage and generosity, even at the cost of blurring the stratification of social health insurance preferred by the Center.

The central-local divergence in health insurance policies is most salient in the stratification dimension. As part of the elite group in the Chinese social welfare system, local leaders enjoy enhanced welfare privileges and share the Center's interest in maintaining the welfare hierarchy and stratification. However, it is also local leaders who bear the financial risk and cost of maintaining such inequitable and fragmented health insurance system. As such, it is not uncommon that despite the Center's relentless efforts to maintain the stratification, some localities undertook incremental reforms to mitigate the inequality and inequity of so-cial health insurance between the privileged groups (e.g., retirees, urban formal workers, and state employees) and others. The qualitative materials presented in this chapter illustrate the central-local interactions, including control and evasion of control, during the stratified expansion of Chinese social health insurance in the first decade of the 2000s.

Chapters 6 and 7 shift from political actors' interests and behaviors to the distributive outcomes. Specifically, Chapter 6 examines the distributive outcomes of China's social health insurance expansion across provinces, while Chapter 7 investigates them across social groups.

6

Understanding Subnational Variation in Chinese Social Health Insurance

In previous chapters, I argued that the Chinese central leaders, whose priority is to maintain regime survival and stability, face a trade-off between control and accommodation of local needs in social welfare provision. The centralized bureaucratic system allows central leaders to control the career advancement of local leaders while delegating substantial discretionary power to local leaders in social welfare policy to accommodate diverse social needs at the local level. With discretionary power in hand, local leaders, who care about their political careers and wish to prevent social unrest from jeopardizing their political career, try to specify and implement social welfare policy in a way that suits local circumstances. In this chapter, I show that diverse local socioeconomic conditions have led to different distributional patterns of social health insurance in subnational China through shaping local leaders' policy priority and choice during the health insurance expansion. Specifically, local leaders in provinces with high social risks are more likely to enlarge the risk pooling of social health insurance, while local leaders in provinces with high fiscal revenues are more likely to enhance the generosity of social health insurance. While leaders in regions with favorable risk profiles (e.g., mass inflow of young labor) and high fiscal revenues become pioneers in promoting substantial expansion of social health insurance, their counterparts in provinces with neither high social risk nor sufficient fiscal resources tend to maintain the status quo of a skimpy and inequitable social health insurance system in their jurisdictions.

The analytical goals of this chapter were threefold. The first was to identify and describe the regional patterns of China's social health insurance in terms of coverage and generosity. In order to clearly identify and characterize the regional patterns of social health insurance in China, I grouped Chinese mainland provinces into four clusters and characterized the social health insurance of each cluster. The second goal of this chapter was to examine the local political economy, especially socioeconomic conditions, underlying the distributional patterns of social health insurance benefits in each cluster of provinces, with particular attention to how these conditions shaped local leaders' policy priority and choice under the framework set by the Center in social welfare provision. To illustrate how local leaders made policy choices regarding health coverage

Social Protection under Authoritarianism. Xian Huang, Oxford University Press (2020). © Oxford University Press.
DOI: 10.1093/oso/9780190073640.001.0001

and generosity according to local political economy, I drew on qualitative evidence from fieldwork conducted between 2009 and 2012 in 16 provinces (including provincial-level cities) covering all four clusters of provinces. The third goal of this chapter was to statistically test the relationships between local socioeconomic conditions and regional patterns of Chinese social health insurance. I compiled and used a provincial-level dataset about local social health insurance and socioeconomic conditions for the statistical analysis.

The rest of the chapter unfolds as follows: Section 6.1 recaps central and local leaders' interests and strategies for social welfare provision and then formulates three hypotheses regarding the distribution of social health insurance benefits across Chinese mainland provinces. Section 6.2 presents the cluster analysis and discusses the regional variations and patterns of social health insurance in China. Section 6.3 elucidates the local political economy behind each of the regional patterns of social health insurance, including socioeconomic conditions and local leaders' corresponding policy priority and choice in social health insurance expansion. Section 6.4 presents the statistical analysis results on the correlations between local socioeconomic conditions and distribution of social health insurance benefits. 6.5 summarizes and concludes this chapter.

6.1. Distributive Implications of the Stratified Expansion of Social Health Insurance in Subnational China

The Chinese central leaders' top priority in social welfare provision is to maintain regime stability. Of special importance for political survival of the Chinese authoritarian regime is maintaining particularly privileged welfare provisions for the elites while preserving an essentially modest social provision for the masses. To achieve this, the central leaders face a trade-off between control and accommodation of social needs. On one hand, they attempt to control who gets what, distributing more benefits to the social groups with the most political connections or importance for regime stability. As Chapter 2 has detailed, the Center's control of the stratification patterns of social welfare works through three channels: social legislation, fiscal transfers, and personnel management. Since the 1990s, through a series of legislative moves the Center has established a social health insurance system in which different social groups are entitled to programs with distinct levels of benefits depending on their socioeconomic status.[1] This fragmented social welfare system is conducive to weakening social groups' capabilities for horizontal mobilization while privileging the groups with political connections or importance to the regime. Moreover, as Chapter 4 demonstrates, the Center allocates large amounts of fiscal transfer to subsidize the privileged groups such as party officials, civil servants, and state-sector formal employees, assuring that they receive higher levels of benefits. Through extensive and centralized personnel control, the Center makes local state agents internalize its political interest—maintaining social stability and order—in making and implementing social policy. In the top-down official evaluation system that governs job assignments, performance appraisals, promotions and demotions, and remuneration for government officials, maintaining social stability is a hard target with veto power (Edin 2003a, 2003b; Whiting 2004).

On the other hand, the Center wants to accommodate most social groups to some extent and hopes to avoid too much of a gap between the haves and have-nots. Since the Center has higher costs to monitor and less expertise in distributing benefits among various social groups in a way that maximizes political returns under changing and diverse subnational circumstances, they delegate discretionary power to local leaders in making and implementing social welfare policy. The Center can do this precisely because it controls the career incentives of local leaders and can control the stratification of social welfare provisions through social legislation and fiscal transfers. In the Social Insurance Law and various administrative regulations,[2] the Center has granted substantial discretion to local leaders in specifying the policy details that directly determine the coverage and generosity of social health insurance, such as eligibility requirements, level of risk pooling (e.g., county, city, or province), reimbursement rates, contribution rates, and conditions for premium exemption.

Chinese local leaders are appointed by the Center, and they care about their political careers in the established system. In order to advance their careers, they must meet a variety of policy targets set by the Center. Aside from maintaining social stability in their jurisdictions, economic development and public goods provision are the main responsibilities assigned to local leaders. In social welfare policymaking, local leaders face various constraints: political, fiscal, and social. First, local leaders' policy choices are constrained by the political principles set by the Center. On the surface, Chinese local leaders manage most of the social insurance funds and responsibilities over social welfare provision,[3] which certainly enhances their power through larger budgets, more personnel slots, and greater regulatory power. Nevertheless, their efforts and performance are monitored by the Center through effective top-down personnel control. In addition, local leaders must abide by the Social Insurance Law and various social insurance statutes that have institutionalized the fragmentation and stratification patterns of social insurance.[4]

The second constraint that local leaders face in social welfare provision is fiscal stringency. Under China's fiscal decentralization or de facto "fiscal federalism,"[5] local governments are the main providers of social welfare: they bear about 70% of the cost of health insurance financing for the non-working population, including peasants, the elderly, students, and children. Some local governments face substantial budget deficits (Oi and Zhao 2007; Wong 2009), so paying the medical bills in full and on time is usually a burden on local budgets for these localities. Thus, local fiscal revenue is an important predictor of local leaders' policy choice regarding the generosity of social health insurance. The degree of fiscal stringency differs across regions depending on local fiscal resources, including fiscal revenue extracted from local sources and fiscal transfers received from the Center. Chapter 4 has shown that the Center's fiscal transfers are politically determined rather than equalization-driven: more fiscal transfers are directed to the provinces with larger elite groups that the Center tries to privilege in welfare distribution, such as party and government officials, civil servants, and public-institute and SOE employees. Since the amount of fiscal transfer a locality expects to receive from the Center is mostly predetermined by its sociopolitical profile, the majority of Chinese localities that don't expect to receive massive fiscal transfers from the Center are dependent on local revenues for social welfare provision. As such, fiscal-revenue-starved localities are less able to expand social health insurance especially the level of benefits.

The third constraint that local leaders face is social risk, which is a function of local demography and socioeconomic development. Social risk is a crucial factor shaping local leaders' policy choice in expanding health insurance coverage for three reasons. First, the nature of social health insurance is to pool and mitigate risks across segments of the population. The performance of social health insurance is thus contingent on the demographic profile of localities. A locality with a younger population faces lower risks in social health insurance, for example, than a locality with an aging population. Second, the lack of nationwide risk pooling and an effective risk-sharing mechanism across regions in China's social health insurance system makes the localities with small populations particularly vulnerable to shocks such as disease epidemics and natural disasters. Third and most important, decades of mass migration accompanying economic reform and openness since the 1980s have profoundly changed the risk profiles of many localities. As detailed in Chapter 3, Deng Xiaoping's strategy for economic reform and openness in the 1980s—"let some people (regions) get rich first" starting from the Special Economic Zones in the coastal region—has created a domestic labor market in which some provinces in the central region continuously "export" labor to the ones in the coastal region. Labor mobility works as a multiplier of social risks, creating strong preferences for local leaders in the regions with high labor mobility to enlarge the risk pooling of local social health insurance.[6] For all these reasons, local leaders facing high social risks (due to demography, labor mobility, etc.) in their jurisdictions have strong motivations to expand the coverage of social health insurance to counteract the risk.

In summary, the Chinese central leadership incorporates both elements of control and accommodation in its strategy of social welfare provision for regime survival and stability. On one hand, the Center relies on social legislation, fiscal transfers, and personal management to maintain a fragmented and stratified social welfare system that ultimately divides the society while privileging certain groups over others. On the other hand, the Center delegates discretionary power to local leaders in policymaking and implementation regarding who is covered and how generous their benefits are in order to accommodate diverse local situations and needs.

Local leaders who want to survive under the top-down bureaucratic system attempt to prevent social unrest from breaking out in their jurisdictions by proactively providing and distributing social welfare benefits in a manner that suits the local conditions and social needs of their constituents. Since local leaders' discretion in social welfare policy lies mainly in coverage and generosity, they have four different choices in distributing social insurance benefits: (1) a generous and inclusive pattern: giving more people generous benefits, (2) a generous yet exclusive pattern: giving certain groups more benefits, (3) a strict yet inclusive pattern: giving meager benefits to more people, and (4) a strict and exclusive pattern: giving only meager benefits to only certain people.

The distributive pattern that local officials eventually choose is determined by the configuration of constraints they face, particularly in terms of fiscal resources and social risks in their jurisdictions. High social risks without adequate fiscal resources at local governments' disposal motivate local leaders to expand health insurance in a strict yet inclusive pattern of benefit distribution (i.e., giving meager benefits to more people); on the contrary, abundant fiscal revenues (whether locally sourced fiscal revenues or fiscal transfers from the central government) combined with low social risks encourage local leaders to expand only the generosity of social health insurance (i.e., giving certain people more benefits). In contrast, a combination of both high fiscal revenues and social risks leads to an expansion of social health insurance with a generous and inclusive pattern (i.e., covering more people with generous benefits); by the same logic, a combination of low fiscal revenues and social risks is conducive to a feigned expansion of social health insurance or an expansion in a strict and exclusive manner (i.e., giving only meager benefits to only certain people).

Observable implications can be derived from the above theoretical arguments. First, the local distribution of social health insurance benefits differs significantly along the dimensions of generosity and coverage where the Center delegates substantial authority to local officials. Second, the generosity and coverage of social health insurance vary with the local political economy, particularly its fiscal and socioeconomic conditions, and this constrains local officials' policy choices. Based on these implications, I formulated the following hypotheses for empirical tests.

Hypothesis 1: The provision of Chinese social health insurance has systematic regional variation in terms of generosity and coverage.

Hypothesis 2: Provinces with more fiscal resources provide more generous social health insurance than others do.

Hypothesis 3: Provinces with higher social risks provide broader coverage in social health insurance than others do.

6.2. Regional Variation in Chinese Social Health Insurance

To test the hypotheses, I compiled a provincial-level panel dataset (1999–2010) using government statistics. In China, all local governments (including provinces, prefectures and counties, but excluding townships) manage certain social health insurance programs.[7] The province is selected as the unit of analysis in the following quantitative studies for two reasons. First, as of the time of writing this book, all available Chinese social health insurance statistics were reported at national or provincial levels. The merit of these statistics is that they cover all Chinese mainland provinces and time periods from 1999 when social health insurance was established in China. However, the drawback is that the statistics are too aggregated to conduct intra-province or inter-prefectural analysis. Considering both the merits and the drawbacks of the data, I decided to use the province as the unit in quantitative analysis while complementing it with qualitative evidence drawn from my field interviews at the other local levels (e.g., prefecture/city, county, and township). Second, for analytical simplicity, the theoretical analysis assumes that the Chinese political structure consists of only two levels, the central and the local levels, and that the logic underlying the interaction between central and local levels is probably applicable to the interactions between upper and lower levels within local governments. Hence, using the province as the unit of quantitative analysis does not contradict the theory, but we need to keep its limits in mind when interpreting the empirical analysis results and their implications.

To examine the local distribution of health insurance benefits, I constructed two variables—generosity and coverage. Generosity is measured as annual per capita expenditures on social health insurance. Coverage refers to the percentage of the population in a particular location covered by social health insurance. Data were compiled from government statistics[8] and were averaged for 2007 through 2010.[9] The results indicate that both coverage and generosity of Chinese social health insurance have remarkable regional variations: health insurance coverage was much higher in the central and coastal regions than in the northeast and western regions; in contrast, health insurance generosity was significantly higher in the western and coastal regions than in the central and northeastern regions.

Based on the coverage and generosity variables, I conducted a cluster analysis[10] to further examine whether it is possible to discern statistically distinct patterns in Chinese social health insurance. All Chinese mainland provincial-level units were ranked according to these two variables, and the rank values for each province on both variables were used as inputs for cluster analysis. The first step of interpreting the cluster analysis results was to determine how many clusters exist among Chinese provinces in terms of generosity and coverage of social health insurance. Based on conventional procedures for cluster analysis,[11] the results (Table 6.1) indicate four

Table 6.1 Determining the Number of Clusters Using the Duda and Hart Method

Number of Clusters	Duda/Hart	
	Je (2)/Je (1)	Pseudo T-squared
1	.6236	17.51
2	.4543	21.63
3	.1848	39.71
4	.5148	9.43
5	.2461	18.38
6	.4007	7.48
7	.4517	4.86
8	.2381	9.60
9	.0000	—
10	.3490	5.60
11	.0268	36.33
12	.4105	4.31
13	.4985	3.02
14	.1172	7.53
15	.2786	2.59

Notes:

1. Je (1) is the squared errors when there is one cluster, and Je (2) is the sum of squared errors within a cluster when the data are broken into two clusters.

2. The conventional rule for deciding the number of groups is to determine the largest Je(2)/Je(1) value that corresponds to a low pseudo-T-squared value that has a higher T-squared value above and below it.

significantly distinct clusters among Chinese provinces in terms of generosity and coverage of social health insurance.

The next step was to examine which provinces fall into each cluster and what characteristics each cluster has. Table 6.2 reports the province members of each cluster and their ranks of generosity and coverage. Cluster 1 consists of five provinces in the coastal region (Shandong, Jiangsu, Zhejiang, Fujian, and Guangdong) and one ethnic autonomous region—Tibet. Cluster 2 includes three provincial-level municipalities (Beijing, Shanghai, and Tianjin) and three ethnic minority-concentrated provinces in China's northwest—Xinjiang, Ningxia, and Qinghai. Cluster 3 covers most northern provinces (Heilongjiang, Jilin, and Liaoning, Shanxi, Shaanxi, Hebei) and several southern provinces (Hubei, Guangxi, Yunnan, and Hainan) in the central region. Cluster 4 is composed of other central and western provinces such as Henan, Anhui, Jiangxi, Hunan, Sichuan, and Chongqing.

Computing the cluster average ranks on the two indicators makes the features of each cluster readily apparent: cluster 2 and cluster 4 are starkly distinct from one another. Provinces in cluster 2 clearly privilege generosity over coverage in health insurance expansion, all of them having high ranks on generosity but low ranks on population coverage. Provinces in cluster 4 are just the opposite. Moreover, provinces in cluster 1 appear to favor both coverage and generosity in health insurance expansion, as they rank relatively high on both. In contrast, provinces in cluster 3 have low values on both generosity and coverage. Based on the characteristics of these clusters, provinces in cluster 2 are referred to as "the privileging type," because they place an emphasis on generosity in health insurance expansion. Provinces in cluster 4 are labeled "the risk-pooling type," as they prioritize coverage over generosity in health insurance expansion. Since provinces in cluster 1 favor both generosity and coverage in health insurance expansion, they are referred to as "the dual type." By contrast, average generosity and coverage are both relatively low in provinces of cluster 3, reflecting the status quo of social health insurance before expansion, and hence cluster 3 is called "the status-quo type."

The cluster analysis results not only validate Hypothesis 1 but also suggest that the regional variation of social health insurance correspond well to regional socioeconomic differences. To demonstrate this, the clustering is presented on a map of mainland China (Figure 6.1). The map reveals that the northeast and the southwest regions are predominantly of the status-quo type. Their counterparts in the east coastal region are mainly of the dual type. The populous provinces along the Yangtze River in the central region, such as Sichuan, Hunan, Hubei, Jiangxi, and Anhui, are of the risk-pooling type. Meanwhile, Chinese metropolises, namely, Beijing, Tianjin, and Shanghai, and the ethnic minority autonomous provinces in the northwest are of the

Table 6.2 Clustering of Chinese Mainland Provinces by Social Health Insurance Attributes

Cluster	Province	Coverage	Generosity
1	Shandong	11	12
1	Jiangsu	8	9
1	Zhejiang	16	7
1	Fujian	12	10
1	Guangdong	17	6
1	Tibet	10	3
cluster average		*12*	*8*
2	Beijing	28	1
2	Shanghai	29	2
2	Tianjin	30	5
2	Xinjiang	27	8
2	Ningxia	21	11
2	Qinghai	25	4
cluster average		*27*	*5*
3	Heilongjiang	31	25
3	Jilin	22	30
3	Liaoning	23	13
3	Inner Mongolia	26	19
3	Hebei	19	23
3	Shanxi	24	17
3	Shaanxi	15	20
3	Hubei	13	26
3	Guangxi	14	27
3	Hainan	20	24
3	Yunnan	18	14
cluster average		*21*	*22*
4	Henan	3	29
4	Anhui	1	21
4	Jiangxi	7	31
4	Hunan	6	22
4	Gansu	5	18
4	Sichuan	4	15
4	Chongqing	2	16
4	Guizhou	9	28
cluster average		*5*	*23*

Notes: The cluster analysis results are calculated using the *cluster linkage* command in STATA/IC 12.0 for Windows. Ward's linkage is used as the agglomerative linkage method in this cluster analysis. The stopping rule is the Duda/Hart Je(2)/Je(1) index stopping rule. Ranks are rounded to the nearest integer to facilitate comparability.

privileging type. Overall, the results from the cluster analysis support the first hypothesis that systematic and different patterns of social health insurance exist among Chinese provinces.

6.3. Local Political Economy and Regional Variation of Social Health Insurance

The clustering of Chinese mainland provinces in social health insurance shown in Figure 6.1 appears to correspond to the key differences of regional economies in the coastal, central, northeastern, and western regions outlined in Chapter 3. The dual type provinces are mostly in the coastal region where the China's manufacturing and export centers are concentrated. Export-oriented development of labor-intensive manufacturing in this region not only has generated high fiscal revenues for local governments but has also attracted millions of young migrant workers from the provinces in the central and western regions with large

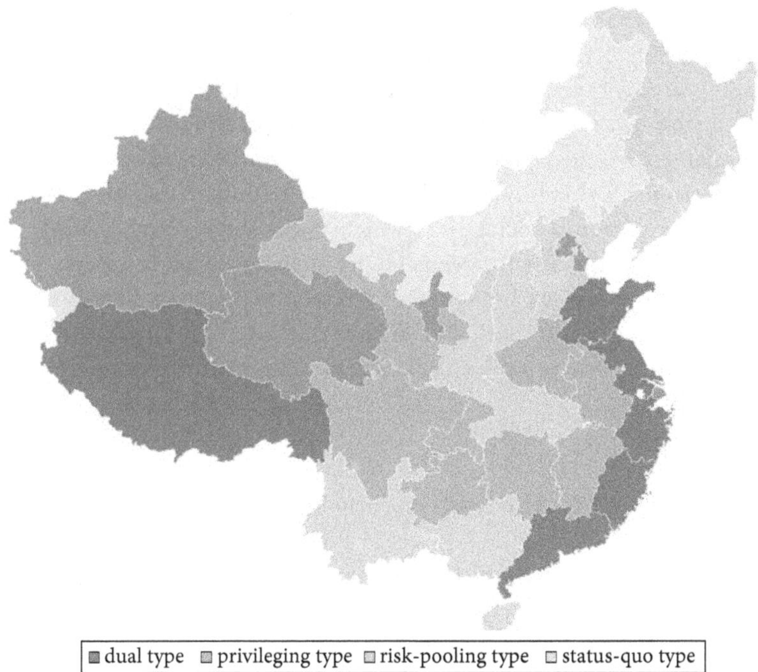

Figure 6.1 Clusters of Chinese Mainland Provinces by Social Health Insurance Attributes

Data source: China Human Resources and Social Security Yearbooks, 2007–2010.

Mainland agricultural sectors and populations. The status-quo type provinces are mostly in the northeast and southwest regions with a less developed economy.

However, regional economies can't fully explain the clustering and the regional variations of Chinese social health insurance. Within each cluster of provinces shown in Table 6.2 and Figure 6.1, the economic differences across provinces are considerable and even prominent in some cases. For example, the privileging type cluster comprises both economically advanced metropolises in the coastal region (Beijing, Tianjin and Shanghai) and the underdeveloped ethnic minority provinces in the western region (Xinjiang, Ningxia). The economic contrasts between these two are stark: in 2010 the coastal region's GDP per capita was three times that of the western region; the coastal region's per capita local government revenue was five times the western region's; the coastal region's total foreign trade was over 16 times the trade of the western region. Obviously economic factors alone can't explain the convergence of local leaders' distributive choices in social health insurance between the coastal metropolises and the western ethnic minority regions. It is the Center's fiscal transfers, based on political consideration and calculations, that fill the shortfall in fiscal revenues of the poor ethnic minority regions to facilitate continuous increase of social health insurance generosity in provinces like Tibet, Ningxia, and Xinjiang. As such, it is more sensible to consider regional economic factors combined with political leaders' interests, strategies, and policy choices elucidated in previous chapters to understand the regional clustering and variations in Chinese social health insurance.

Regional economic factors (GDP, industrialization, urbanization, trade) contribute to the formation of the local socioeconomic conditions (e.g., fiscal affluence or constraint, social risk) which influence political leaders' policy choices that shape the distributive outcome of social health insurance we have observed across provinces. In the rest of this section, I rely on the fieldwork that I conducted between 2009 and 2012 to illustrate the conditions in the local political economy that shape policy choices in local health insurance expansion for each type of province.

6.3.1. The Risk-Pooling Type Provinces

Provinces whose urban social health insurance is categorized as "the risk-pooling type" are Gansu, Sichuan, Chongqing, Henan, Hunan, Hubei, Jiangxi, Anhui, and Guizhou. They are in the central-west and central-south of China. Many local initiatives for expanding social health insurance coverage in China were found in these risk-pooling type provinces. One of the prominent features in the political economy of these provinces is mass labor outflow since the 1990s.

Most Chinese migrant workers in the east coastal region—the powerhouse of the Chinese economy—come from these provinces in the central region. According to China's national population census data between 1995 and 2010 (Table 6.3), Henan, Sichuan, Hunan, and Anhui are the provinces with the largest labor outflows. Mass outflows of labor exert tremendous pressures on local social health insurance funds because those who stayed, especially in the rural areas, are mainly elders and children who are more likely to need health care.[12] In this circumstance, social health insurance of the risk-pooling type provinces generally has large population coverage but lower level of benefits, indicating that the priority was to enlarge risk pooling during social health insurance expansion. This priority is exemplified by these provinces' desire for using larger risk pooling to address existing or potential deficits in local social health insurance funds.

Through my interviews in the risk-pooling provinces, I often found that local officials there shared strong concerns about existing or looming deficits in local health insurance funds. These concerns stemmed from the outflow of millions of young laborers from these regions in the three decades after 1978. Because of labor outflow, the dependency ratio in all these provinces, except Hubei, was above the national average in 2010; this generated high financial pressure on local health insurance and thus the political imperative of social health insurance expansion. As an administrator of social health insurance in Zhengzhou city of Henan province put it, "Failure or delay in [health insurance reimbursement] payments will give rise to public grievances and risk collective protests. No local officials dare to take the risk."[13] This concern drove local officials in the risk-pooling provinces to prioritize expanding social health insurance coverage over generosity in order to obtain a larger risk-sharing pool for social health insurance funds. Every year, when the health insurance enrollment period starts, local officials in the risk-pooling provinces intensively utilize propaganda and social media, such as microblogs and mobile-phone text message, to mobilize people—especially young people—to join local social health insurance programs.[14] Moreover, the requirement of holding local *hukou* was often ignored or de-emphasized by local officials in the risk-pooling provinces to obtain higher enrollment of social health insurance.[15]

In 2004, coastal manufacturing centers in China began to report labor shortages as factories struggled to attract enough young migrant workers onto their production lines (Gallagher 2016). The shortage became more severe over time. Since the economic downturn due to the global financial crisis in 2008, an increasing number of Chinese migrant workers who were already in their 30s or 40s began returning to their hometowns or home provinces in the central and the western regions. Local officials of these provinces actively targeted the returning laborers, arranging special handling (e.g., temporary lower premiums, combining work injury, maternity, and health insurance together) to induce

Table 6.3 Internal Migration by Province during 1995–2010

Province	1995–2000 migration (10,000 persons)			2005–2010 migration (10,000 person)		
	Inflow	Outflow	Inflow-Outflow	Inflow	Outflow	Inflow-Outflow
Eastern China	**2466.64**	**597.48**	**1869.16**	**4357.92**	**1193.36**	**3164.56**
Beijing	188.97	17.44	171.53	382.78	40.6	342.18
Tianjin	49.20	10.43	38.77	149.71	21.34	128.37
Hebei	76.99	87.22	−10.23	92.41	201.74	−109.33
Shandong	90.41	87.82	2.59	133.56	201.50	−67.94
Liaoning	75.48	37.99	37.49	117.19	68.54	48.65
Shanghai	216.78	16.29	200.49	490.05	40.10	449.95
Jiangsu	190.84	124.10	66.74	488.73	189.35	299.38
Zhejiang	271.47	96.98	174.49	837.29	133.94	703.35
Fujian	134.62	62.45	72.17	244.99	111.37	133.62
Guangdong	1150.11	43.80	1106.31	1387.44	161.29	1226.15
Hainan	21.77	12.96	8.81	33.77	23.59	10.18
Central China	**353.93**	**1743.59**	**−1389.66**	**606.61**	**2941.43**	**−2334.82**
Guangxi	28.75	183.81	−155.06	59.78	282.05	−222.27
Anhui	31.35	289.30	−257.95	82.21	552.56	−470.35
Shanxi	38.27	33.36	4.91	49.82	79.37	−29.55
Inner Mongolia	32.55	44.11	−11.56	82.77	64.76	18.01
Jiangxi	23.59	268.06	−244.47	69.84	348.33	−278.49
Jilin	25.40	52.93	−27.53	33.84	85.39	−51.55
Heilongjiang	30.12	93.98	−63.86	32.19	146.32	−114.13
Henan	46.99	230.90	−183.91	42.97	543.04	−500.07
Hubei	60.65	221.02	−160.37	84.35	380.42	−296.07
Hunan	36.26	326.12	−289.86	68.84	459.19	−390.35
Western China	**400.61**	**883.61**	**−483**	**525.67**	**1358.39**	**−832.72**
Sichuan	58.96	439.55	−380.59	105.28	498.81	−393.53
Chongqing	44.78	110.31	−65.53	73.56	184.41	−110.85
Guizhou	26.15	123.19	−97.04	59.19	268.08	−208.89
Yunnan	73.27	39.81	33.46	62.09	108.91	−46.82

Table 6.3 *Continued*

Province	1995–2000 migration (10,000 persons)			2005–2010 migration (10,000 person)		
	Inflow	Outflow	Inflow-Outflow	Inflow	Outflow	Inflow-Outflow
Shaanxi	42.30	71.93	−29.63	73.4	134.75	−61.35
Gansu	20.36	56.08	−35.72	26.02	104.69	−78.67
Qinghai	7.69	12.32	−4.63	18.25	15	3.25
Ningxia	12.88	8.74	4.14	23.9	15.07	8.83
Xinjiang	114.22	21.68	92.54	83.98	28.67	55.31

Notes: 1995–2000 migration data are compiled from China's 5th Population Census Statistics (2000); 2005–2010 migration data are from China's 6th Population Census Statistics (2010).

them to register for local social insurance. Some local leaders of the risk-pooling provinces went further, negotiating with their counterparts in the coastal region to transfer back the money in the returning migrants' personal health insurance saving accounts that had been opened in the coastal provinces when the persons were working there.[16] These initiatives and tactics commonly seen in the risk-pooling-type provinces have resulted in higher population coverage of social health insurance compared to other provinces.

6.3.2. The Dual Type Provinces

The provinces whose social health insurance is characterized as the dual type, meaning both high generosity and coverage, are predominantly the prosperous provinces in the coastal region of China, such as Jiangsu, Zhejiang, Guangdong, Fujian, and Shandong. The benefits provided through social health insurance in these provinces, though not the highest in the country, are all above the national average level. Pioneers of social health insurance integration across social groups are also found among the local leaders in these provinces. For example, social health insurance expansion in these regions was made inclusive, with working migrant workers entitled to employment-based and even residency-based health insurance. In 2010, the social health insurance enrollment of migrant workers experienced negative growth in half of Chinese provinces while it steadily increased in the dual type provinces such as Jiangsu, Fujian, Zhejiang, and Guangdong.[17] The high generosity and coverage of social health insurance in the dual type provinces can be attributed to their strong local fiscal capacity and high labor mobility. The developed economies of these provinces, indicated by high levels of GDP per capita, economic openness, industrialization, and urbanization, generated abundant fiscal resources for social welfare development. Between 1999 and 2010, the per capita government revenues of these coastal provinces were almost twice the national median. Also, the Center's fiscal transfers account for less than 5% of social health insurance financing in these provinces. As local officials in Dongguan city of Guangdong province in southeast China noted, "We received nothing from the Center for social health insurance, and the prosperous local economy is sufficient to support it [local social health insurance]."[18]

In the dual type provinces, benefits of social health insurance have increased as coverage has expanded. For example, since 2008 the local government in Dongguan, a prefectural city in Guangdong province, has been generously subsidizing not only the local population but also "outsiders," such as rural-to-urban migrants and peasant workers, to help them enroll in local social health insurance. This constitutes a stark contrast with the health insurance expansion in the risk-pooling type provinces where local officials usually hold conservative and sometimes adverse views toward increasing benefits when coverage expands. When talking about local social health insurance, a local official in Kunshan, a county-level city with remarkably successful manufacturing sectors in a dual type province, Jiangsu, commented that "the prosperity of the local economy is impossible without the contributions of the migrant workers [so they deserve the increased benefits]." This official continued, "But those young people rarely go to hospitals, so that [despite high generosity] we have been running a surplus in social health insurance funds for years."[19]

Given that the local economy in the dual type provinces relied heavily on the inflow of migrant workers for labor-intensive manufacturing, the local officials there determined to build a large risk-sharing pool in social insurance to counter the high risks associated with market fluctuation and the potential of large labor outflows. Over time, these coastal provinces with high labor mobility have accumulated a huge amount of surplus in local social health insurance funds (see Figure 6.2), an indication of local officials' successful efforts to incorporate young labor into local social health insurance coverage. The surplus further mitigates the policy trade-off commonly faced by Chinese local leaders between expanding coverage and increasing benefits. As both fiscal and labor resources are conducive to health insurance expansion in the dual type provinces, the implementation of health insurance expansion in both coverage and generosity is greater here than in the other types of provinces.

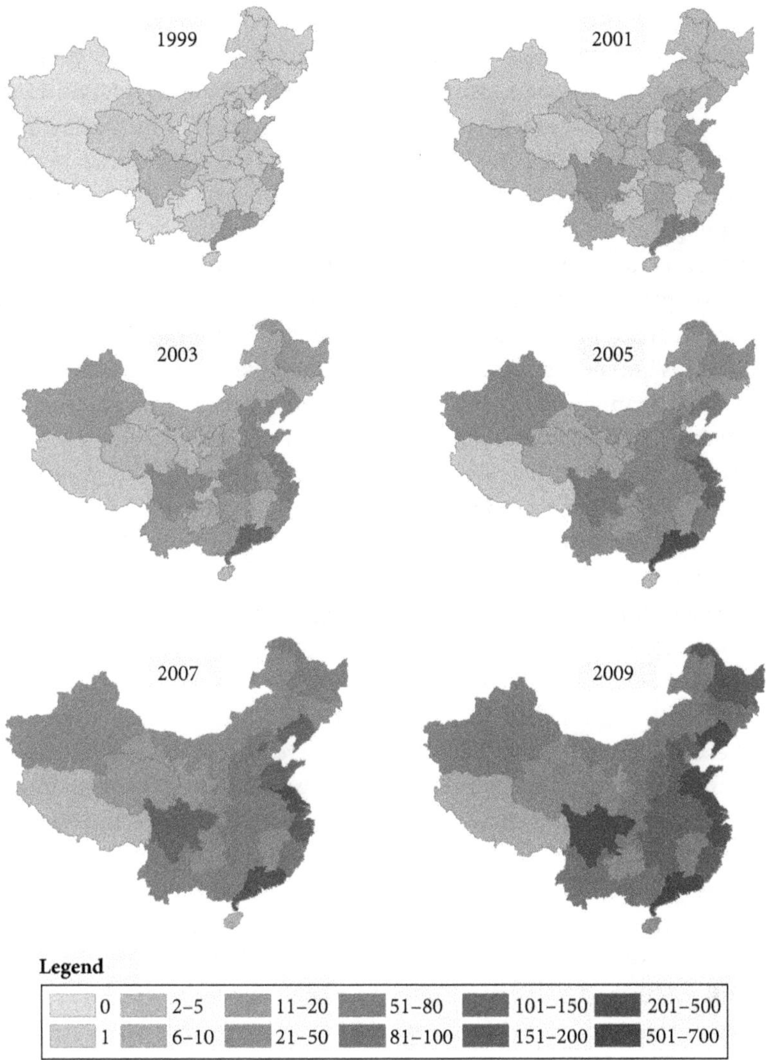

Figure 6.2 Urban Employee Basic Medical Insurance Fund Surplus by Province
Note: Unit is billion yuan; data from Local Financial Statistics *(di fang cai zheng tong ji zi liao hui bian)*.

6.3.3. The Privileging Type Provinces

Provinces whose social health insurance is categorized as "the privileging type" by the cluster analysis are Beijing, Tianjin, Shanghai, Xinjiang, Qinghai, and Ningxia. The first three are Chinese province-level municipalities locating in the coastal region and the last three are ethnic minority provinces in remote areas of China's Northwest. The social health insurance systems of both regions are characterized by generous yet exclusive benefits, revealed by their high ranks in generosity but relatively low ranks in coverage. Their priority of increasing benefits to certain people indicates the inclination of these local governments to overspend on the social welfare of selected groups; it also reflects the abundant fiscal transfers or political favors[20] these provinces receive from the Center.

Like their counterparts in the dual type provinces, local officials in the privileging type provinces were pioneers in raising the generosity of social health insurance. A trend of "double reimbursement" (*er ci baoxiao*) in social health insurance was initiated in some of the privileging type provinces such as Beijing, Tianjin, and Shanghai in 2010. "Double reimbursement" means that social health insurance beneficiaries can receive another reimbursement for their medical expenses at a reimbursement rate of over 50%, if local social health insurance funds have or are expected to have a surplus by the end of the year.[21] In the provinces that allowed "double reimbursement," individuals' or households' out-of-pocket medical expenses were lower, indicating more generous benefits from social health insurance. It is worth noting that the "double reimbursement" benefit is not conditional on increased premium payments by individuals or households; instead, it is based on local leaders' projection of a surplus of funds in social health insurance or just a government budget surplus. Given the advanced economies and abundant local fiscal revenues in the metropolises like Beijing and Shanghai, it is not a surprise that they initiated "double reimbursement" in social health insurance to enhance generosity. As for the other privileging type provinces, mainly the ethnic minority autonomous regions whose economies are relatively underdeveloped, expansionary spending initiatives and experimentations were not uncommon in local social health insurance.[22] The heavy dependence of local public finance on the Center's fiscal transfers and grants reduces these provinces' incentives for spending forbearance.

The privileging type provinces clearly differ from the dual type provinces in that the generous health insurance benefits in the privileging type provinces were exclusive and designated for only certain groups such as party officials, civil servants, selected formal state-sector employees, or in general, people with local urban *hukou*. During field interviews in the privileging type provinces and municipalities such as Ningxia and Beijing, I found that the local officials were reluctant to sponsor non-locals or labor-market outsiders to participate in local social health insurance out of fear that broad inclusion would dilute the fiscal favors received from the Center for the targeted and concentrated privileged groups. Local social health insurance administrators in these provinces relentlessly stress local *hukou* and/or long-term local employment as crucial prerequisites for social entitlements and welfare benefits, a stark contrast to the slack enforcement of the local *hukou* requirement in social health insurance enrollment in the risk-pooling provinces like Anhui and Hunan.

Provincial-level municipalities like Beijing and Tianjin tend to have larger elite groups (civil servants, SOE and public-sector employees) while the ethnic minority autonomous regions in China's northwest hold more concentrated and religious ethnic minority groups (e.g., Uygurs, Tibetans, and Hui). Concentration of the elite or privileged groups in these provinces induce greater fiscal transfers from the Center to these provinces for co-opting and placating these groups. The heavy weight of the Center's fiscal transfers in financing social health insurance in the ethnic minority autonomous regions further impedes local incentives to creatively broaden the coverage of social health insurance.[23] As a social insurance official in Ningxia Hui Minority Autonomous Region put it frankly, "We have been receiving a lot of fiscal transfers from the Center, and we want to use that money only on the designated groups."[24]

The low or restricted labor mobility in the ethnic minority autonomous regions and the metropolises also partially accounts for the lack of motivation for the local leaders to expand social insurance coverage to outsiders. In China, the criteria for admitting migrants to the local *hukou* population category in cities are mostly set by local governments, as opposed to the central government (Chan and Buckingham, 2008). The locally set entry requirements in the metropolises such as Beijing, Shanghai, and Tianjin, namely, college degrees, stable employment and income, paying social insurance premiums for at least five years, have no relevance to the great majority of migrants with rural origins who tend to be low skilled and work in informal sectors (Wallace 2014; Chan 2010). Since *hukou* policy is closely related to social insurance policy and welfare entitlements, such restrictive *hukou* policy in the privileging provinces/municipalities reflects their local governments' reluctance to expand social spending and welfare provisions beyond the insiders.

6.3.4. The Status-Quo Type Provinces

The social health insurance in the remaining provinces, such as Guangxi, Yunnan, Hainan, Shanxi, Shaanxi, Hebei, Heilongjiang, and Jilin, are categorized as the "status-quo type." In a stark contrast to the dual type provinces where social health insurance has high generosity and population coverage, the status-quo type provinces have relatively low generosity and population coverage in social health insurance. Unlike the risk-pooling type and the dual type provinces, the status-quo type provinces did not have high labor mobility in the reform era that would significantly magnify local social risks and drive local officials to enlarge risk pooling strategically. Thus, local officials in the status-quo type provinces lacked a strong motivation to enlarge the risk pooling of social health insurance. In the status-quo type provinces such as Guangxi and Heilongjiang provinces, my fieldwork found that underspending on social welfare was quite common and that expansion of social health insurance was often perfunctory (e.g., using "double counting" in health insurance enrollment to boost the health insurance coverage rate on paper as elaborated in Chapter 5).

Unlike the privileging type provinces that usually receive fiscal or political favors from the Center, the status-quo type provinces with meager local revenues receive only moderate fiscal transfers from the Center, which prevented them from overspending in social health insurance. In my field interviews in Guangxi and Heilongjiang provinces, fiscal straits were commonly mentioned as a reason local officials in the status-quo type provinces took "inaction" (*wu zuo wei*) in social health insurance expansion. As one municipal official in Nanning city of Guangxi province pointed out, "Some of our local governments cannot even pay their staff's salaries on time, let alone provide generous social health insurance benefits [to people]."[25] For local officials in the provinces with low social risks and dire fiscal straits, maintaining the status quo of the skimpy social health insurance is a less costly choice; consequently, their expansion of social health insurance is half-hearted and sometimes just on paper (e.g., distributing scant lump-sum cash to individual houses as NRCMS "reimbursement" for outpatient services, elaborated in Chapter 5).

In sum, local officials' policy priorities and choices in social health insurance expansion vary markedly across regions with diverse local political economies and thus give rise to the different regional patterns of Chinese social health insurance. The goal of this section is not to make strict causal inferences but to understand the regional variation of social health insurance and its correlation with local socioeconomic conditions. As Section 6.2 suggests, two local socioeconomic conditions, fiscal resources and social risks, exert important impacts on the coverage and generosity of social health insurance. This section shows that the impacts of these socioeconomic conditions affected local leaders' policy priorities and choices in social health insurance expansion. The next section turns to a more rigorous test of the correlations between local socioeconomic conditions and the distributional patterns of social health insurance among Chinese provinces.

6.4. Local Socioeconomic Conditions and Regional Variation of Chinese Social Health Insurance

The coverage and generosity variables in the cluster analysis (Section 6.2) continue to be used as dependent variables in the regression analysis that follows.

The explanatory variables are levels of local social risks and fiscal resources, respectively. Two factors are used as proxies for social risks: (1) labor mobility and (2) dependency ratio. Labor mobility is measured by the ratio of migrants to provincial total population. Since the measure of migrants is defined as the absolute value of the difference between provincial total population and local population (i.e., population with local *hukou*), it focuses on the magnitude of province-to-province migration;[26] the dependency ratio is measured by the ratio of people aged above 65 or below 15 to the working population (between 15 and 65). The other key explanatory variable is local fiscal resources, consisting of (1) locally sourced fiscal revenue measured by per capita local budgetary revenue and (2) fiscal transfers, measured by per capita central-to-local transfers.[27] I expected to see in the regression results that the level of social risks is positively correlated with health insurance coverage, and that the level of fiscal resources is positively correlated with health insurance generosity.

A number of economic and political control variables are included in the regressions: (1) economic development, using the logarithm of GDP per capita; (2) urbanization, using percentage of urban residents in the total population; (3) political standing of provincial governors, as measured by the bureaucratic integration score (BINT) coded according to local leaders' past career trajectories;[28] the BINT variable controls for local leaders' personal ambitions in politics; (4) unobserved year- or region-specific situations, using year and province dummies. Summary statistics of all variables are presented in Table 6.4.

The data cover 31 Chinese mainland provinces (including provincial-level municipalities and ethnic autonomous regions) from 1999 to 2010 to take advantage of the large cross-provincial variations in social health insurance and local socioeconomic conditions. Since the data are constructed as a panel dataset, panel-corrected standard errors are applied in the ordinary least squares (OLS) regression analysis.[29] The regression results are reported in Table 6.5. For each dependent variable, Model 1 reports the results of the baseline model that includes only the key explanatory variables, Model 2 presents the results when control variables including year and province dummies (fixed effects, FE) are added,[30] and Model 3 reports the results when control variables and the one-year lagged dependent variable (LDV) are included.[31]

Overall, the regression results lend support to the main theoretical predictions in Hypotheses 2 and 3. The first finding is that social risks (measured by labor mobility and the dependency ratio) are significantly and positively associated with health insurance coverage. According to Model 2, all else being constant, moving from minimal to maximal labor mobility increases coverage by nearly 30 percentage points; according to Model 3, likewise, the dependency ratio increases coverage by 19 percentage points. In the FE model (Model 2), the coefficient for labor mobility is larger and more significant than the coefficient for

Table 6.4 Descriptive Statistics of Variables in the Regional Variation Analysis

Variable	Definition	Obs	Min	Max	Mean	Standard Deviation
Coverage	$\dfrac{\text{population insured}}{\text{total population}} \times 100$	343	.02	102.57	42.50	32.63
Generosity	$\dfrac{\text{annual health insurance expenditure}}{\text{population insured}}$	354	18.56	3204.43	666.26	461.67
Labor mobility	$\dfrac{|\text{total population} - \text{local population}|}{\text{local population}} \times 100$	372	.02	63.04	6.32	9.34
Dependency	$\dfrac{\text{population above 65 or below 15}}{\text{population between } 15-65} \times 100$	372	20.94	64.49	39.66	7.48
Urbanization	$\dfrac{\text{urban population}}{\text{total population}} \times 100$	358	21.99	99.40	47.07	17.74
GDP	GDP per capita	372	2475.30	75074.00	17197.79	14116.20
Fiscal transfer	$\dfrac{\text{annual central} - \text{to} - \text{local transfer}}{\text{population}}$	372	165.86	17641.20	1463.97	1850.25
Fiscal revenue	$\dfrac{\text{annual local budgetary revenue}}{\text{population}}$	371	104.75	12490.34	1548.45	1986.00

Fiscal resource	fiscal transfer + fiscal revenue	371	377.11	18858.80	3014.11	2856.02
Ethnic region	"1" for ethnic minority autonomous region, "0" for otherwise	372	0	1	.16	.37
BINT	Huang (1996), pp. 210–211	372	1	3	1.14	.55

Notes:

1. Local population is defined as people holding local residency (*hukou*).

2. The maximum of coverage exceeds 100% because of duplicate enrollment problems (i.e., some people are enrolled in more than one social health insurance program).

Data sources: China Statistical Yearbook (2000–2011), *China Labor Statistics Yearbook* (2000–2009); *China Human Resources and Social Security Yearbooks* (2009–2011); *China Population Statistics Yearbook* (2000–2011); *China Finance Statistics Yearbook* (1999–2011); *Local Finance Statistical Data* (2000–2010).

Table 6.5 Determinants of Social Health Insurance Coverage and Generosity

	DV: Coverage			DV: Generosity		
	1	2	3	1	2	3
Labor mobility	.704***	.498***	.183	4.786	4.539	6.859**
	(.158)	(.115)	(.123)	(4.194)	(4.037)	(2.731)
Dependency	.387	.289	.432***	4.430	7.029**	3.538
	(.315)	(.266)	(.143)	(3.469)	(3.228)	(3.382)
Fiscal resource	.003***	.003***	.001	.056***	.055***	.049***
	(.001)	(.001)	(.001)	(.020)	(.015)	(.013)
Log (GDP per capita)		23.899***	15.859***		5.006	159.331**
		(5.971)	(3.943)		(71.390)	(74.837)
Urbanization		−.263***	−.312***		2.048***	1.981
		(.044)	(.074)		(.649)	(1.509)
BINT		1.221	.669		.746	−7.210
		(.821)	(.446)		(10.452)	(14.257)
Lagged DV			.757***			.249***
			(.089)			(.079)
Year dummy	Yes	Yes	No	Yes	Yes	No
Province dummy	Yes	Yes	No	Yes	Yes	No
R-squared	.942	.950	.837	.854	.856	.677
Observation	342	342	307	353	341	313

Notes:

1. Results are estimated using a cross-section time-series regression model with panel-corrected standard errors (PCSEs); standard errors are in parentheses.

2. To economize on space, values of intercept and year/province dummy variables are not reported.

3. *** p<.01, ** p<.05, * p<.10.

4. DV = Dependent Variable.

the dependency ratio, indicating that once we control for unobserved year- or province-specific situations, labor mobility better captures the effect of social risks on coverage. By contrast, in the LDV model (Model 3), in which we control for a province's previous level of health insurance coverage, the dependency ratio better captures the effect of social risks on the annual change of health insurance coverage. In addition, health insurance generosity is positively correlated with labor mobility and dependency ratio in the FE and LDV models, respectively.

The second finding is that fiscal resources (the sum of local-sourced fiscal revenues and central-to-local fiscal transfers) are significantly and positively associated with the generosity of social health insurance. According to Models 2 and 3, with all else held constant, moving from minimal to maximal fiscal resources increases health generosity per beneficiary by 681 *yuan* and 607 *yuan,* respectively. These correlations are significant at the 99% confidence level in all model specifications. In addition, the regression results indicate a positive correlation between fiscal resources and social health insurance coverage. However, the positive relationship loses statistical significance in the LDV model, indicating that given a province's previous level of health insurance coverage, fiscal resources are no longer predictive of the coverage.

As for the control variables, the level of GDP per capita is significantly and positively associated with health insurance coverage and generosity in most model specifications. This lends some support to the economic explanation of the regional variation that provinces with a more advanced economy can cover more people and provide more benefits. By contrast, urbanization is significantly and negatively correlated with health insurance coverage, though it is positively correlated with health insurance generosity. These results are in line with the observation about the Chinese society that despite a continuously increasing number of people living in cities (i.e., the high urbanization rate), due to the rigid household registration system and its anachronistic associations with social entitlements, only a portion of the urban residents (usually those with state-sector employment and local urban *hukou*) have full access to urban social health insurance, which has markedly higher level of benefits than rural health insurance.[32] In addition, the unobserved year- and region-specific situations (the year and province dummies) account for about 50% of the variation in health coverage and 25% in health generosity. Overall, these findings suggest the limitations of a purely economic or modernization explanation of Chinese social welfare expansion: the regional variations in health insurance coverage and generosity can't be fully explained by economic factors.[33]

It is worth noting that BINT—the measure of provincial governors' personal ambition in politics based on their prior career trajectories—has no significant impact on social health insurance, suggesting that local leaders' distributive choices in social health expansion were shaped mainly by the socioeconomic conditions in their jurisdictions rather than by their personal political ambition or connections. Nonetheless, the small variation in the BINT variable across provinces and years in this study might contribute to the insignificance of this variable in the results.

In sum, the statistical results indicate significant correlations between local socioeconomic conditions and local distributive patterns of social health insurance measured by coverage and generosity. All other things being equal, regions with higher social risks tend to cover more people under social health insurance, while regions with more fiscal resources tend to provide more generous health insurance benefits. As summarized in Figure 6.3, based on the results of cluster

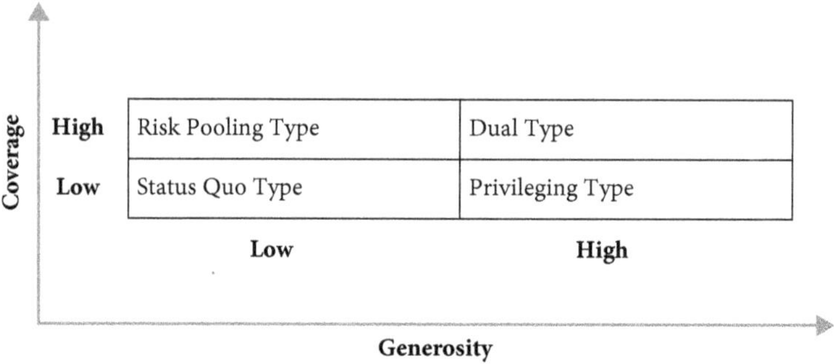

Figure 6.3 Four Types of Social Health Insurance in China

and regression analyses, high social risks without adequate fiscal resources at the local governments' disposal motivate local leaders to focus their efforts on the coverage of social health insurance during expansion, as seen in the risk-pooling type provinces; on the contrary, abundant fiscal revenues (whether locally sourced or transfers from the central government) combined with low social risks encourage local leaders to expand the generosity of social health insurance exclusively for the elite, as exemplified by the privileging type provinces. In contrast, a combination of high fiscal revenues and high social risks gives rise to dual type provinces where social health insurance is expanded to cover more people and provide generous benefits; by the same logic, a combination of low fiscal revenues and low social risks results in the status-quo type provinces where social health insurance expansion lags greatly, with fewer people covered and receiving meager benefits.

These regional variations, corresponding to regional political economies, especially local fiscal resources and social risks, are tolerated by the Center, which attempts to accommodate local situations and social needs as long as its preferred pattern of welfare stratification (generous benefits for the elite) is observed to help ensure regime survival and stability. In China's decentralized fiscal and social welfare systems, the Center uses abundant fiscal transfers to enhance the local fiscal revenues of the periphery regions with the concentrated ethnic minority groups (e.g., Xinjiang, Ningxia, Tibet) so that they can provide welfare benefits to local residents (including Han civil servants and state-sector employees) that are as generous as the benefits provided in the major cities (e.g., Beijing, Shanghai, Tianjin). Meanwhile, the Center allows plenty disparities to exist in social health insurance expansion in the other regions, where the local governments must rely on local resources and socio-economic conditions to meet local welfare needs and maintain social stability as much as they can.

6.5. Conclusion

This chapter has focused on the regional variations in Chinese social health insurance. First, it identified and described the diverse regional patterns and variations in Chinese social health insurance during the expansion in the 2000s. Then it mapped those regional patterns and variations to the central and local leaders' distributive strategies and policy choices developed under varying regional fiscal and socioeconomic conditions. Chinese central leaders, who care about regime survival and stability, delegated substantial discretionary authority to local leaders for making choices for social health insurance coverage and generosity in order to accommodate diverse local circumstances while maintaining a hierarchy in social welfare provision that favors the groups with political connections and importance. Under the framework set up by the Center, Chinese local leaders with discretionary power proactively implemented social welfare policy according to local conditions; in doing so, they prevented social unrest in their jurisdictions, which could jeopardize their political careers in the centralized personnel system. Therefore, the local profile of social health insurance differed drastically in generosity and coverage, the two dimensions in which the Center delegated discretionary authority to local leaders. Differences across provinces in health insurance generosity and coverage reflect the diverse local conditions, particularly local fiscal resources and social risks, under which local distributive plans and choices were made.

To characterize the distributive outcome of the Center's stratified expansion of social welfare provision in the subnational context, I utilized a provincial-level panel dataset (1999–2010), which showed the regional variations in Chinese social health insurance and their correlations with local socioeconomic conditions. In addition, I drew on qualitative evidence from my fieldwork in the four clusters of provinces including interviews with local officials to describe the local political economy underlying the regional patterns and variations in Chinese social health insurance. The distributive implications and outcomes of the Chinese authoritarian regime's stratified expansion of social welfare provision was also investigated and demonstrated at the individual level. This is reported in Chapter 7.

7

Who Gets What, When, and How from Chinese Social Health Insurance Expansion?

Chapter 6 described in detail how local governments adjusted their policies for social health insurance according to local conditions, resulting in significant variations in the distributive pattern of social health insurance benefits. The regional variation in social health insurance persisted during the social health insurance expansion in the 2000s, and as a result, people living in different provinces of China received different levels of health care benefits and protection. Given the significant regional variation of social health insurance presented in Chapter 6, this chapter examines the distributive implications and outcomes of the stratified expansion of social health insurance at the individual level. The main finding that emerges from the data analysis in this chapter is that the expansion of Chinese social health insurance in the 2000s did extend access to basic social health insurance to most people; yet the expansion not only failed to correct health inequalities resulting from the burgeoning market economy but also reinforced existing social cleavages inherited from the socialist past, such as the rural-urban divide, in the social health insurance. Moreover, the fragmented health insurance programs and increasing benefit disparities in the expansion have created new divides within certain social groups including urbanites and the workforce. As such, the distribution of expanded health insurance benefits significantly stratifies the Chinese society, reflecting and reinforcing existing social inequalities and cleavages.

The inequalities in China's social policies are manifested in at least four aspects. First, the risk pooling and benefits of social insurance are confined to individual subnational units such as cities and counties. As Chapter 6 showed, coverage and generosity of social health insurance vary markedly across localities. Most state-provided social welfare benefits are still contingent on local and specific (e.g., agricultural or non-agricultural) *hukou* status, which is mostly inherited from family. Second, since the Maoist era, rural and urban China have operated under quite distinct systems, with urbanites consistently receiving preferential treatment over their rural counterparts regarding social insurance. This urban-rural divide has been reinforced in several social welfare reforms (such as reforms of

Social Protection under Authoritarianism. Xian Huang, Oxford University Press (2020). © Oxford University Press.
DOI: 10.1093/oso/9780190073640.001.0001

pension, health insurance, and social assistance) in the post-Mao era. Third, in urban China, the working class or labor market insiders[1] enjoy various types of social benefits not available to those outside of the labor market because of skill shortcomings, disease, disability, or age. In this sense, the stratified social insurance system established in the 2000s is market-conforming and productivist. Fourth, even within the urban workforce, the Chinese social health insurance system is so fragmented that those with government employment or working in state sectors enjoy higher benefits than those in other sectors of the economy, especially in the informal sector where increasing numbers of migrants work.[2] Thus, China's remarkable expansion of social health insurance in the 2000s seems to have institutionalized the socioeconomic status and regional differences in the social welfare system rather than correcting social inequalities.

At first glance, a highly unequal provision of social welfare benefits might be unexpected in the context of contemporary China with its strong party-state claiming to be committed to socialism. However, stratification of social welfare provision is less surprising when we consider China's authoritarian and decentralized governance. The multiplicity and complexity of social divisions embedded in China's social welfare expansion in the 2000s reflect the authoritarian leaders' "divide and rule" strategy for maintaining social control. The fragmented social welfare provision enables multiple social cleavages to crosscut society without following a single and deep class line. As Chapter 4 elucidates, of special importance for the Chinese authoritarian regime to survive is the maintenance of particularly favorable welfare provisions for the urban and state-sector employees while establishing and preserving an essentially modest social provision for many other social groups. The distribution of China's expanding social health insurance benefits reveals a paradox: the impressive expansion of social health insurance enrollment and the increased number of social health insurance programs have not reduced but rather have reinforced socioeconomic inequalities. Instead of leveling the social playing field, the changes in social health insurance have continued to link social benefits to citizens' socioeconomic and residency status that are essentially determined by their political positions and relations with the Chinese authoritarian state. Therefore, the expansion has significantly reinforced rather than mitigated social cleavages by institutionalizing the existing and emerging social divides in the social health insurance system.

The analytical purpose of this chapter is to empirically examine the distribution of social health insurance benefits among different groups of individuals in China. The chapter unfolds as follows. Given the main argument that the Chinese authoritarian regime adopts and implements a stratified expansion strategy in social welfare provision for political survival and stability, Section 7.1 develops hypotheses regarding the relationship between individuals' socioeconomic status and the social health insurance benefits they receive from the government.

Section 7.2 illustrates with descriptive data who are the beneficiaries of China's social health insurance expansion and what kinds of health insurance benefits they received during the expansion in the 2000s. Special attention is given to the distributive implications of the expansion, which manifest the highly stratifying nature of China's social health insurance expansion. Sections 7.3 and 7.4 draw on two individual-level surveys to further examine the stratification of Chinese social health insurance benefits through two lenses: (1) distribution of the most generous employment-based social health insurance benefits in the society, and (2) distribution of different social health insurance benefits among social groups. Examination of these distributions shows that the social health insurance expansion not only strengthens and deepens existing social cleavages but also creates new divides in Chinese society. Section 7.5 concludes this chapter.

7.1. Social Stratification as a Political Strategy

Politics is about who gets what, when, and how (Lasswell 1936). The essence of social welfare policy is political as it decides who is included and who is excluded, as well as who pays and who benefits. Although there is a line of literature taking a functionalist view of social welfare policy positing that social welfare policy largely responds to changing societal conditions such as industrialization (Rimlinger 1971) and modernization (Flora and Alber, 1981), the most prominent approach in the literature of the welfare state is political: focusing on the conflicts and coalitions of different social groups with distinct economic interests and policy goals, such as labor versus capital (Esping-Andersen 1990; Korpi 1983), poor versus rich (Meltzer and Richard 1981), or employers versus employees (Mares 2003; Swenson 2002). In this literature, a counterintuitive finding persists, namely, that "social welfare is not just a mechanism that intervenes in, and possibly corrects, the structure of inequality; it is, in its own right, a system of stratification. It is an active force in the ordering of social relations" (Esping-Andersen 1990, 23). Esping-Andersen's seminal work *Three Worlds of Welfare Capitalism* demonstrates that different welfare state regimes create different forms of social inequality and stratification. Conservative welfare states such as Germany, Austria, Italy, and France consolidated divisions among wage-earners by legislating distinct social programs for different occupations and status groups, while liberal welfare states such as Great Britain and most of the Anglo-Saxon world allow for a dualism between the state and the market in the form of state-provided means-tested assistance and market-based private welfare plans.

The stratification nature of social welfare policy is not limited to democracies. In an autocratic setting that lacks open and competitive elections to reveal opposition, public opinions, and policy preferences, political leaders face greater uncertainties of the power, loyalty, and intention of the elite and the mass groups. Given these uncertainties, autocratic leaders often stratify social welfare provision to "divide and rule" the society, distributing benefits and resources to different groups strategically to maintain social control. In this circumstance, the importance of social welfare policy as a strategy for political purposes (e.g., cooptation, mobilization or demobilization, social control) is heightened. As a political strategy, stratification of social welfare provision serves to tie different social groups' loyalties and benefits to the state while marginalizing redistributive bargaining across groups.

By the same logic, social stratification is a running theme underlying Chinese social welfare policy throughout both the Mao (or socialist) and the post-Mao (or reform) eras, no matter what the government's rhetoric indicates. As chapters 4 and 5 show, the stratification of Chinese social welfare provision was created in a top-down process and manner, and redistributive conflict and bargaining mainly took place during policy implementation and at the local level. Moreover, the stratified provisions complicated the dynamics of redistribution in the context of contemporary China, as redistribution entailed not only a dualistic conflict between the poor and the rich, or the haves and the have-nots, but spread tensions across a multitude of various regions and social groups. Under the Chinese stratified social welfare system, one's benefit and security are not just a function of individual or household income but also of political connections and one's importance to the regime, indicated by one's socioeconomic and sociopolitical status such as *hukou*, communist party membership, and type and ownership of one's work unit or employer. The relative positions of these different types of status in the social structure and their associated benefits and security are defined by the regime. Although it should be noted that in the reform era, market forces can affect the positioning of status to some extent independent of deliberate state policies, many of the salient socioeconomic statuses in contemporary China, such as urban *hukou*, state sector, and permanent/formal employment are state-constructed and the benefits associated with them politically and economically are determined by the state.

One might question whether China's social insurance expansion in the 2000s was just restoring the comprehensive social welfare provision that existed in the socialist era under Mao. Nara Dillon's detailed research on the Maoist welfare state breaks this illusion: social welfare under Mao was neither broad nor equitable among different social groups (Dillon 2015). As Dillon notes, "The narrow reach of the Maoist welfare state served to increase the gaps between city and countryside, industry and agriculture, and men and women. One of the bitter ironies of the Chinese Communist Revolution is that the most important social program [welfare state] for workers did not eliminate inequality; it entrenched it" (Dillon 2015, 1). The labor insurance program that constituted the core of the Maoist welfare state embedded several salient social cleavages (Dillon 2015). First, peasants were the majority of the Chinese population in Mao's era but were excluded from the program. Second, among urban residents, a significant share of whom were covered by the labor insurance program, the most fundamental cleavage was between permanent employees in the state and the non-state sectors. Third, even within state-owned enterprises there were divisions between permanent and temporary workers, not to mention differences between genders and different generations (Dillon 2015).

The social cleavages produced in the Maoist welfare state are expected to persist, reproduce, and even increase in the reform era for three reasons. First, despite spectacular economic openness and liberalization in the post-Mao era, the authoritarian nature of the Chinese regime doesn't change. The uncertainties for the Chinese regime have increased as social groups have become more diverse and affluent during the market economy reform and development since 1978. This can be seen from the new terms and emphasis on governance, such as social management (*she hui guan li*), building a harmonious society (*gou jian he xie she hui*), and stability maintenance (*wei wen*) which were prevalent in Chinese central leaders' speeches and government documents during the 2000s. In these circumstances, the political importance of social welfare policy for cooptation, (de)mobilization, and social control is heightened.

Second, the stratified expansion of social welfare provision in the reform era is market-conforming. By privileging the state sector over others, labor market insiders over outsiders, and urbanites over peasants, the stratified social insurance system installed in the 2000s worked seamlessly with the "state capitalism" (Liebman and Milhaupt, 2016) or "commanding heights economy" (Huang 2008) thriving at the same time in China. State economic and social policies greatly favored the urban economy, especially large firms in the state sector; they were given much more in resources, privileges, and preferential treatment than rural and private sectors (Huang 2008; Wallace 2014). In 2009, SOEs made up around 80% of the value of the stock market in China; the profit made by China's two giant SOEs, China Mobil and China National Petroleum Corporation, totaled more than its other most profitable private companies combined,[3] and the sectoral differences in social welfare benefits reflect the privileged position of SOEs.

Third, groups having vested interests in the social welfare system, such as civil servants, state-sector employees, and retirees who received various health care and pension privileges, have been entrenched since the 1950s. The bureaucratic frictions and resistance coming from these groups during social welfare reforms constitute great obstacles to reforming or integrating social welfare provisions across regions or social groups (Huang and Kim 2020; Duckett 2003; Hsiao

2007). This resembles the "feedback effect" of social welfare policy on support for social welfare reform found in Western democracies: social security programs were backed up by powerful interest groups (Pierson 1996). Similarly, Linda Cook (2007) found in Russia and Eastern Europe that the bureaucratic welfare stakeholders who were left over from the communist period played a large role in impeding social welfare reforms and policies that aimed to reduce entitlements and subsidies in the 1990s.

Studies of Chinese social policy and welfare programs in the reform era have shown clearly that rural people, including peasant workers and rural migrants in cities, and labor market outsiders, such as informal employees in the private sector, are disadvantaged and discriminated against in the provision of social welfare benefits (Solinger 1999; Gao et al. 2012; Gallagher et al. 2015). Rising inequality in social policy has been commonly explained as an economic outcome or phenomenon. However, this book's argument about the stratified expansion strategy of Chinese authoritarian leaders demonstrates that these inequalities were the outcome of deliberate state policies. Consequently, the social welfare expansion in the 2000s perpetuated rather than corrected the social cleavages and inequalities. To empirically test and demonstrate this, hypotheses regarding the relationships between people's socioeconomic/sociopolitical status and their health insurance benefits were formulated as follows.

Hypothesis 1: All other things being equal, urban hukou *holders receive more generous health insurance benefits than rural* hukou *holders.*

The *hukou* system is China's basic institution for allocating socioeconomic resources and opportunities. It was created in the 1950s and has been maintained since by the Chinese regime. Categorizing individuals by socioeconomic status (agricultural or non-agricultural; in other words, rural or urban) and residential location (local and non-local), the *hukou* system serves multiple purposes for the regime. First, the system helps maintain the urban bias, a prominent feature of the state-led development and industrialization model that the Chinese regime adopted and has maintained since the early 1950s. In the heyday of Soviet-style industrialization in the 1950s, investment in the country was taking place in cities and industrial sites while the agricultural sector was falling back on older, more labor-intensive practices (Chan 1994). While preventing peasants from flowing into cities, the regime extracted intensively from the countryside and peasantry to feed urbanites and fuel urban industries. Jeremey Wallace commented on China's *hukou* system as "a thoroughly modern and dictatorial solution to problems inherent to industrialization" (Wallace 2014, 74).

Second, the *hukou* system allows the regime to control the pace and process of urbanization. From the Chinese authoritarian regime's perspective, urbanization is economically beneficial as it promotes and generates economic growth; nonetheless, urbanization is politically dangerous as high concentrations of urban populations resulting from urbanization breed political instability (Wallace 2014). In the reform era after 1978, restrictions on rural-to-urban migration were relaxed (Solinger 1995). Nonetheless, rural migrants were not allowed to freely convert their *hukou* status to local and non-agricultural, especially in large cities. As a result, rural migrants live and work as second-class citizens in cities. China's urbanization is thus considered incomplete (Chan 2010). From time to time, the Chinese government has experimented with piecemeal *hukou* reforms when it needed to stimulate economic growth, mitigate labor shortages, and generate fiscal revenues. But these reform initiatives have deliberately been limited to small and medium-sized cities (Wallace 2014).

Third, the *hukou* system enables the regime to treat its urban workers and residents with preferential policies and exclusive benefits, maintaining higher living standards in cities without inducing massive migration into cities. While most people working and living in the countryside were granted agricultural *hukou*, state employees were granted non-agricultural *hukou* regardless of their urban or rural location and as such were provided better benefits. To begin with, job placement in the state sector is highly associated with one's *hukou* status being urban and local (Xiao and Bian 2018). Hence, urban *hukou* is more of an exclusive socioeconomic status than a geographic notion in China.

In short, China's *hukou* system is a key mechanism and source of social stratification motivated by the regime's political concerns and interests. Differences in *hukou* status (urban or rural, local or non-local) correspond to distinct levels of benefits, opportunities, and resources provided by the state to individuals.

Hypothesis 2: All other things being equal, state-sector employees receive more generous health insurance benefits than non-state-sector employees.

Hypothesis 3: All other things being equal, formal employees and retirees receive more generous health insurance benefits than informal ones.

Hypothesis 4: All other things being equal, employees of large-sized employers receive more generous health insurance benefits than do employees of small- and medium-sized employers.

Besides *hukou*, labor market status (namely, employment sector and status, type of labor contract, and employer size) is another important mechanism and source of social stratification in China. The state sector, comprising government agencies, public institutions, and state-owned enterprises, continually provides significantly higher social benefits and security to its employees. This preferential arrangement was brought about by the state socialism model under Mao to prioritize heavy manufacturing sectors for centrally planned industrialization. This distributive pattern still holds despite the "differentiation and de-empowerment of the working class" in the post-Mao era (Bian 2002) when China reoriented to more market-driven and open economic development. Starting in 1980, labor markets gradually re-emerged in the cities with the decline of bureaucratic control over labor and state assignments of jobs, which was dominant and prevalent in the planned economy. Since 1992 when China's economic openness and reform resumed after the 1989 Tiananmen protest, the labor market has expanded gradually. Employment relations became flexible and fluid. Layoffs in the state sector became routine during SOE reform and restructuring in the late 1990s. Meanwhile, informal and atypical employment became commonplace as the private sector grew tremendously, being the main source of jobs for both rural migrants and laid-off workers from the state sector. The social stratification by labor market in the form of state/non-state sectoral divide was unique to state socialism in China, but the stratification process and pattern in post-Mao China that embraced formal/informal segmentation or dualism in the labor market are commonly seen in capitalist economies (Hodson and Kaufman 1982; Esping-Andersen 1999).

In a market economy, individual merit traits such as educational attainment, skill level, and entrepreneurship are usually the main determinant of one's earning capability and thus one's labor market status such as occupational prestige, job security and position, and career mobility. Decades of economic openness and reform in China since 1978 make researchers wonder if the economic transformation also shifts resource allocation from state to market domination that leads to the decline of political power and the rise of human capital and entrepreneurial abilities (Nee 1989; Bian 2002; Zhou 2004). The debate among researchers is ongoing, and the literature shows that both mechanisms of market and political power are at work in post-Mao China. On one hand, research has found that income return from human capital has increased in both China's rural and urban settings (Nee and Cao 1999), though these increases are smaller than in advanced capitalist economies (Parish and Michelson 1996). On the other hand, there is also strong evidence that political power persists in allocating resources and opportunity across social groups by determining individuals' income (Zhou 2000), fringe benefits (Zhou 2004), and career mobility (Bian 2009) in the post-Mao era.

As of 2003, assignments by the state, including assigning jobs to school graduates, reallocating job holders, and hiring employees' children or relatives, still accounted for a quarter of all jobs; moreover, the jobs that were delivered through state authority were more likely to lead to upward career mobility (Bian 2009). Based on a detailed study of channels and chances of job change using

China General Social Survey (CGSS) 2003 data, Bian Yanjie found that men, Communist Party members, and the highly educated are more likely than their counterparts to use the state or hierarchical channels, rather than the market, for job hunting and change (Bian 2009). He thus commented that "after 25 years of economic reform, the path to some of the most desirable jobs in the country are still controlled and monopolized by the government hierarchy" and "it will remain as long as the CCP is the ruling party of China" (Bian 2009, 188).

Hypothesis 5: All other things being equal, CCP members receive more generous health insurance benefits than nonmembers.

An extension of the preceding debate regarding state or market domination in resource allocation in China's reform era can be found in the discussion of whether it is human capital (e.g., education) or political capital (e.g., political membership) that determines individuals' economic benefits, opportunities, and resources. In Mao's time, the CCP enjoyed a near monopoly on the distribution of goods and resources, such as jobs, housing, access to education, health care, and scarce consumer goods (Dickson and Rublee 2000). In the post-Mao era, the market emerged as an alternative source of resources, opportunities, and goods for individuals in China. In this circumstance, scholars found that education, an indicator of human capital, had a greater impact on a person's income than did CCP membership (Walder 1995; Xie & Hannum 1996). However, the CCP's grip on crucial resources in the economy and society remains and continues to grow steadily. According to the 1988 China Household Income Project (CHIP) survey, CCP members were concentrated in the most influential and most prestigious jobs: 84% of responsible officials and 77% of factory managers and directors are CCP members (Dickson and Rublee 2000). By analyzing the CHIP data, Dickson and Rublee found that both political (CCP memberships) and human capital (e.g., college degrees) matter in determining one's income and occupational prestige in the reform era; more important, they demonstrate an interesting cohort effect of human/political capital: the older cohort's income was more dependent on political than human capital; for the young cohort, the advantage of having both political and human capital is the highest for holding a prestigious job such as professional/technical jobs or becoming an official. This echoes the observation that in post-Mao China most young people joined the CCP not for ideological reasons but for material ones, such as advancing career, social status, and income (Rosen 1990; Dickson 2016).

Human and political capital, however, are less easily separated than the existing studies seem to assume, and they became more intertwined in the post-Mao era than ever before. Bian (1994) found that education did not improve a person's chances of attaining CCP membership in the Maoist era, but in the post-Mao era those with higher education have a better chance of gaining CCP membership. This is an intentional outcome of the CCP's cooptation strategy and move to expand party membership among highly educated, high-tech specialists, and certain private sectors that "represent the most advanced productive forces" for purposes of political survival, stability, and adaptation. In the 2000s, the CCP has focused on college campuses as the main source of new members, and roughly 40% of new recruits are college students when they join the party (Dickson 2016). Since a considerable portion of urban state-sector employees and urban skilled workforce are CCP members, the impact of CCP membership is widely diffused and confounded with labor market status such as one's employment sector and formal contract. Hence, while we expect that CCP members were still privileged in some benefit provisions and resource allocation in the 2000s, we also expect that compared to other individual merit traits like education and labor market status, the effect of CCP membership might not be the most significant or largest influence overall in the reform era.

7.2. Inequalities in Chinese Social Health Insurance

As Chapter 3 details, China's social welfare reform since the 1980s has gone hand in hand with its economic reform and openness. The impact of social welfare reform on the distribution of benefits has been no less dramatic than that of economic reform in China. Social welfare reforms such as "socializing" the previous work-unit-based health care, housing, education, and pensions have not only led to an abandonment of the "Iron Rice Bowl" and establishment of contributory payroll-based social insurance for the urban industrial working class, but have also generated new social inequalities and regional disparities. Both individual-level survey data and provincial-level statistics demonstrate that China's social health insurance coverage has dramatically expanded in the 2000s. According to data from the China Health and Nutrition Survey (CHNS), an international collaborative, multi-waved panel survey project in China,[4] the coverage of social health insurance (including UEBMI, URBMI, and NRCMS programs) in nine Chinese provinces increased from 37.39% in 2000 to 89.5% in 2009 on average (see Figure 7.1).

Based on eligibilities, Chinese social health insurance programs can be categorized into two types: employment-based programs (e.g., GIS, UEBMI) and residency-based programs (e.g., URBMI, NRCMS).[5] Employment-based social health insurance is financed by defined contributions from employers and sometimes employees as well, while residency-based social health insurance programs are financed mostly by general taxes in addition to individuals' premium payments. Government subsidization accounts for up to 70% of financing responsibilities for residency-based social health insurance in some provinces.[6]

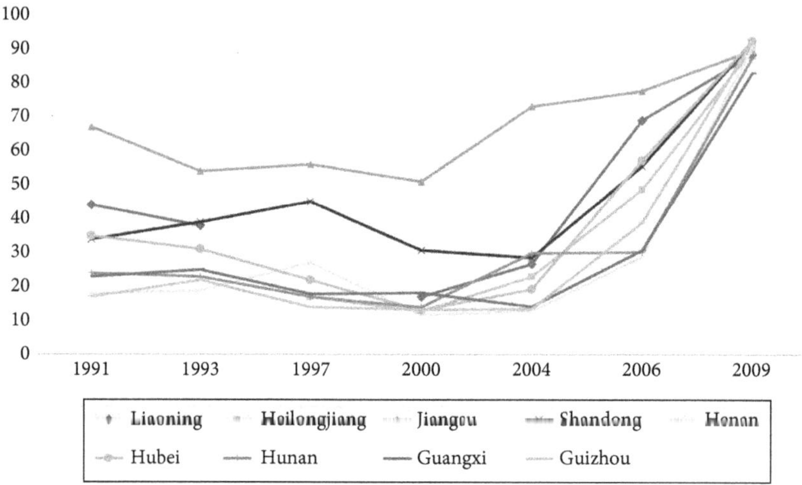

Figure 7.1 Health Insurance Coverage (% Insured) in Nine Chinese Provinces
Data source: China Health and Nutrition Survey.

According to the CHNS data, the landscape of Chinese social health insurance changed dramatically from 2000 to 2009 (Figure 7.2). In 2000, before social health insurance expansion, employment-based health insurance programs such as GIS and UEBMI were the dominant social health insurance programs in China, enrolling and supporting approximately 80% of overall social health insurance beneficiaries. By contrast, in 2009, after the social health insurance expansion, as many as 40% of social health insurance beneficiaries were covered by residency-based health insurance programs such as URBMI and NRCMS. It is noteworthy that the government's free medical care (GIS), which had previously covered party and government officials and civil servants, shrank to one of the smallest health insurance programs in 2009, as it was transformed into a subsidiary or supplementary scheme under the UEBMI framework in half of Chinese provinces. Shares of commercial and other health insurance programs remained residual and decreasing in China from 2000 to 2009, especially during the social health insurance expansion that has significantly squeezed the space for private insurance.

In terms of the generosity of social health insurance, an internal report of MoHRSS in 2010 disclosed that the UEBMI's inpatient reimbursement rate is notably higher than the URBMI's, except in three metropolises (Beijing, Shanghai, and Tianjin) (see Figure 7.3). The provincial average of inpatient reimbursement rates is 67.68% of medical expenses for UEBMI beneficiaries (mainly urban state-sector employees), down to 55.32% for URBMI beneficiaries (mainly urban non-working people including the elderly, children, and students).

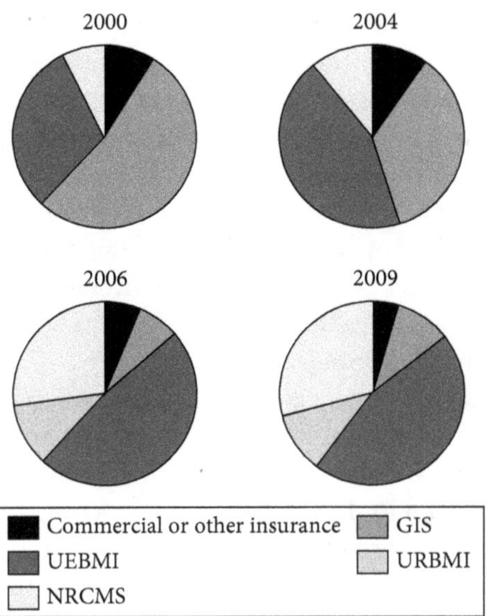

Figure 7.2 Distribution of Health Insurance Program in China Health and Nutrition Survey Sample by Year

Note: "Commercial or other insurance" refers to private and other health insurance; GIS refers to Government Insurance Scheme; UEBMI refers to Urban Employee Basic Medical Insurance; URBMI refers to Urban Resident Basic Medical Insurance; NRCMS refers to New Rural Cooperative Medical Scheme.

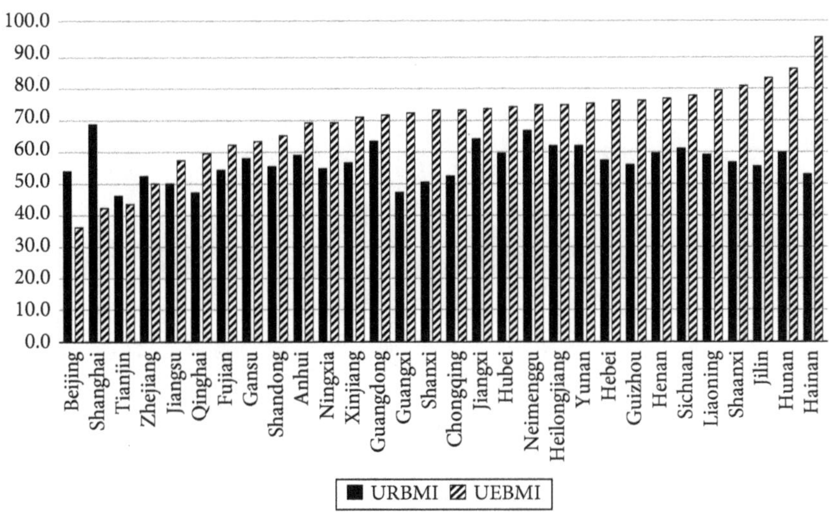

Figure 7.3 Inpatient Reimbursement Rates of Urban Health Insurance by Province (2010)

Note: The reimbursement rate refers to the percentage of inpatient expenses reimbursed by Urban Employee Basic Medical Insurance (UEBMI) and Urban Resident Basic Medical Insurance (URBMI); data are from Urban Social Basic Health Insurance Report, Ministry of Human Resources and Social Insurance (MoHRSS) 2011.

A similar pattern can be found for outpatient reimbursement, with a few exceptions (see Figure 7.4). The provincial average of outpatient reimbursement for UEBMI beneficiaries is 98.23 yuan per patient, one third higher than for URBMI beneficiaries. Despite the lack of comparable data for the NRCMS program, both my research and secondary literature (e.g., Meng and Tang 2010) suggest that the NRCMS's reimbursement rates are even lower than the URBMI's. Hence, the employment-based social health insurance programs provide the most generous yet exclusive benefits to urban formal employees, while the residency-based social health insurance programs supply inclusive yet limited benefits to other groups in society.

Another way to capture the inequalities in Chinese social health insurance is through comparing the medical facilities and services that are associated with the different social health insurance programs. Most Chinese hospitals are state-owned and categorized into three types: primary, secondary, and tertiary. This categorization of hospitals is not based on the types of medical services that the hospitals supply but the quantity of beds and personnel of the hospitals. Primary hospitals are township or community clinics with about 20–99 beds with a minimum of 3 doctors and 5 nurses, while secondary and tertiary hospitals have 100–499 and over 500-plus beds, respectively, with a minimum of .88 and 1.03 health workers per bed (Qian and Blomqvist 2014). Besides larger size, the tertiary hospitals, which are usually located in capital cities, are equipped with

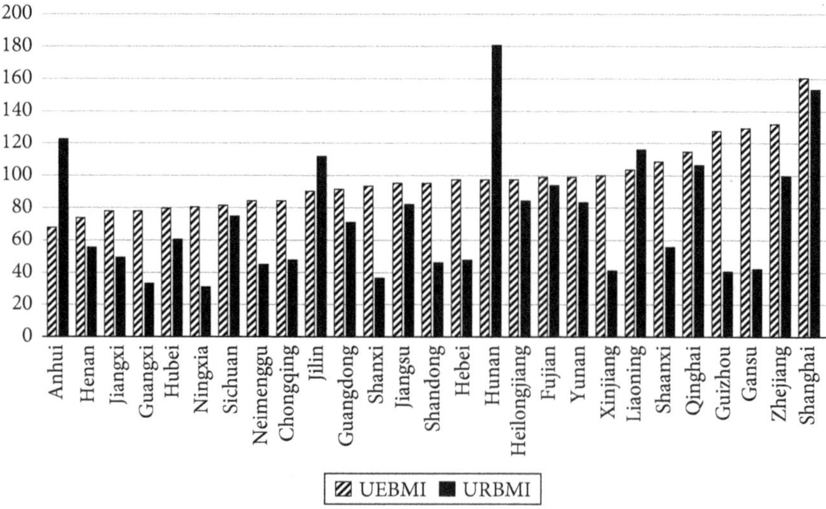

Figure 7.4 Outpatient Reimbursement Amount of Urban Health Insurance by Province (2010)

Notes: Unit is yuan/person; UEBMI refers to Urban Employee Basic Medical Insurance; data are from Urban Social Basic Health Insurance (URBHI) Report, Ministry of Human Resources and Social Insurance (MoHRSS) 2011.

much more advanced and high-quality facilities and more highly experienced medical professionals (Figure 7.5).

The associations between types of hospitals and reimbursement rates in the social health insurance programs indicate the de jure differences of health care that respective social groups receive. A general rule applies to all social health insurance programs that the higher the level of hospital, the lower the reimbursement rate of social health insurance. However, the reimbursement rates that differ by the different health insurance programs for medical services provided by the higher level of hospitals (e.g., tertiary hospitals) are arbitrarily set by the state. For the best health care (presumably supplied by the tertiary hospitals), beneficiaries of NRCMS program (i.e., peasants or rural residents) can get only 30% of their expenses reimbursed while beneficiaries of UEBMI (i.e., urban formal workers and state employees) can get 70% to 90% of expenses reimbursed. Also, the differences in health care that different social groups receive show a similar pattern that is biased in favor of urban formal workers. An internal report by MHRSS shows that in 2010, more than 90% of UEBMI expenditures were made to the tertiary and secondary hospitals (specifically, around 60% on tertiary and 30% on secondary), indicating that most medical services and treatments enjoyed by the UEBMI beneficiaries—urban formal workers, state employees—are provided by those hospitals with better personnel and more advanced equipment and facilities. Since the tertiary hospitals are concentrated in the economically advanced or capital cities,[7] rural people,

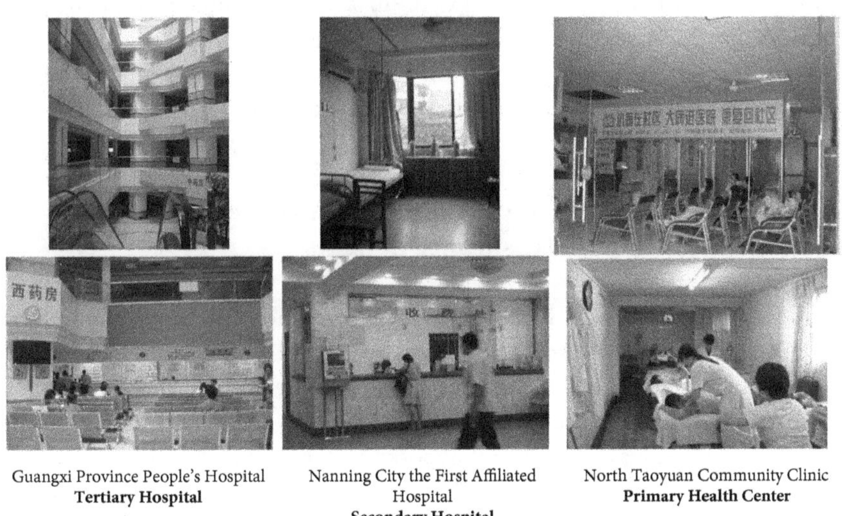

| Guangxi Province People's Hospital
Tertiary Hospital | Nanning City the First Affiliated
Hospital
Secondary Hospital | North Taoyuan Community Clinic
Primary Health Center |

Figure 7.5 Different Types of Hospitals in China

Note: Photos taken by the author during fieldwork in Chinese cities in 2011.

especially those from the periphery or remote areas, who wish to obtain high-quality or special health care in the tertiary hospitals, not only have to pay much more out of pocket but also bear the extra costs of traveling to and living in the large cities.[8]

To sum up, this section delineates a nuanced picture of the beneficiaries and benefits of Chinese social health insurance expansion. On the one hand, social groups such as peasants and urban poor who are unemployed or informally employed, and migrant workers who were previously excluded from the urban employment-based social health insurance programs, have gradually been insured through the residency-based health insurance programs (mainly URBMI and NRCMS). On the other hand, the benefits these newly insured groups have received were quite limited in both quantity and quality and rely heavily on government subsidization for financing (half from the central government and half from the local government in the western and inland provinces). Such policy design generates certain consequences with important distributive implications. First, the residency-based social health insurance programs that rely heavily on fiscal transfers from multiple levels of government are especially vulnerable to fiscal cutbacks, especially when the local governments—the major sponsors of social health insurance in China—are unable to meet these financial obligations. Second, the employment and non-employment divide in the social health insurance programs identifies beneficiaries with labor market participation and status. In this way, it continues to marginalize labor market outsiders—people unable to work due to age, sickness and disability, and people employed in the informal sectors of the economy. Third, the urban-rural divide is maintained and embedded into the social health insurance expansion. Evidence in this section supports the general conjecture that the expansion of Chinese social health insurance reinforces rather than mitigates social inequalities.

7.3. Distribution of Employment-Based Health Insurance Benefits

The stratification of social health insurance throughout the expansion period can be examined in two aspects: (1) coverage or distribution of the most generous employment-based social health insurance benefits in the society; and (2) distribution of different social health insurance programs among social groups. Section 7.2 lays out several hypotheses positing that both the coverage of employment-based social health insurance and the distribution of different social health insurance programs among social groups are highly correlated with people's socioeconomic, sociopolitical, and labor market status. This section presents empirical evidence regarding the coverage of employment-based health insurance, and the next section focuses on the distribution of various health insurance programs among social groups.

The analysis of employment-based social health insurance coverage is based on a national survey, the China General Social Survey (CGSS),[9] which has collected data from individuals in 28 Chinese mainland provinces in multiple rounds since 2003. For cross-time comparison, this analysis relies on CGSS data collected in 2003, 2006, and 2008. The dependent variable (*medinsu*) is binary, constructed from respondents' answer to the question, "Does your work unit/company provide any kind of medical insurance?" in the CGSS questionnaire. The independent variables are at the individual level and concentrate on respondents' socioeconomic and employment status. The socioeconomic and sociopolitical factors included are respondent's education level (*educ*), annual income (*log_indiv_income*), household registration status (*urban hukou*), migration status (*migrant*), and CCP membership (*CCP*). The employment factors included are respondents' employment status (*unemployed*), employment type— whether they have signed a legal labor contract with their employer (*formal*), employment sector (*SOE, COE, POE, FOT, other*),[10] and employer size (*employer size*). Control variables are respondents' demographic factors such as age (*age*) and gender (*female*). Given the regional variation or pattern of social health insurance presented in Chapter 6, the types of provinces (i.e., dual, risk-pooling, privileging, or status-quo type) where the respondents resided are included in the regressions as dummy variables (with the status-quo type being the omitted category to avoid multicollinearity). A descriptive summary of the data is provided in Table 7.1. A logistic regression model is employed in this analysis.

The logistic regression results, presented in Table 7.2, strongly support the stratification hypotheses. Using the "divide by four" rule for interpreting logistic coefficients,[11] holding other conditions constant, urban *hukou* increased one's probability of being covered by employment-based health insurance by about 29% in 2003, but the magnitude of this effect decreased over the time period studied. Migrants had a lower probability of being covered by employment-based health insurance until 2008, when migration's negative effect on social health insurance coverage was found to be trivial and statistically insignificant. Moreover, CCP members were more likely to be covered by employment-based health insurance in 2003 and 2006, but the positive effect of party membership disappeared in 2008.

While we can conclude from the above results that the impacts of socioeconomic and sociopolitical status such as *hukou* and CCP membership on employment-based social health insurance coverage were declining in terms of significance and magnitude from 2003 to 2008 (but still statistically significant throughout the years studied), the effects of employment situations were increasing over the same period. Again, using the "divide by four" rule

Table 7.1 Descriptive Statistics of Variables in the CGSS Data

	Mean	Median	Minimum	Maximum	Observation
medinsu*	.62	1	0	1	9940
age	45.11	44	16	90	9991
female*	.52	1	0	1	9991
edu	4.74	5 (high school)	0 (no formal education)	11(graduate school or above)	9983
Log(indiv_income)	9.29	9.29	3.00	13.85	8475
CCP*	.16	0	0	1	9914
urbanhukou*	.90	1	0	1	9991
migrant*	.10	0	0	1	9991
unemployed*	.14	0	0	1	9991
formal*	.52	1	0	1	8306
employer size	3.61	4 (100–499 employees)	1(1–10 employees)	8 (10000+ employees)	9252
SOE*	.52	1	0	1	9991
COE*	.13	0	0	1	9991
POE*	.13	0	0	1	9991
FOE*	.02	0	0	1	9991
Other*	.02	0	0	1	9991
Risk-pooling type	.23	0	0	1	9991
Dual type	.22	0	0	1	9991
Privileging type	.26	0	0	1	9991

*means the variable is binary with 1 referring to "yes" and 0 referring to "no."

for convenience, while holding other conditions constant, unemployment decreased one's probability of being covered by the employment-based social health insurance by approximately 20% in 2008, though this rate was lower in 2003 and 2006, meaning that unemployed people were increasingly cut off from the employment-based social health insurance programs during the 2008 global financial crisis. By contrast, formal employees (those who have a legal labor contract with their employer) increasingly benefited from employment-based social

Table 7.2 Logistic Regression Results about Employment-Based Health Insurance Coverage

	2003	2006	2008	Total
female	.046 (.148)	−.042 (.110)	.059 (.118)	.034 (.074)
age	.017** (.008)	.038*** (.005)	.029*** (.006)	.031*** (.004)
edu	.173*** (.037)	.143*** (.049)	.187*** (.034)	.151*** (.025)
log(indiv_income)	.625*** (.092)	.709*** (.077)	.306*** (.072)	.485*** (.058)
CCP	.464** (.202)	.610*** (.188)	−.264 (.210)	.203** (.103)
urban hukou	1.120** (.531)	.990*** (.189)	.374 (.244)	.764*** (.149)
migrant	−.617** (.255)	−.583** (.236)	−.074 (.238)	−.466*** (.174)
unemployed	−.765** (.368)	−.603*** (.187)	−.801** (.204)	−.398** (.111)
formal employment	1.340*** (.185)	1.424*** (.178)	2.242*** (.212)	1.209*** (.108)
employer size	.594*** (.048)	.233*** (.042)	.138*** (.037)	.257*** (.033)
Employment sector: SOE	.902*** (.250)	1.639*** (.171)	.904** (.451)	1.061*** (.125)
Employment sector: COE	−.318 (.264)	.671*** (.175)	.288 (.493)	.268** (.136)
Employment sector: FOE	1.505* (.807)	.461 (.354)	.149 (.579)	.519** (.235)
Employment sector: POE	−.555* (.293)	.050 (.146)	−.483 (.494)	−.431*** (.124)
Employment sector: Other	−.347 (.728)	1.180** (.512)	−.316 (.676)	−.165 (.374)
Dual type	.515 (.397)	.318 (.313)	.215 (.141)	.263 (.198)
Privileging type	.613** (.292)	.569** (.259)	.210 (.167)	.501** (.177)
Risk-pooling type	.141 (.224)	.316 (.194)	−.228 (.219)	.066 (.137)

Continued

Table 7.2 *Continued*

	2003	2006	2008	Total
Constant	−11.610*** (1.318)	−11.154*** (.751)	−6.880*** (.834)	−8.624*** (.639s)
N	1486	3601	2029	7116
Pseudo R^2	.376	.358	.339	.300

*** p<.01, ** p<.05, * p<.10

health insurance from 2003 to 2008. In effect, formal employment (*formal*) turns out to be the largest and most significant factor in determining one's probability of being covered by employment-based social health insurance in all model specifications. As for employment sectors, the state sector is consistently and significantly associated with higher probabilities of being covered by employment-based health insurance. On the contrary, working in the private sector decreases one's probability of being covered by employment-based social health insurance, though this negative effect was not significant in 2006 and 2008. A large-sized employer is also more likely to provide employment-based health insurance, although this effect was strongest in 2003 and gradually decreased thereafter.

Regarding the results about province types, all other things being equal, individuals living in the privileging type of provinces were more likely to be covered by the generous employment-based social health insurance than their counterparts in other types of provinces (e.g., risk-pooling type, dual type). This finding supports the arguments in previous chapters about the Center's interests in stratifying the expansion of social health insurance (chapters 2 and 4).

To summarize the results from the CGSS data, an individual's chance of being covered by employment-based social health insurance was determined significantly by both the person's socioeconomic and sociopolitical status, such as *hukou* (Hypothesis 1), CCP membership (Hypothesis 5), and employment situations such as employment status (Hypothesis 2), employment sector (Hypothesis 3), and employer's size (Hypothesis 4). The urban-rural divide has existed in Chinese society for decades due to the rigid household registration system stemming from the command economy prior to 1978. The divides between the state and non-state sectors and between formal and informal employees in the coverage of employment-based social health insurance, as shown in the CGSS data, reflect new social inequalities associated with China's burgeoning market economy. It was also found that employment-based health insurance coverage continues to privilege those advantaged in the market economy—the high-income and highly educated groups. Thus, it is fair to conclude that the expansion of employment-based social health insurance hardly corrects socio-economic inequalities; instead, it reinforces labor market cleavages. The Chinese state that has been remarkably successful in supervising the transition from a command economy to a market economy has failed to correct the existing and emerging social inequalities in its social welfare policy.

7.4. Distribution of Different Health Insurance Benefits

It was shown that employment-based social health insurance provides much more generous benefits to a relatively small group of beneficiaries—urban formal and state sector employees. The social health insurance expansion that entrenched the vested interests of urban formal state employees while incorporating other societal groups into newly created separate health insurance programs further stratified the society by reinforcing existing social cleavages and generating new divides within social groups. Section 7.3 provides empirical evidence for the stratification in terms of employment-based social health insurance coverage in the society. This section uses another individual-level social survey, the China Health and Nutrition Survey (CHNS), collected in nine Chinese provinces (Liaoning, Heilingjiang, Jiangsu, Shandong, Henan, Hubei, Hunan, Guangxi, and Guizhou) in multiple waves between 2000 and 2009, to demonstrate how people with differing socioeconomic and labor market status were "selected" into different health insurance programs with distinct levels of benefits. To better compare the stratification of social health insurance before and after the social health insurance expansion, I used CHNS data collected in urban areas in the years of 2004 and 2009, respectively.

The dependent variable, health insurance program (*prog*),[12] consists of five categories: "commercial or other health insurance," "GIS," "UEBMI," "URBMI," and "NRCMS." Except for the first one, the others are social health insurance programs. The rank of generosity of these social health insurance programs is GIS>UEBMI>URBMI>NRCMS. Other than social health insurance, a small portion of the population (9.87% and 2.97% of urban adult respondents in the 2004 and 2009 samples, respectively) joined non-social health insurance programs such as commercial or other health insurance programs, but non-social health insurance continues to be residual in terms of coverage and generosity in China. The focus of the analysis lies on the social health insurance programs. Since the dependent variable is multinomial, a multinomial logistic regression model was applied to this analysis. I used "commercial or other health insurance" as the baseline category in the multinomial logistic regression.

The independent variables cover two dimensions of individuals' attributes: socioeconomic status and employment situations. The socioeconomic factors included are household registration status (*urban hukou*)[13] and education level (*edu*).[14] The factors pertaining to a respondent's employment situations include employment status (*employsta*),[15] employment sector or employer ownership (*employown*),[16] and employer size (*employsz*).[17]

Province types (dual, risk-pooling, status-quo)[18] are also included in the regressions as dummy variables (with status-quo type being the omitted category to avoid multicollinearity). Summary statistics of all variables are in Table 7.3.

Descriptive data of the dependent variables (Figures 7.6–7.9) show that the distribution of various health insurance programs among individuals differs dramatically with people's socioeconomic and employment situations (i.e., *hukou*, employment status, employment sector, and employer size) both before and after the expansion (in 2004 and 2009, respectively). In addition, several discernible trends stand out from cross-time comparison of the descriptive data. First, social health insurance programs became more diverse, especially for the urban population. Second, the share of non-social health insurance, such as commercial and private health insurance, shrank significantly from 2004 to 2009. Third, the share of government free medical care (GIS) became smaller in 2009 compared to 2004. This does not mean that the health care privileges of civil servants and government officials disappeared; rather, GIS was integrated into the UEBMI program as a subcategory or supplementary insurance program for the privileged groups in two thirds of the Chinese provinces.[19]

Regression results using the 2004 data are presented in Table 7.4, and results using the 2009 data are summarized in Table 7.5. As expected, highly educated people were more likely to become the beneficiaries of urban employment-based

Table 7.3 Descriptive Statistics of Variables in the CHNS Data

	Mean	Standard Deviation	Minimum	Maximum	Observation
prog	3.40	1.17	1	5	4017
edu	2.17	1.52	0	6	6093
urbanhukou	.71	.45	0	1	5869
employsta	2.40	1.49	1	5	5753
employown	3.14	1.48	1	6	2707
employsz	1.94	.85	1	3	2357
Risk-pooling type	.22	.42	0	1	6321
Dual type	.23	.42	0	1	6321
Status-quo type	.55	.50	0	1	6321

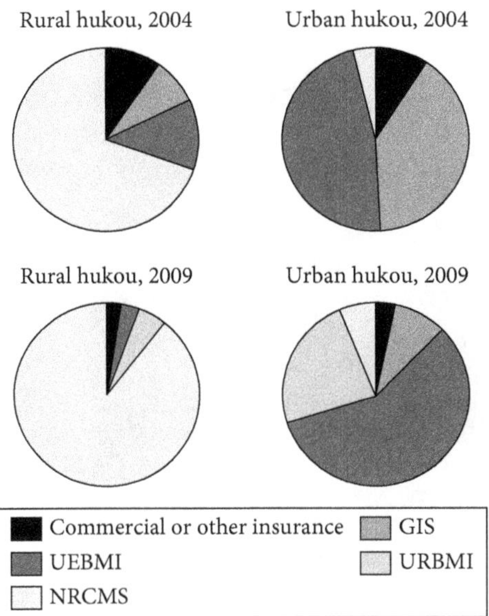

Figure 7.6 Distribution of Health Insurance Programs by *Hukou* and Year

Note: UEBMI = Urban Employee Basic Medical Insurance; NRCMS = New Rural Cooperative Medical Scheme; GIS = Government Insurance Scheme; URBMI = Urban Resident Basic Medical Insurance

Data source: China Health and Nutrition Survey, 2004 & 2009.

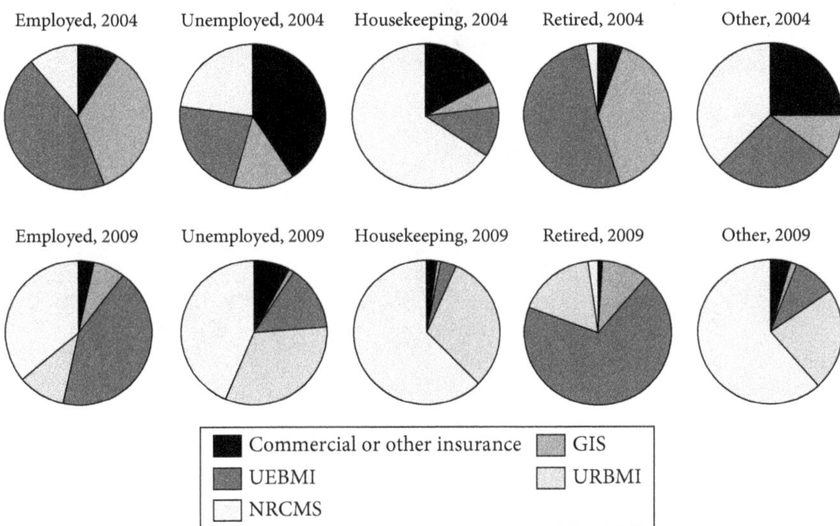

Figure 7.7 Distribution of Health Insurance Program by Employment Status and Year

Note: UEBMI = Urban Employee Basic Medical Insurance; NRCMS = New Rural Cooperative Medical Scheme; GIS = Government Insurance Scheme; URBMI = Urban Resident Basic Medical Insurance

Data source: China Health and Nutrition Survey, 2004 & 2009.

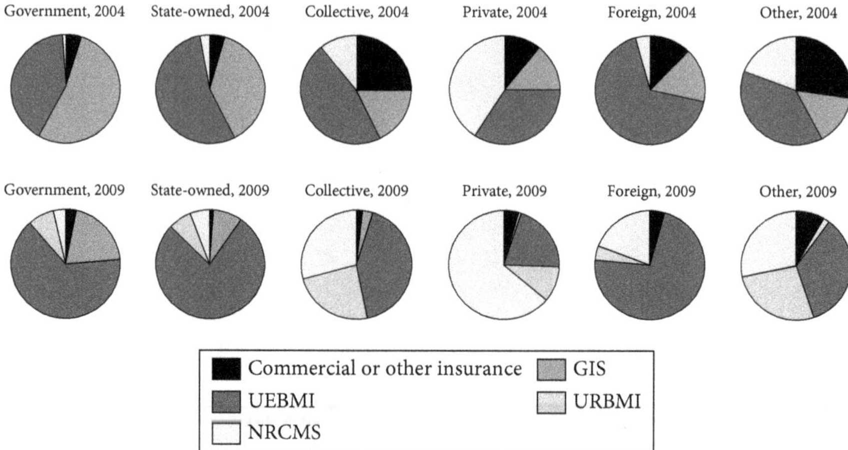

Figure 7.8 Distribution of Health Insurance Programs by Employer Ownership and Year

Note: UEBMI = Urban Employee Basic Medical Insurance; NRCMS = New Rural Cooperative Medical Scheme; GIS = Government Insurance Scheme; URBMI = Urban Resident Basic Medical Insurance

Data source: China Health and Nutrition Survey, 2004 & 2009.

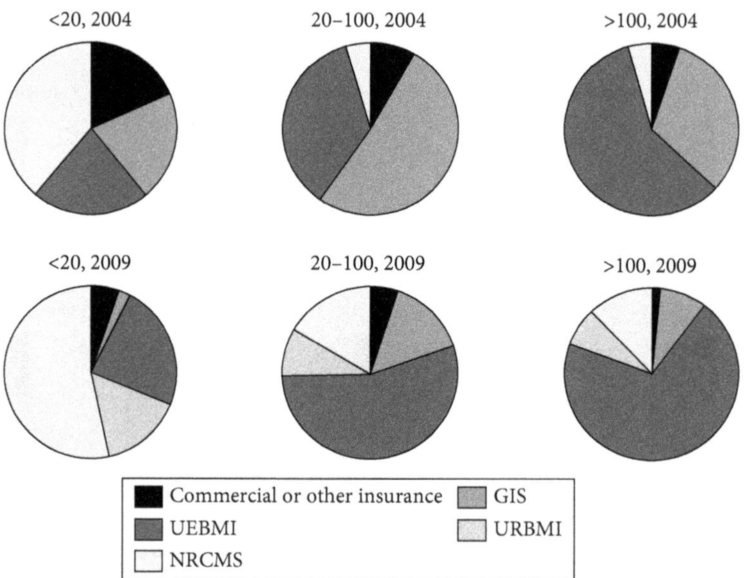

Figure 7.9 Distribution of Health Insurance Programs by Employer Size and Year

Note: UEBMI = Urban Employee Basic Medical Insurance; NRCMS = New Rural Cooperative Medical Scheme; GIS = Government Insurance Scheme; URBMI = Urban Resident Basic Medical Insurance

Data source: China Health and Nutrition Survey, 2004 & 2009.

Table 7.4 Multinomial Logistic Regression Results about Health Insurance Program Choice in 2004

	(1)			(2)		
	GIS	UEBMI	NRCMS	GIS	UEBMI	NRCMS
Edu	.264**	.201**	−.589***	.126	.100	−.435**
	(.094)	(.091)	(.138)	(.152)	(.146)	(.210)
Urban hukou	1.056**	.906*	−2.769***	−.255	−.399	−3.092***
	(.538)	(.492)	(.488)	(.944)	(.900)	(.937)
Employment status: employed	baseline					
Employment status: unemployed or student	−2.762***	−2.889***	−1.298			
	(.737)	(.728)	(.800)			
Employment status: housekeeping	−3.083**	−2.238**	−.374			
	(1.124)	(.760)	(.646)			
Employment status: retired	1.019***	1.025***	−1.020**			
	(.318)	(.312)	(.516)			
Employment status: others	−1.840**	−1.088**	−.650			
	(.651)	(.506)	(.588)			
Employment sector: government or public				Baseline		
Employment sector: SOE				−.873	−.502	.809
				(.668)	(.665)	(1.330)
Employment sector: COE				−2.852***	−1.392**	.385
				(.668)	(.631)	(1.284)
Employment sector: POE				−2.193***	−.899**	1.620
				(.647)	(.631)	(1.223)
Employment sector: FOE				−2.635**	−1.017	−.028
				(.932)	(.822)	(1.704)
Employment sector: others				−3.428**	−1.439*	−.03
				(.870)	(.752)	(1.70)
Employer size				.360	1.031***	.385
				(.275)	(.265)	(.354)
Dual type	−1.602***	−1.408***	−.437	−.780*	−.921**	.382
	(.307)	(.301)	(.444)	(.467)	(.453)	(.689)
Risk-pooling type	−.897**	−.635*	−.688	−1.019*	−.519	.265
	(.369)	(.359)	(.480)	(.555)	(.542)	(.775)
Constant	−.396	.825	3.761***	2.425	.612	1.442
	(.616)	(.573)	(.613)	(1.275)	(1.239)	(1.726)
Pseudo R^2	.191			.246		
N	1014			529		

*** p<.01, ** p<.05, * p<.1

Table 7.5 Multinomial Logistic Regression Results about Health Insurance Program Choice in 2009

	(1)				(2)			
	GIS	UEBMI	URBMI	NRCMS	GIS	UEBMI	URBMI	NRCMS
Edu	.207*	.014	−.298***	−.694***	.077	.070	−.151	−.578***
	(.115)	(.102)	(.104)	(.113)	(.175)	(.149)	(.161)	(.178)
Urban hukou	2.452***	2.882***	1.292***	−2.372***	2.193**	2.365***	1.176**	−2.715***
	(.616)	(.415)	(.378)	(.359)	(.899)	(.573)	(.568)	(.523)
Employment status: employed	baseline							
Employment status: unemployed or students	−2.542**	−1.841***	.419	−.140				
	(1.105)	(.543)	(.492)	(.531)				
Employment status: housekeeping	−15.179	−2.118***	.852*	.405				
	(586.082)	(.541)	(.462)	(.470)				
Employment status: retired	2.038***	1.960***	1.632***	−.472				
	(.571)	(.548)	(.560)	(.642)				
Employment status: other	−1.796**	−1.911***	−.057	−.081				
	(.711)	(.459)	(.429)	(.439)				
Employment sector: government or public					baseline			
Employment sector: SOE					13.732	14.562	14.402	14.665
					(918.025)	(918.025)	(918.025)	(918.025)

Employment sector: COE					13.472 (1427.015)	14.676 (1427.015)	16.276 (1427.015)	16.608 (1427.015)
Employment sector: POE					−3.317*** (.708)	−1.074** (.494)	.170 (.557)	.901 (.661)
Employment sector: FOE					−17.332 (1224.994)	−.728 (.876)	−−.527 (1.337)	1.260 (1.150)
Employment sector: others					−2.641** (1.263)	−.968 (.806)	.416 (.864)	−.108 (1.051)
Employer size					.732** (.333)	.826*** (.286)	.288 (.310)	.049 (.326)
Dual type	−1.017** (.360)	−.952** (.316)	−.393 (.323)	−1.296*** (.370)	−.375 (.510)	−.398 (.434)	−.460 (.479)	−1.351** (.570)
Risk-pooling type	.245 (.481)	.611 (.428)	.782* (.429)	.215 (.427)	−.042 (.759)	.731 (.678)	1.534** (.694)	.773 (.695)
Constant	−1.707** (.677)	.191 (.476)	1.090** (.447)	5.040*** (.426)	−1.544 (1.304)	−.973 (.973)	.349 (1.025)	3.617*** (1.059)
Pseudo R²	.394				.415			
N	2272				893			

*** p<.01, ** p<.05, * p<.1

social health insurance programs (GIS and UEBMI) rather than commercial or other health insurance in 2004. However, this effect decreased in terms of magnitude and significance in 2009. By contrast, urban *hukou*'s effect increased substantially in both magnitude and significance from 2004 to 2009. Specifically, urban *hukou* significantly increased the odds of individuals having urban employment-based social health insurance (i.e., GIS or UEBMI) relative to having commercial health insurance in 2009, while such effects were weaker or insignificant in 2004. This indicates that urban *hukou* rather than individuals' human capital (e.g., education) has become an increasingly important prerequisite for obtaining urban health care benefits (including GIS, UEBMI, and URBMI) since 2004. It also implies that the distribution of social health insurance benefits is skewed to urbanites more than to high-income groups in general.

According to Tables 7.4 and 7.5, the quantitative results on employment status lend support to the stratification hypotheses of social health insurance expansion. Specifically, the odds of an individual participating in employment-based health insurance (i.e., GIS or UEBMI) relative to participating in commercial health insurance decreased significantly if his/her employment status changed from being employed to being unemployed. On the contrary, the odds of an individual joining urban social health insurance (i.e., GIS, UEBMI, or URBMI) relative to joining commercial health insurance increased significantly if his/her employment status changed from being employed to retired. These results can be interpreted to mean that, as compared to employees, unemployed people (including students and housekeepers) were generally excluded from the generous social health insurance programs such as the GIS and UEBMI, while retirees increasingly benefited from various urban social health insurance programs, from employment-based social health insurance (i.e., GIS, UEBMI) to residency-based social health insurance (i.e., URBMI) throughout 2004–2009.

As for the effects of employment sector (measured by employer's ownership), the results in Table 7.4 and 7.5 show that there was no significant difference in terms of the odds of one joining social health insurance relative to joining commercial and other health insurance if one's employment sector changed from government institutes to SOEs in 2004 or 2009. This implies that no significant gap of social welfare benefits existed between government employees and SOE employees in those years. However, the odds of individuals joining employment-based health insurance relative to joining commercial and other health insurance significantly decreased if their employment sector moved from government institutes to private-owned enterprises in 2004 and 2009. This suggests that, compared to government and state-sector employees, private-owned-enterprise employees were less likely to benefit from the employment-based social health insurance than from commercial or other forms of health insurance. It is also noteworthy that private-owned-enterprise employees' disadvantage in obtaining employment-based social health insurance benefits became more substantial in 2009 than in 2004. Moreover, the odds of individuals having employment-based health insurance relative to having commercial or other health insurance significantly decreased if their employment sector changed from government institutions to foreign-owned or collective-owned firms in 2004, though such an effect disappeared in 2009, implying an expansion of employment-based social health insurance coverage among foreign-owned and collective-owned firms in 2009.

In addition, the effect of an employer's size on employment-based social health insurance coverage was positive as expected. Working for a large-sized employer significantly increased the odds of one having UEBMI relative to having commercial or other health insurance in both 2004 and 2009, which means that large-sized firms or work units in China continued to insure employees through UEBMI rather than commercial or other health insurance programs.

Although the CHNS data do not cover all Chinese provinces, the coefficients of province types show that all other things being equal, individuals living in the dual type or the risk-pooling type provinces (e.g., Jiangsu, Shandong, Hunan and Guizhou) were less likely to be enrolled in generous employment-based social health insurance programs (e.g., GIS, UEBMI) as opposed to commercial or other health insurance in 2004; but such effects seem to subside in 2009. Moreover, individuals living in the risk-pooling type of provinces were significantly more likely to be enrolled in the residency-based social health insurance programs such as URBMI in 2009. These results combined suggest that in the provinces where local governments took expansive social health insurance policies to obtain larger risk pooling, the social health insurance whose coverage was drastically expanded was mainly the residency-based programs (e.g., URBMI), which usually provide less generous benefits than the employment-based health insurance programs (e.g., GIS, UEBMI). Given local governments' different interests and policy choices for social health insurance expansion (elaborated in chapters 5 and 6), the uneven expansion of social health insurance across programs designated for different social groups, as presented in Table 7.4 and 7.5, is not surprising.

To sum up the results from the CHNS data in 2004 and 2009, people of different socioeconomic status and employment situations were enrolled into different health insurance programs. Other factors being equal, people with urban *hukou* were likely to be covered by the social health insurance programs with generally greater benefits (Hypothesis 1). Moreover, people of different employment situations were covered by different social health insurance programs. Retirees and incumbent employees were covered by the generous GIS or UEBMI programs, while unemployed people (including students and housekeepers) were either uninsured or insured by the programs with meager benefits, such as URBMI and NRCMS (Hypothesis 2). Furthermore, employees in private sectors or in small-sized firms tended to be enrolled in the social health insurance programs with the lowest benefits, such as NRCMS (Hypothesis 3 and 4). Hence, social health insurance after expansion stratified Chinese society along three cleavage lines: (1) urban versus rural; (2) labor market insiders versus outsiders; and (3) state versus non-state sectors. These cleavages are not exclusive to one another. On the contrary, they are interwoven in such a way as to fragment the society and privilege some groups over others without breaking society into a single and deep class line.

7.5. Conclusion

The questions this chapter empirically addresses can be summarized as "who gets what, when, and how from China's recent social welfare expansion." This chapter presents an in-depth investigation of the distribution pattern of social health insurance benefits among social groups in China. Based on analysis of individual-level survey data, I found that China's social health insurance expansion from 2003 to 2009 did significantly expand people's access to social health insurance. Peasants and urban non-working people who were previously excluded from the urban employee health insurance are now covered by separate and different social health insurance programs. However, the expanded social health insurance coverage and benefits are not only fragmented but also highly stratified across three cleavage lines: (1) rural versus urban, (2) labor market insiders versus labor market outsiders, and (3) state versus private sectors. The social health insurance expansion since 2004 has reflected and reinforced social inequalities based on individuals' labor market participation and socioeconomic status. Hence, the achievement of near universal health insurance coverage has not fundamentally solved the problems of health care access (*kan bing nan*) and affordability (*kan bing gui*) in China.

The findings of this chapter highlight the existence and complexity of multiple social divisions embedded in China's social health insurance system, which, it is worth noting, also characterize the distribution of other social welfare benefits in China, such as pensions (Frazier 2010). The fact that China's social welfare expansion strengthens rather than attenuates social stratification resonates with the authoritarian regime's stratified expansion strategy in social welfare provision.[20] It serves the authoritarian leaders' interests in maintaining regime stability by consolidating divisions among social groups to prevent alliances that could challenge the regime while tying social groups' loyalties directly to the state authority. The regime solicits cooperation from state employees and urban formal workers in key sectors while generally neglecting the much larger workforce in the informal and non-state sectors and rural areas, with the primary aims of containing urban riots, reinforcing divisions between social groups (e.g., between labor market insiders and outsiders), and promoting political cooptation (among labor market insiders). Under such a fragmented social welfare system, horizontal mobilization among societal groups—including cross-regional, cross-class, or cross-sectoral coalitions—becomes even more difficult as people's preferences and interests are divided in a complicated way so that their abilities of aggregating and organizing appeals to the state are weakened.

8

Conclusion

8.1. Summary of Arguments, Findings, and Contributions

Who gets what, when, and how from China's authoritarian welfare state? This is the core question that motivates this book. Although an extensive literature examines the welfare state in affluent democracies, we know less about the politics and policies of social welfare provision in authoritarian countries. Contrary to the conventional wisdom that the welfare state is a feature of democracies, my research demonstrates that an authoritarian country might dramatically expand social welfare provision without democratization. This book, using a combination of individual-level survey data and government statistics, employs quantitative analysis along with extensive fieldwork and qualitative research to explore the nuances of social welfare policy and to explain the political rationale for the policy design, implementation, and distributive pattern of social health insurance under Chinese authoritarianism in the first decade of the 2000s.

Chinese social health insurance underwent a dramatic expansion from 1999 to 2011 without significant political reform or democratization in the country. Accompanying the expansion was a sharp stratification of health care benefits across social groups and subnational regions. A seeming contradiction thus arises: the remarkable expansion of social health insurance coverage and generosity and the increased number of social health insurance programs did not reduce but rather reproduced and reinforced social inequalities in China. Instead of leveling the social playing field, the changes in social health insurance continued to link welfare benefits to citizens' sociopolitical status, employment, and residency. To address this puzzle, I developed a theoretical framework that takes into account authoritarian leaders' distributive trade-off, the decentralized multilevel governance setting, and the diverse local political economy in China.

Authoritarian leaders are fundamentally interested in regime survival and stability. As threats to the regime can emerge from both elites and masses, authoritarian leaders must strategically distribute resources between them. Doing so in a manner that efficiently balances benefits between elites and masses to maximize the leaders' survival prospects constitutes a choice with potential costs. When authoritarian leaders concentrate too many benefits on elites, they are vulnerable not only to unrest from the discontented masses but also to threats from within the empowered elites who can replace the incumbent leaders. Yet when authoritarian leaders reduce the privileges of elites and empower the masses by universalizing benefits, they risk betraying the very elites on whom they rely to ensure political survival. One strategy the Chinese authoritarian regime has adopted is to maintain a particularly privileged welfare provision for elites while preserving an essentially modest social provision for the masses. Under the conditions of political centralization and fiscal decentralization, the Chinese central leaders, on one hand, have established and maintained a highly stratified social welfare system to achieve a "divide and rule" situation that privileges the elite groups over others. On the other hand, the central leaders have sought to delegate discretionary power to local leaders regarding the coverage and generosity of social welfare distribution in order to accommodate diverse local and social needs and co-opt local leaders into the policymaking process.

Given the Center's strategy, Chinese local leaders, who owe their political careers to the Center rather than to the general public, proactively design and provide welfare benefits in a manner that suits the socioeconomic needs of their jurisdictions and thus contribute to social stability—a well-known priority target in the Center's assessment, appointment, and promotion of local leaders. My study points out that the local leaders encounter different constellations of constraints such as fiscal stringency and social risks in social policymaking and implementation. High social risks without adequate fiscal resources at local governments' disposal motivate local leaders to focus their efforts on expanding the risk pooling of social health insurance, resulting in a strict yet inclusive model of health insurance expansion (i.e., giving meager benefits to more people); on the contrary, abundant fiscal revenues (whether locally sourced fiscal revenues or fiscal transfers from the central government) combined with low social risks incentivize local leaders to enhance the benefits of social health insurance exclusively, leading to a generous yet exclusive model of health insurance expansion (i.e., giving certain groups more benefits). In contrast, a combination of both high fiscal revenues and social risks gives rise to a generous and inclusive expansion of social health insurance (i.e., giving more people generous benefits); by the same logic, a combination of both low fiscal revenues and social risks is conducive to a strict and exclusive expansion (i.e., only giving certain people meager benefits) or maintaining the status quo of social health insurance that is characterized by low coverage and generosity.

To explain the strategy, pattern, and subnational variation of social health insurance expansion in China, I conceptualized the distribution of social health insurance benefits in three dimensions— generosity, coverage, and stratification. Generosity captures the average level of benefits or spending per individual. Coverage, in terms of the proportion of people insured in the total population, represents the spread of social health insurance benefits among individuals. Stratification, measured by the inequality of benefits that different groups receive, describes the distributive pattern of social health insurance benefits across social groups within the population.

In the empirical parts of the book, I provided evidence for (1) the formation of the stratified expansion strategy and policies of Chinese authoritarian leaders in social welfare provision and the underlying central-local relations and interactions; (2) the expanded yet stratified distribution of social health insurance benefits among Chinese regions and social groups. Specifically, I first examined the Chinese regime's stratified expansion strategy in social welfare provision by drawing qualitative evidence from Chinese central leaders' speeches to local or ministerial officials and from central work conference memos, and quantitative evidence about the central-to-local fiscal transfers from 1998 to 2009 (Chapter 4). Then I employed subnational comparative case studies, drawing on 148 field interviews conducted in 16 Chinese provinces from 2009 to 2012, to uncover the local interpretation and implementation of the Center's stratified expansion strategy, especially how local socioeconomic conditions and the dynamics of central-local relations have shaped local leaders' policy preferences and choices regarding the distribution of social health insurance benefits (Chapter 5). After that, I conducted in-depth quantitative analyses to examine the distribution of social health insurance benefits across subnational regions and social strata in China: I utilized a provincial-level panel dataset from 1999 to 2010 to identify the subnational variations in Chinese social health insurance coverage and generosity as well as their correlations with local socioeconomic conditions (Chapter 6); I further used both government statistics and individual-level national survey data to recover the stratification pattern of Chinese social health insurance benefits among social groups (Chapter 7).

The main empirical findings regarding the distribution of Chinese social health insurance benefits are threefold. First, the Chinese social health insurance system is highly stratified across three social cleavage lines: (1) urban versus rural; (2) labor market insiders versus labor market outsiders; and (3) state versus non-state sectors. These social cleavages, which crosscut class differences, have been institutionalized in China's social welfare system and legitimized by the Center through a bundle of social legislation and finally by the Social Insurance Law, promulgated in 2010. Moreover, the Center makes use of fiscal transfers and top-down personnel control to maintain its preferred stratification pattern in social welfare distribution. The main stratification pattern of social health insurance persists across localities: urban state-sector employees receive far more benefits than other urban residents and rural dwellers in most Chinese provinces.

Second, generosity and coverage of social health insurance differ dramatically across localities, indicating that local leaders choose different models of social welfare expansion according to the specific profile of constraints they encounter in local circumstances. Specifically, local leaders in regions with high levels of social risk tend to expand the coverage of social health insurance, while local leaders in regions with high levels of fiscal revenue are more likely to enhance the generosity of social health insurance benefits. While local leaders in regions with high social risks and fiscal prosperity have been pioneers in promoting substantial social health insurance expansion, their counterparts in regions with neither high social risks nor fiscal prosperity tend to defend the status quo—a fragmented and inequitable social health insurance system—in their jurisdictions.

Third, the diverse local choices for social health insurance expansion sometimes conflict with the Center's most preferred stratification of social health insurance. This further compels and constrains the Center to enforce stratification of social health insurance. The distribution of health benefits in China during the first decade of the 2000s was thus a dynamic mix of both expansion and stratification with the central-local tensions and interactions standing at the core of the politics on the supply side.

This book contributes to the studies of social welfare development in non-democracies, the political economy of authoritarian regimes, and Chinese politics in the following ways. First, the book demonstrates that social welfare expansion, in some cases, is not a result of democracy but of resilient authoritarianism. Social welfare is one of the tools employed by authoritarian leaders to maintain regime stability. The political motivation for social welfare provision is different in non-democracies—it comes more directly from top-down pressure to maintain social order and stability than from bottom-up demands as in democracies—but this does not mean that non-democracies provide less social welfare than democracies do. This resonates with the findings about the generosity of social welfare benefits in some comparative studies of social welfare in the developing world (Haggard and Kaufman 2008). This book emphasizes that the stratification or inequalities of social welfare under authoritarian rule are largely attributable to the authoritarian leaders' political interest and strategy for maintaining regime survival and stability. The analysis in this book employs and develops a multidimensional conceptualization of welfare distribution—coverage, generosity, and stratification—to provide a more fine-grained and comprehensive framework for understanding authoritarian leaders' strategies and policy choices in social welfare provision.

Second, while the study of authoritarian regimes typically emphasizes the role of formal institutions such as elections, legislature, and political parties in authoritarian survival and adaptability (Magaloni 2008; Gandhi 2008; Boix and Svolik 2013), this study considers another important yet insufficiently studied tool that authoritarian leaders also utilize to prevent threats to regime stability: social welfare policy. It contributes to the study of political economy of authoritarian regimes by theorizing the trade-off authoritarian leaders confront when distributing benefits among different social groups for regime survival and stability. In this book, I explained the stratified expansion strategy that authoritarian leaders may adopt to manage the distributive trade-off in social welfare provision—maintaining a privileged provision for elites while expanding a modest provision for masses—and substantiated this strategy in the context of the Chinese authoritarian regime.

Third, in specifying the regularity, conditions, and policy outcomes of the interactions between Chinese central and local leaders in social welfare provision, the book sheds light on how political leaders in an authoritarian country with a multilevel governance structure respond and adapt to social needs. The analysis of subnational politicians' incentive structure and policy choices in social welfare provision demonstrates an "indirect accountability" built into the Chinese politics. This "indirect accountability,"[1] evidenced by the non-elected local leaders' proactive accommodation of social and local needs in policy-making and implementation under the formal upward-accountability or centralized cadre evaluation system, partially accounts for the puzzling resilience and adaptability of the Chinese authoritarian regime.

8.2. Looking Forward: Integration of Social Health Insurance in China

From 1999 to 2011, the Chinese authoritarian regime was engineering and maintaining a fragmented yet expansive social welfare system. One might question whether "stratified expansion" is still an accurate description of Chinese social welfare reform in the following decade given the rapid changes in social welfare policies. In 2009, the Chinese central government unveiled a three-year plan for health reform, claiming to provide affordable and equitable basic health care for all. In addition to the expansion of social health insurance, another change in the 2009 health reform plan was a trend toward merging various social health insurance programs; this seems odd as it appears contradictory to the Center's interests and its previous efforts of maintaining the fragmentation and stratification of social welfare benefits. The government claimed that integrating social health insurance would help reduce the unequal entitlements in social health insurance that were common across localities and social groups as determined by individuals' sociopolitical status.

Recall that Chinese social health insurance is fragmented in three ways. The first is the urban-rural divide. Citizens with urban *hukou* and those with rural status are entitled to different and separate health insurance programs, with the former providing more generous benefits than the latter. The second is regional segmentation. Chinese social health insurance programs were established at the district level in cities and the county level in rural areas. By 2010, about half of social health insurance programs were still operated by county-level governments. Regional disparities of health insurance regulations and benefits are so pronounced that it is hardly feasible for individuals to continue their current health insurance enrollment if they move to other localities beyond their hometown where their households are registered. The third is social stratification. Chinese health insurance programs are designed and organized around social groups: state employees, urban formal workers, urban non-working residents, and rural residents are each included in different programs with distinct contribution and benefit rates. Individuals basically have no right to choose—they cannot join the programs whose designated beneficiaries are above their own status (e.g., the rural residents cannot join the urban programs; urban unemployed residents cannot join the urban employees' health insurance; non-state employees cannot join the state employees' health insurance, etc.).

In these circumstances, social health insurance integration will lead to income redistribution and risk sharing among subnational regions and social groups. Specifically, pooling an individual social health insurance program (UEBMI, URBMI or NRCMS) across subordinate localities within a geographical unit (e.g., across counties and city districts within a prefectural-level city, or across cities within a province) will redistribute income and share risk across areas (i.e., interregional redistribution) while pooling together the various social health insurance programs (UEBMI, URBMI and NRCMS) within a geographical unit (e.g., city or province) will redistribute risks and benefits across social groups (i.e., intergroup redistribution).

Given the Center's primary interest in maintaining the hierarchy, or privileges for elite groups in social welfare provision, I predicted that the Center would tolerate health insurance integration across regions (interregional redistribution) more than integration across social groups (intergroup redistribution) because regional integration should bring the Center more functional benefits of economic integration and urbanization, such as accelerating labor mobility and increasing supplies of rural labor and land. In fact, the progress of interregional integration of social health insurance had become more prominent at the end of the first decade of the 2000s. In 2007, the Center picked Chengdu and Chongqing cities in the central region as the experimental zones (*shi dian*) in which to launch a pilot scheme entitled "urban-rural integrative development" (*cheng xiang tong chou fa zhan*), of which the most prominent reforms in the social domain were *hukou* and social welfare reforms. These local governments unified urban and rural *hukou* into one single local resident category so that "all residents would possess the same *hukou* status by 2011, and would thus gain equal access to social insurance programs previously only open to urban residents."[2] They also merged the urban resident social health insurance, URBMI, and the rural social health insurance, NRCMS, into a single program—the Urban and Rural Resident Basic Medical Insurance (URRBMI)—in 2008. Since then, the stratification of social health insurance benefits based on *hukou* status has been abolished in Chengdu and Chongqing cities, at least on paper.[3] In January 2016, the Center further called for the urban-rural integration of social health insurance nationwide, requiring all cities to integrate the URBMI and NRCMS programs in their respective jurisdictions by the end of 2016.

Despite some encouraging signs in the central directives to promote social health insurance integration across urban and rural areas, strong commitment on the part of the Center had not materialized—in introducing fiscal assistance to integrate social health insurance at higher levels or across more social groups—by 2017. Rather than promoting citizens' equal social rights, the Center's genuine intention is to facilitate urbanization, as the new central leadership headed by Xi Jingping starting in 2013 considers this to be a new engine for China's economic growth in the coming decade. Politically, the Center is cautious about pushing for full integration of social health insurance. Certain efforts for partial integration of social health insurance, such as the urban-rural integration, are beneficial to the regime as they help mitigate increasing regional disparities and social inequality, which have been generating increasing social grievances and breeding political instability since the mid-1990s. However, a fully integrated social health insurance would destroy the hierarchy in social welfare provision and eliminate the elite groups' health care privileges, and this move would contradict the authoritarian leaders' core interest of maintaining the elites' welfare privileges for regime stability. Like social health insurance expansion in preceding years, integration of social health insurance presents a political dilemma for the Chinese authoritarian leaders. It is thus not a surprise to find that despite frequent discussion of social welfare integration in government documents, no laws have been promulgated to enforce it.[4] In Xi Jinping's keynote speech at the CCP's 19th Congress in 2017, a meeting commonly considered a key indicator of the central leadership's policy priorities for the next five years, no substantially new initiatives or directives were presented concerning social health insurance beyond the urban-rural integration.

At the local levels, as with social welfare expansion, some localities have experimented with various schemes for social health insurance integration (e.g., urban-rural pooling, city-level pooling) while some have shown no interest or even resistance to the idea (Huang and Kim 2020; Muller 2017). The Center retains veto power and the right to intervene in any local health insurance integration that it perceives as having gone too far and as impairing the Center's interests in maintaining regime survival and stability. Therefore, at least in the foreseeable future, the integration of social health insurance in China will remain partial and confined to those health insurance programs designated for the masses. Meanwhile, the Center will relentlessly promote and develop supplementary health insurance programs for elite groups to ensure their loyalty and political support in the face of further social insurance expansion and integration. As long as the Chinese political regime remains autocratic, the hierarchy in the distribution of social welfare benefits, which helps ensure the CCP's survival and stability, is likely to persist.

8.3. Implications

Implications of this book concern the prospects for social stability and regime change in China. China's expansive yet stratified social welfare system has mixed implications for the prospects of the Chinese authoritarian regime. On the one hand, the current social welfare system reinforces social inequalities and entrenches the elite groups' benefits and status, which might foster resentment and demands for change from the masses whose living standards have experienced less increase. The institutional fragmentation of the welfare system and the inequality of social benefits are commonly deemed by the media and intellectuals as one of the largest obstacles to China's deeper economic restructuring and urbanization.[5] In a focus group study of public opinion on social policy in six Chinese cities, participants in all the cities noted that officials received far better benefits than ordinary urban workers (Frazier 2011). Based on a national representative stratified sample, Neil and Duckett (2015) found that Chinese citizens' satisfaction with the health care system is positively correlated with having health insurance but negatively correlated with the perception of unequal access. These empirical studies reveal the emerging awareness among Chinese citizens of the inequity of the welfare system. This awakening could trigger more demand in the general public for greater expansion of welfare provision. Given the increasing public demands and the limited capacities and willingness of the authoritarian regime to respond to and satisfy them, it is possible that in the long run the stratified expansion strategy of social welfare provision will be detrimental rather than beneficial to the stability of the Chinese authoritarian regime, whose legitimacy has relied heavily on good governance and economic performance.

On the other hand, China's social welfare system, as detailed in this book, seems to contribute to its "authoritarian resilience" (Nathan 2003; Shambaugh 2008). Under the Chinese fragmented and stratified social welfare system, horizontal mobilization among societal groups—including cross-regional, cross-class, or cross-sectoral coalitions—remains difficult as people's preferences and interests are divided in a complicated way so that their abilities to aggregate and organize appeals to the state are weakened. Moreover, the Chinese social welfare system continuously expands coverage and generosity so that its main beneficiaries—urban formal workers and state employees, or the majority of the middle class—who lack an alternative to the state provision of social welfare and services have an increasing stake in keeping the status quo. A report based on a national public survey, China Family Panel Study, suggests that most members of the Chinese middle class appear satisfied with the status quo (Li et al. 2015).[6] However, given the regime's struggles in balancing the different ends in society, which this book documents, the resilience of the Chinese authoritarian regime may be impermanent and could be vulnerable in the future.

Returning to the main argument of this book—that the Chinese authoritarian regime uses social welfare expansion as a tool to maintain regime survival and stability—one may wonder how effective this tool really is and how it complements other measures the regime is adopting for social stability. Social welfare expansion was not and will not be the only tool the Chinese regime utilizes to ensure its survival and stability. Like many other autocracies, the Chinese regime uses some combination of "carrots" (i.e., measures that build public support through the distribution of rents and patronage, programmatic redistribution, and broad-based economic growth) and "sticks" (i.e., coercive or repressive measures) (Gallagher and Hanson, 2009) to garner public support for the regime. In the first decade of the 2000s when the expansion of social welfare provisions including health care, education, pension, and subsistence allowances was ongoing (Huang 2014, Lü 2014; Frazier 2010), the Chinese regime was also well known for regularly using repression, censorship, and coercion to maintain political and social order (Huang and Yang 2004; King, Pan and Roberts 2013; Deng and O'Brien 2013). Empirical assessment of the political effectiveness of social welfare expansion indicates that the expansion does play an important role in boosting public support for the Chinese central and/or local governments (Lü 2014; Huang and Gao 2018, 2019). These policy effects are likely to encourage the regime's decision to further expand social welfare provision, though the distribution of the expanded benefits will continue to be structured to stratify the society according to the regime's political interest.

A broader implication of this book is that in authoritarian countries such as China, the specific political economic factors that drive the social welfare development or policies do not necessarily differ from those of democratic countries. As shown in this book, fiscal constraints and social risks that affect social welfare development in democracies (Beramendi 2012; Hauserman 2010; Rehm 2016) are also important predictors of local leaders' social policy choices in China. However, this does not mean that there is no difference between democracies and autocracies in social welfare provision. A key difference between the Chinese welfare state and the conventional welfare state in liberal democracies is that in China, social welfare policy is viewed as a means to achieve political stability and economic development rather than an intrinsic social right of individuals. Hence, the distribution of social welfare benefits, or "who gets what, when, and how" in China is heavily shaped by the political interests and calculation of the regime, whose social policies reflect the various (political, economic, social, and demographic) conditions and challenges it encounters.

8.4. Looking Beyond China

Compared with other Asian countries, China's social welfare expansion over the past decade is outstanding. According to the Asian Development Bank (ADB)'s Social Protection Index (SPI) data,[7] the breadth (coverage) of Chinese social protection in 2009 was .798 (meaning that 79.80% of the eligible population were actual beneficiaries of social welfare), ranked only after Japan (.905) and South Korea (.886) among 37 Asian and Pacific countries.[8] Given that social protection coverage in China was only .448 in 2005 (compared to .950 in Japan and .842 in South Korea at the time), this figure suggests remarkable progress by the Chinese government in social welfare expansion.

In a stark contrast to its remarkable achievement in terms of social welfare expansion, the general generosity (depth) of Chinese social welfare provision is lower than the expected level given its economic development and income level. According to the ADB's SPI data, the depth of Chinese social welfare in 2009 was .174 (meaning that the average benefit level of Chinese social welfare was only about .04 % of its GDP), which places China between Thailand (.153) and the Kyrgyz Republic (.196).[9] This trend also appears in the other East Asian countries, where the score for social protection breadth is considerably higher than the score for social protection depth: according to the ADB's SPI data, the average depth (generosity) of social protection in East Asia in 2009 was much lower than the average in Central and West Asia (.461), South Asia (.360), and the Pacific (.899), and barely higher than in Southeast Asia (.284).

As for stratification or inequality in social protection, China's level is above the mean in other Asian countries and stays at a relatively high level compared to other East Asian countries (all of them are democracies). As Chinese authoritarian leaders rely less directly on a majority of the population to stay in power compared to democratic leaders, they tend to concentrate welfare benefits and allocate more resources to elites or to small groups with political clout and connections.[10]

The final question concerns the extent to which the stratified expansion strategy in authoritarian social welfare provision, as seen in China, is generalizable beyond the China case. In past decades, it was not uncommon for non-democratic governments to expand social welfare provision dramatically. In the

Middle East and North Africa (MENA), the autocratic rulers expanded various transfer programs during the Arab Spring. For instance, Bahrain's King Hamad ibn Isa Al-Khalifa gave each Bahraini family the equivalent of US $2,650;[11] The Syrian government of Bashar al-Asad froze electricity prices and announced a 72% rise in heating-oil benefits for public workers;[12] and the Saudi government announced an increase in subsidies for new marriages, homeowners, and businesses.[13] Iran's largest revolutionary welfare foundation, the Imam Khomeini Relief Committee, provides a wide range of services, including financial aid, health insurance, interest-free loans for housing scholarships, and stipends for the elderly poor in rural areas. A 2010 report reveals that in the small Iranian town of Shahar Babak in Kerman province with a population of just over 50,000, 3,800 families received monetary allowances of $20 to $30 per month and nearly 700 students received some form of stipend (Harris 2013). In Latin America since the 1990s, the semi-democratic government of Mexico has pioneered targeted and conditional cash transfer programs (PROGRESA) for vote-buying (De La O 2013; Diaz-Cayeros et al. 2016); a similar expansion of social transfers or benefits for "outsiders" occurred in Chile, Argentina (Garay 2016), Venezuela (Haggard and Kaufman 2008), and Brazil (Zucco Jr. 2013). These policies are mostly transfers of income (in the form of cash, subsidies, price regulation, land reform, and programmatic redistribution) from the government to a targeted segment of the population for political cooptation. In contrast, China's expansive social welfare initiatives in the 2000s, including expansion of health insurance, pensions, and education, are more permanent social entitlements offered by the state with distinct political implications.

Compared to the one-time or conditional cash transfers in MENA and Latin American countries, the expanded social entitlements in China such as social health insurance, pensions, and education have put a powerful restraint on future retrenchment for two reasons. First, these entitlements are relatively broadly targeted in China and signal the CCP's long-term commitment to social protection. The entitlements, as a "social contract" between government and people, generate public expectations for the benefits the government will deliver. Reneging on these social entitlements is particularly dangerous for an authoritarian government like China whose legitimacy relies heavily on good governance and economic performance. This is distinct from the distributive efforts motivated by clientelism such as cash payments or in-kind goods distribution, which dominate in other developing countries during electoral contests.

Second, the expanded social entitlements in China are non-discretionary in the sense that they are administered through professional bureaucracies and distributed according to formulated rules and regulations by local states. Moreover, those expanded social welfare benefits are mostly contribution-based and financed by payments from employers, individuals, and different levels of government. Their implementation has been integrated into the Chinese political and economic system, by cadre evaluation, inter-government fiscal transfers, and social legislation. The institutional arrangements of social welfare expansion, such as the fiscal transfers and administrative decentralization, further distinguish the political battles over social policy in China from those in other countries.

However, this doesn't mean that the Chinese stratified social welfare expansion, born of the regime's political interest in balancing distribution between elites and masses, is unique in the world. In Iran, oil revenues do not automatically lead to welfare expansion for purposes of social leveling, class reshuffling, and balancing the rural-urban divide; instead, social welfare or transfers were expanded by the intertwined forces of elite competition and popular mobilization (Harris 2017). In Latin American cases, large-scale social welfare expansion took place when the incumbents faced credible challenges from political opponents in addition to intense social mobilization (Garay 2016; Diaz-Cayeros et al. 2016). What we need to pay more attention to is the conditions when applying the stratified expansion findings developed from the Chinese case to other authoritarian countries.

I anticipate that the stratified expansion strategy for social welfare provision is most likely to be found in those authoritarian countries with a broad power base, strong commitment to economic development, and necessary state capacity (e.g., fiscal and administrative capacity) to provide basic social protection. The need for a broad power base to survive makes the balancing between elites and masses in benefit distribution a salient consideration for the authoritarian leaders' distributive decisions and social welfare policy. The presence of a strong commitment to economic development moderates the authoritarian rulers' predatory tendency and makes it possible for social welfare development to appear on the leaders' agenda. Also, the state must have the capacity to realize the political and economic interests of authoritarian leaders in social welfare provision; after all, to implement an expansive and stratifying social welfare provision requires considerable financial and administrative capabilities.

These conditions narrow down the number of authoritarian countries for which the stratified expansion of social welfare provision is feasible: they exclude the rentier states with narrow fiscal and political bases, the predatory states that survive mostly via terror and repression, and the low-income or post-conflict countries in the developing world in which the states simply lack the capacity and infrastructure to provide basic social protection. This is not to suggest that there are no social services in those countries, but they lack institutionalized welfare commitments and provision by the state.[14] In all other authoritarian countries, the distribution of social welfare benefits, characterized by the trade-off of balancing between elites and masses in resource allocation, is likely to fall on a spectrum where at one end there is severe stratification favoring the top elites and at the other end there is broader and more inclusive expansion benefiting the masses.[15]

In the long run, without regime change, welfare expansion in authoritarian countries is unlikely to develop into a universalistic and rights-based welfare system. As the Chinese case shows, social welfare expansion under authoritarianism is not merely an economic choice but a political dilemma with distributive trade-offs for the authoritarian leaders.

APPENDIX A

Data Sources

The data used in the analysis in this book were collected from multiple sources: archives, fieldwork, interviews, and national representative surveys. As such, they came with the advantages and limitations associated with the respective data source or collecting method, but the sources also complement each other to present a relatively complete picture of the design, enforcement, and distributive outcome of the Chinese social health insurance expansion. The empirical analysis used both qualitative and quantitative data. On the qualitative side, I completed a total of 148 field interviews with government officials, social insurance administrators and experts, health care providers, and health insurance beneficiaries holding different socioeconomic status in 16 Chinese provinces between 2009 and 2013. The 16 provinces that I visited for the interviews cover the four clusters of Chinese provinces in terms of distribution of social health insurance benefits identified by the cluster analysis in Chapter 6 of this book. Details about the interviews cited are shown in Appendix B.

The qualitative data also included primary documents about social health insurance collected from government and library archives, such as government internal reports, political leaders' speeches and memoirs, central work conference and ministerial meeting memos, and government-sponsored conference publications. The qualitative materials included secondary-source literature in Chinese and English on China's social welfare development during the Maoist and the post-Mao eras; these helped create a historically grounded account of the formation and evolution of the Chinese social health insurance system.

On the quantitative side, three datasets were analyzed in this book. The first concerns the central government's fiscal transfers to local governments. The central-to-local fiscal transfer data were compiled from the Chinese government publication *Local Fiscal Statistics* (*di fang cai zheng tong ji zi liao*), published annually by the Ministry of Finance by the China Finance and Economy Press; this dataset provides a valuable perspective on the Center's distributive strategy in this period. It consists of various measurements of elite groups in provinces and the sociopolitical and socioeconomic conditions of the provinces from 1998 to 2010. Analysis of this data uncovers the pattern and determinants of the central-to-local fiscal transfers throughout social health insurance expansion.

The second dataset contains individual-level data from national social surveys, the China General Social Survey (CGSS) and the China Health and Nutrition Survey (CHNS), about Chinese citizens' health insurance participation and benefits. Both surveys collected data at the individual level every two to three years from 2000 to 2011. The CGSS sample covers more than 4,000 adult Chinese citizens in 28 of 31 Chinese mainland provinces, and the CHNS covers 9 provinces in total (4 in Eastern China, 3 in Central China, and 2 in Western China). These survey data show clearly the systematic stratification of social health insurance benefits across social strata. More information about the CGSS can be found at http://www.chinagss.org/ or http://www.ust.hk/~websosc/survey/GSS_e.html. More information about the CHNS can be found at their website: http://www.cpc.unc.edu/projects/china.

The third dataset, compiled from government statistical yearbooks such as the *China Labor Statistics Yearbook* (1999–2007), the *China Human Resources and Social Security Yearbooks* (2008–2011), and various provincial statistical yearbooks, has information on provincial social health insurance expenditure and population coverage, and the socioeconomic conditions of provincial units (including four provincial-level municipalities and five ethnic autonomous regions) from 1999 to 2010. This administrative dataset complements the individual-level survey datasets in delineating the distributive profile, especially the coverage and generosity, of Chinese social health insurance across provinces over time and in examining the relationship between the local political economy and the expansion of social health insurance benefits.

One might question the accuracy of the Chinese government's statistics insofar as local governments may misrepresent their social health insurance expenditures or beneficiaries to impress the Center. To cross-validate the accuracy of the government statistics used in this study, I computed and compared the enrollment rates (coverage) of China's major social health insurance programs using both government statistics and public survey data from CHNS and CGSS. The comparison shows little significant difference between the two sets of results, which, to some extent, validates the government statistics on social health insurance coverage.

List of Interviewees Cited in Chapters

	Position	Institution	Location	Date
1	Official	Township Social Insurance Bureau	Lidu, Jiangxi	6/2/2011
2	Official	Municipal Social Insurance Bureau	Nanning, Guangxi	6/8/2011
3	Official	Ministry of Human Resources and Social Security (MoHRSS)	Beijing	6/16/2011
4	Official	District/County Social Insurance Bureau	Taizhou, Zhejiang	6/21/2011
5	Official	County Social Insurance Bureau	Yuhuan, Zhejiang	6/22/2011
6	Official	Municipal Social Insurance Bureau	Dongguan, Guangdong	6/27/2011
7	Official	Municipal Social Insurance Bureau	Shenzhen, Guangdong	6/29/2011
8	Official	Municipal Social Insurance Bureau	Zhuhai, Guangdong	7/1/2011
9	Official	Provincial Social Insurance Bureau	Nanning, Guangxi	7/15/2011
10	Official	District/County Social Insurance Bureau	Nanning, Guangxi	8/5/2011
11	Official	County Social Insurance Bureau	Xing'an, Guangxi	8/10/2011
12	Official	Municipal Social Insurance Bureau	Guilin, Guangxi	8/10/2011
13	Official	Provincial Social Insurance Bureau	Nanning, Guangxi	3/31/2012
14	Official	Municipal Social Insurance Bureau	Chengdu, Sichuan	4/13/2012
15	Official	Provincial Social Insurance Bureau	Chongqing	4/16/2012
16	Scholar	Provincial Academy of Social Science	Chengdu, Sichuan	4/17/2012
17	Official	Provincial Social Insurance Bureau	Lanzhou, Gansu	4/20/2012
18	Official	Provincial Social Insurance Bureau	Yinchuan, Ningxia	4/24/2012

Continued

	Position	Institution	Location	Date
19	Official	Municipal Social Insurance Bureau	Zhengzhou, Henan	5/14/2012
20	Official	Provincial Social Insurance Bureau	Hefei, Anhui	5/17/2012
21	Official	Provincial Social Insurance Bureau	Wuhan, Hubei	5/22/2012
22	Official	Municipal Social Insurance Bureau	Wuhan, Hubei	5/23/2012
23	Official	Municipal Social Insurance Bureau	Changsha, Hunan	5/25/2012
24	Official	Municipal Social Insurance Bureau	Harbin, Heilongjiang	6/11/2012
25	Official	Municipal Social Insurance Bureau	Shenyang, Liaoning	6/14/2012
26	Official	Municipal Social Insurance Bureau	Dalian, Liaoning	6/18/2012
27	Official	Municipal Social Insurance Bureau	Kunshan, Jiangsu	7/9/2012
28	Official	Municipal Social Insurance Bureau	Kunshan, Jiangsu	7/10/2012
29	Official	Provincial Social Insurance Bureau	Nanning, Guangxi	3/15/2013
30	Official	Ministry of Human Resources and Social Security (MoHRSS)	Beijing	7/3/2013

Notes

Chapter 1

1. The story of Li Jing and Wang Nan is based on a media report by the Bin Dian Weekly in *Beijing Youth Daily*, April 18, 2012, p. 12. The original report can be found at http://zqb.cyol.com/html/2012-04/18/nw.D110000zgqnb_20120418_1-12.htm#, accessed on November 29, 2016.

2. A *hukou* is a record in the system of household registration required by law in China. The household registration system was officially promulgated by the Chinese Communist Party in 1958 to control the movement of people between urban and rural areas. Individuals held either agricultural (rural) or non-agricultural (urban) *hukou* based on their hometown and parents' status, so people were broadly categorized as "rural" or "urban" and "local" or "non-local" persons. Nowadays this anachronistic system of household registration has resulted in tremendous discriminations in public services and welfare provision against rural and non-local populations.

3. These numbers in comparison are calculated or drawn from administrative data compiled by the PRC's Bureau of Statistics.

4. I assume, without loss of generality, that there is always a resource limit for social welfare provision. Under this constraint, giving more benefits to the masses means that the amount of benefits available to the elites will decrease.

5. When the rulers need a large subset of the "selectorate" or population "whose endowments include the qualities or characteristics institutionally required to choose the government's leadership and necessary for gaining access to private benefits doled out by the government's leadership" (Bueno de Mesquita et al. 2003, 42) to take and stay in power, the rulers have an incentive to provide more public goods; otherwise, the rulers are likely to distribute private goods to the important few who support them.

6. Specifically, Mares and Carnes (2009) posit that if an autocracy counts on terror, torture, and purges to survive politically, one should see little or no social policy legislation within the regime. Conversely, if an autocratic state relies on the organizational cooptation of a small group of critical supporters, they will enact "restrictive" social policies characterized by narrow coverage and generous benefits. In contrast, if an autocrat is brought to power by a broad coalition of interests and chooses a strategy based on organizational proliferation, social policy will be characterized by high levels of institutional fragmentation on the one hand, and broader coverage on the other.

7. This is an assumption commonly adopted in the literature of autocracy which argues that public goods provision including social welfare, like repression and terror, is a tool for autocracies to stay in power. See B. Bueno de Mesquita et al. 2003; Tullock 1987; Wintrobe 1998; Haber 2007.

8. Health expenditure is the sum of public and private health expenditure. It covers the provision of health services (preventive and curative), family planning activities, nutrition activities, and emergency aid designated for health but does not include provision of water and sanitation.

9. The Jiang Zemin administration put more emphasis on increasing economic efficiency through economic reform and openness, such as restructuring SOEs and joining the World Trade Organization (WTO), while the Hu Jintao administration put more attention on addressing social issues such as income inequality and urban-rural disparities. Compared to their predecessors, the Xi Jinping administration has been more concerned with political issues, such as anti-corruption, ideology, and foreign policy.

10. This expansion of both coverage and generosity of social health insurance is unprecedented in Chinese history.

Chapter 2

1. Svolik (2012) presents an exception in this regard: he uses "authoritarian control" and "authoritarian power-sharing" to refer to these two relationships, respectively, and recognizes that these two are interconnected. But the work doesn't elaborate how these two relationships interact and how the interaction influences autocrats' policy choice with respect to distribution of resources.

2. This finding is based on Haggard and Kaufman's permissive coding of the "distributive-conflict" transition. There are two types of regime transitions that have been commonly established in the literature of democracy, authoritarianism and regime change: distributive-conflicts-driven (or bottom-up) transition and elite-led (or top-down) transition. Haggard and Kaufman (2016, 37–38) code "distributive conflict" transitions as ones in which two conditions occurred: (1) the mobilization of redistributive grievances on the part of economically disadvantaged groups or representatives of such groups (parties, unions, NGOs) posed a threat to the incumbency of ruling elites; (2) mass mobilization directly ousts incumbents, or the rising costs of repressing these demands force elites to make political compromises in favor of democratic challengers, typically indicated by a clear temporal sequence (mass mobilization followed by authoritarian withdrawal). They code "elite-led transitions" for all cases in which the threats from below did not occur at all or appeared to play only a marginal causal role.

3. Wallace (2014) is one of a few exceptions in this regard that specifically explores the Chinese authoritarian regime's distributive politics and policy in the post-1949 period.

4. The Center's *nomenklatura* regulates the appointment and promotion of party and state main leading cadres and other important positions.

5. As defined in this book, the elites in China were estimated to be at least 50 million in 2008; they were civil servants (formal employees of the government and the party) and public sector employees (e.g., doctors, teachers). They accounted for about 3%–4% of the Chinese population. In contrast, the "elites" defined in the traditional view (e.g., members of the CCP's central committee) are several hundred top leaders from

the government and the party agencies. They account for less than 0.000001% of the Chinese population.

6. Before the expansion of social welfare, people complained about the lack of benefits; after the expansion, people expressed dissatisfaction with the inequality and unfairness of the benefits, as everyone gets something but in different amounts.

7. Perry and Heilmann (2011) characterize the decentralized policymaking style of the Chinese Communist Party generally as "guerrilla policy style": intentionally relying on flexibility and discretion while maintaining the Center's freedom and power of control.

8. "Veto point" here means that the local officials who fail to keep social order in their jurisdictions will probably not receive a promotion no matter how well they perform in other policy areas. See Edin 2003a, 2003b; Whiting 2004.

9. For a detailed examination of autocratic leaders' concerns and strategies for political survival, see Bueno de Mesquita et al. 2003; Magaloni and Kricheli 2010; Svolik 2012; Haber 2007.

10. *New York Times*, October 13, 2016, "Xi Jinping Reminds China's State Companies of Who's the Boss," http://www.nytimes.com/2016/10/14/world/asia/china-soe-state-owned-enterprises.html?emc=eta1&_r=0, accessed on October 14, 2016.

11. This term was first used by Haber (2007). It refers to the organized groups that dictators need to take power and run the country, such as the military, political party, and bureaucrats.

12. Mares and Carnes (2009) attributed this distributional pattern of social welfare to a particular strategy of autocratic leaders for regime survival: organizational proliferation and cooptation.

13. For segmentation of the Chinese social classes and its political implications, see Ma (2010) and Walder et al. (2013).

14. See National Development and Reform Commission (2013), *Guan yu 2013 nian shen hua jing ji ti zhi gai ge zhong dian gong zuo yi jian de tong zhi [Decisions on deepening economic reform priorities in 2013*, State Council #30, retrieved from http://www.gov.cn/zwgk/2013-05/24/content_2410444.htm on December 12, 2016.

15. For more detail on China's tax sharing reform and the intergovernmental transfer system, see Zhang and Martinez-Vazquez 2002 and Wong 2000.

16. To my knowledge, the Center's exact formula, if one exists, for making fiscal transfers is not publicly accessible. Zhang and Martinez-Vazquez (2002) provide valuable information about how to calculate some kinds of central-to-local fiscal transfers.

17. The statutes included *tiaoli, guize, xize* (regulations and rules), *banfa* (means and ways), *fangan* (plans), and *biaozhun* (standards) and some legally binding administrative circulars such as *jueding* (decisions) and *yijian* (directives).

18. For examples of these statutes, see State Council, *Guowuyuan guan yu jian li chengzhen zhi gong ji ben yi liao bao xian zhi du de jue ding (Decision about establishing urban employee basic medical insurance)*, Beijing, State Council Decree #44, 1998. State Council, *Guowuyuan guan yu kai zhan cheng zhen ju min ji ben yi liao bao xian shi dian de zhi dao yi jian (Directives about establishing urban resident basic medical insurance)*, Beijing, State Council Decree #20, 2007. Ministry of Finance, Ministry of

Health, and Ministry of Agriculture, *Guan yu jian li xin xing nong cun he zuo yi liao zhi du de yi jian (Directives about establishing new rural cooperative health insurance)*, Beijing, State Council Decree #3, 2003.

19. The state propaganda and media have widely reported this change in official evaluation. For example, *Yangtze Daily*, "Abolishing GDP Indicator in Nanjing Official Evaluation" [nanjing guanyuan zhengji kaohe quxiao GDP zhibiao] 2011 [accessed November 13, 2013], available from http://www.chinanews.com/gn/2011/08-08/3239847.shtml; *Foshan Daily*, "Official Evaluation Emphasizes Improving People's Livelihoods" [guanyuan kaohe qingxiang minsheng], 2012 [accessed November 13, 2013], available from http://epaper.citygf.com/szb/history/html/2012-01/17/content_460174013.htm; Hu Mengmeng, "Social Development Indicators Included in Guangdong Official Evaluation," *Dongfang News* 2013 [accessed November 13, 2013], available from http://news.eastday.com/c/20130718/u1a7529742.html; *Beijing News*, "New Regulations on Cadre Evaluation" [zhengji kaohe xin guiding], 2013 [accessed December 10, 2013], available from http://economy.caijing.com.cn/2013-12-10/113668865.html.

20. This is similar to the logic of delegation between legislators and bureaucrats in democracies. For a comprehensive review of the delegation theory, see Huber and Shipan (2008).

21. Heilmann (2008) examines the regulations dealing with the economy (including health service and social insurance reform) during the first two decades of China's economic reforms and finds that throughout this period, well above 30% of the total were marked in their titles as provisional or experimental or as regulating experimental points and zones.

22. Officials from provincial governors and below are appointed for time-limited terms, and reappointments and promotions depend critically on performance evaluations that are regularly carried out by the upper levels.

23. The term "social risk" is used here as a compound of different risks that are covered by or related to social health insurance. For example, localities with more dependent populations (such as elderly, children, and the disabled) have higher health risks than others. For another example, localities with larger labor-intensive manufacturing sectors have higher risks of workplace injury and sickness than others.

24. The demographic profile of a population is often used to estimate the potential demand for particular social services such as education, elder care, and health care. See Gandhi 2008, 133.

25. China's unprecedented internal migration and urbanization since the 1980s is incomplete because the *hukou* status of the majority of migrant workers is kept intact (i.e., it remains a non-local status). Because of this, the majority of migrants can claim social welfare benefits (e.g., pension, social health insurance) only from their hometowns (labor-outflowing regions) rather than in their current residential areas (labor-inflowing regions). As local governments in the labor-outflowing regions usually have difficulty collecting sufficient social insurance premiums, they have difficulty paying beneficiaries.

26. The central government's subsidization of these health insurance programs also has large regional variations: the eastern coastal provinces receive few or no fiscal transfers or subsidies from the central government for social health insurance, while western provinces receive large portions (up to 70% of health insurance revenue) from the Center.

Chapter 3

1. In China, all public institutes can be called "work units" (*danwei* in Chinese) and these usually consist of state-owned enterprises, government agencies, and public institutes such as schools, universities, and hospitals. Work units are "mediating organizations," serving not only economic but also political, administrative, and social functions. See Lü and Perry (1997).
2. The 1951 Labor Insurance Regulations mandated work units to provide comprehensive social security benefits covering retirement, health care, and work injury.
3. An example drawn from Huang (2013, 45) shows that in Changyang county, a harbinger of the CMS, the CMS fund came from the annual peasant contribution (one yuan per capita) and the brigade subsidy (0.5 yuan per capita).
4. In the traditional planning system during Mao's era, peasants were organized into production teams (groups of households) and given by the state a quota of goods to produce; they received compensation by meeting the quota. Going beyond the quota rarely produced a sizable economic reward.
5. In the 1990s, only some 6.6% of the rural population belonged to a CMS; the remaining 87.3% were completely uninsured and had to pay the full cost of any medical care and drugs out of their own pockets. See Qian and Blomqvist (2014), 9.
6. China News Center, 2005, "State Council DRC's Assessment and Recommendations on Medical Care Reform (in Chinese)," www.china.com.cn/chinese/health/927874.htm, accessed on September 24, 2016.
7. See "Corruption and Food Safety Top Netizen Concerns" by Li Jingrong, published on March 5, 2009, retrieved from http://www.china-embassy.org/eng/zt/zgrq/t540617.htm on December 16, 2016.
8. Recent years have seen increasing violence against doctors and hospitals in China. Since 2002, attacks have increased by nearly 23% a year according to the China Hospital Management Society. A survey across 10 provinces revealed that over half of health professionals have been verbally abused, almost one third have been threatened, and 3.9% have been physically assaulted by patients or their families. Additional statistics revealed a staggering 17,243 incidents of *yi nao* (medical disputes) in 2010, skyrocketing from 7,000 cases five years ago. The government has ordered armed task forces to guard hospitals to prevent assaults on health providers with instructions to "use weapons against potential attackers if necessary." See "Armed Police Guard Hospitals to Prevent Violence against Doctors by Patients in China" by Vi-Jean Khoo on October 21, 2016, retrieved from http://today.mims.

com/topic/armed-police-guard-hospitals-to-prevent-violence-against-doctors-by-patients-in-china on December 16, 2016.

9. See *Allocation of Govenment Funding for Health*, 2010, by the Ministry of Finance of the People's Republic of China, retrieved from http://ys.mof.gov.cn/2010juesuan/index.html on September 12, 2011.

10. It is debatable whether China's current social health insurance coverage, after expansion in 2003, is universal. On paper, every Chinese citizen is entitled to social health insurance of a certain kind, and the enrollment rate for China's social health insurance reached over 80% by 2010. However, the health insurance benefits, as shown here, are not universal, and out-of-pocket payments are still as high as 34%. I use the term "universal" to describe China's social health insurance after expansion mainly based on its de jure universal coverage; "universal" corresponds to the term *quan min* (全民) commonly used in the Chinese government's documents.

11. Even so, for ordinary Chinese the out-of-pocket expenses for health care are still burdensome. Given a hypothetical situation in which a person was hospitalized, required surgery and the care of a specialist, the vast majority of respondents in the Public Goods and Political Support Survey in 2010 and 2014 said they would have difficulty finding care and paying for it. Specifically, 78% of the respondents said they would have some or major difficulty paying for these medical expenses. See Dickson (2016), 194–195.

12. Data are drawn from Urban Social Basic Health Insurance Report, MoHRSS 2011.

13. The term "fragmented authoritarianism" was developed by Kenneth G. Lieberthal and Michael Oksenberg in their book about China's bureaucratic politics and decision making in Post-Mao era (Liberthal and Oksenberg 1988).

14. See "China's New Health Care Reform Has Stepped into a Critical Stage" by Xin Gu, published on May 24, 2011, retrieved from http://news.china.com.cn/2011-05/24/content_22633046.htm on December 16, 2016.

15. One prominent example is the Shanghai Social Insurance Agency (SIA) scandal in which pension funds became the chief source of financing for at least a dozen of the property developers in the city and their high-profile real estate projects. The Shanghai pension fund financed many of the landmark real estate developments and commercial plazas in the city. See Frazier (2010), 15–16.

16. For details of the market-oriented health care reform measures in the 1990s (Reform Period I), see Huang (2013), 57–63.

17. Between 2013 and 2018, MoH was reorganized and named the National Health and Family Planning Commission; in 2018, it was renamed the National Commission of Health.

18. "Production regime" denotes "the organization of production through markets and market-related institutions" (Soskice 1999, 101).

19. In 1992, China's then paramount leader, Deng Xiaoping, reinvigorated economic reform and openness after the Tiananmen Square Protests of 1989.

20. In 1994, China launched a profound fiscal reform, recategorizing many government revenues and expenditure items including taxes. Therefore, comparing taxes before and after 1994 is not recommended.

21. Tom Orlik, "Charting China's Economy: 10 Years under Hu," *Wall Street Journal*, November 16, 2012, https://blogs.wsj.com/chinarealtime/2012/11/16/charting-chinas-economy-10-years-under-hu-jintao/, retrieved on August 1, 2017.

22. See Wen Jiabao's speech at the 2009 Summer Davos in Dalian on September 11, 2009, retrieved from http://www.fmprc.gov.cn/eng/zxxx/t583527.htm on November 20, 2016.

23. See, for example, "Basic Medical Insurance Should Be Low in Level but Broad in Coverage," comment by Zhu Rongji after the report by Peng Peiyun, director of the State Council, leading a group on local experimentation for urban employee social health insurance, October 27, 1997, from *Zhu Rongji on the Record*, Vol. 3, 459; "Consolidate Universal Social Health Insurance," speech by Hu Xiaoyi at the national working conference on health insurance on April 7, 2011, from *China Human Resources and Social Security Yearbook*, 2012, Vol. 2 (Beijing: Zhongguo lao dong she hui bao zhang chu ban she).

24. Employers are required to contribute roughly 30% of wages to various social insurance programs including pensions, health, and unemployment insurance. See Chen and Gallagher (2013).

25. "Build Up Universal Health Insurance," speech by Hu Xiaoyi at the national working conference on health insurance on April 23, 2009, from *China Human Resources and Social Security Yearbook*, 2010, Vol. 2, 198 (Beijing: Zhongguo lao dong she hui bao zhang chu ban she).

26. Even before 1997, many workers were laid off under a variety of informal arrangements such as "long vacation." See Hurst 2009, 62.

27. Industrial workers were guaranteed that the state would provide them employment security and comprehensive social welfare in return for their accepting the state's authority, and agreeing to depress their consumption and personal aspirations.

Chapter 4

1. "The Present Situation and Economic Work," speech by Jiang Zemin at the national economic working conference on November 15, 1999, from *Selected Works of Jiang Zemin*, Vol. 2, 433 (Beijing: Foreign Languages Press).

2. "Several Issues Regarding Improving the Social Insurance System," speech by Zhu Rongji at a symposium on social welfare issues on May 26, 2000. From *Zhu Rongji on the Record*, Vol. 3, 504–506 (Beijing: Ren min chu ban she).

3. "Basic Medical Insurance Should Be Low in Level but Broad in Coverage," comment by Zhu Rongji after the report by Peng Peiyun, director of the State Council leading group on local experimentation of urban employee social health insurance, October 27, 1997, from *Zhu Rongji on the Record*, Vol. 3, 459.

4. "Sparing No Effort to Maintain Security for Business and Society," speech by Zhu Rongji at a working conference about social stability issues, April 9, 2002, from *Zhu Rongji on the Record*, Vol. 4, 347–348.

5. "Do a Good Job in Maintaining Business and Social Stability," speech by Hu Jintao at a meeting with provincial leaders on April 9, 2002, from *Selected Works of Hu Jintao*, Vol. 1, 530–532 (Beijing: Ren min chu ban she).

6. "Do a Good Job in Maintaining Business and Social Stability," 540.

7. "Deepening the Study and Implementing the Spirit of the 16th National Congress of CCP, Creating a New Situation for Medical, Work Injury and Maternity Insurances," speech by Wang Dongjin at the national working conference on health insurance on February 18, 2003, from *China Human Resources and Social Security Yearbook*, 2004, Vol. 2, 60 (Beijing: Zhongguo lao dong she hui bao zhang chu ban she).

8. "Sparing No Effort to Maintain Security for Business and Society," 347–348.

9. "Sparing No Effort to Maintain Security for Business and Society," 345.

10. "Basic Medical Insurance Should Be Low in Level but Broad in Coverage," 476.

11. "Place the Promotion of Economic and Social Coordinated Development in a More Prominent Position," speech by Hu Jintao at a national working conference on fighting and preventing SARS on July 28, 2003, from *Selected Works of Hu Jintao*, Vol. 2, 65.

12. Non-state-sector employees include employees of foreign-owned firms, private-owned firms, joint ventures, and small businesses.

13. For example, the fiscal subsidy for urban non-working residents' premiums for URBMI was 40 yuan/person in 2007; it increased to 200 yuan/person in 2011, five times that of 2007.

14. "Consolidate Universal Social Health Insurance," speech by Hu Xiaoyi at the national working conference on health insurance on April 7, 2011, from *China Human Resources and Social Security Yearbook*, 2012, Vol. 2 (Beijing: Zhongguo lao dong she hui bao zhang chu ban she).

15. "Speeding Up the Transformation of the Economic Development Model," speech by Hu Jintao at a symposium with provincial leaders on scientific development and the transformation of the economic development model on February 3, 2010, from *Selected Works of Hu Jintao*, Vol. 3, 352.

16. "Speeding Up the Transformation of the Economic Development Model," 338.

17. "The More Difficult the Time, the More attention to People's Livelihood," speech by Hu Jintao at a central economic working conference on December 8, 2008, from *Selected Works of Hu Jintao*, Vol. 3, 212.

18. "The More Difficult the Time, the More attention to People's Livelihood," 145–156.

19. "The More Difficult the Time, the More attention to People's Livelihood," 147.

20. "Provide Institutional Protection for Health Care of All People," speech by Hu Xiaoyi at the national working conference on health insurance on February 28, 2008, from *China Human Resources and Social Security Yearbook*, 2009, Vol. 2, 146 (Beijing: Zhongguo lao dong she hui bao zhang chu ban she).

21. "Build Up Universal Health Insurance," speech by Hu Xiaoyi at the national working conference on health insurance on April 23, 2009, from *China Human Resources and Social Security Yearbook*, 2010, Vol. 2, 198 (Beijing: Zhongguo lao dong she hui bao zhang chu ban she).

22. State sector here refers to the public sector (e.g., schools, hospitals, media) and the SOEs.

23. "Improve Social Health Insurance System to Build a Socialist Harmonious Society," speech by Wang Dongjin at the national working conference on health insurance on February 23, 2005, from *China Human Resources and Social Security Yearbook*, 2006, 65 (Beijing: Zhongguo lao dong she hui bao zhang chu ban she).

24. "For the People-Oriented Development and Future: Promote the Health Insurance System Reform Move Forward," speech by Wang Dongjin at the national working conference on health insurance on September 23, 2004, from *China Human Resources and Social Security Yearbook*, 2005, 66 (Beijing: Zhongguo lao dong she hui bao zhang chu ban she).

25. "Build Up Universal Health Insurance," 197.

26. "Build Up Universal Health Insurance," 197.

27. "Build Up Universal Health Insurance," 197.

28. Social Insurance Law, 2011, Chapter I, Article 3.

29. "GIS Will Merge into Urban Employee Health Insurance," http://misc.caijing.com.cn/templates/inc/webcontent.jsp?id=110145226&time=2009-04-15&cl=100&page=all, accessed on August 3, 2017.

30. "Why Did Beijing Adopt GIS Reform? Unbearable High Expense," http://view.news.qq.com/a/20130115/000006.htm, accessed on August 3, 2017.

31. "Reimbursement Rate Gets Higher after Beijing GIS Reform," blog.sina.com.cn/s/blog_6004a97e010121q9.html, accessed on August 3, 2017.

32. "Supplementary Health Insurance: Another GIS," http://view.news.qq.com/a/20130115/000005.htm, accessed on August 3, 2017.

33. "Is GIS dead yet?," *In Touch Today*, Issue 2307, January 15, 2013, http://view.news.qq.com/zt2013/gfyl/index.htm, accessed on August 3, 2017.

34. "Build Up Universal Health Insurance," 198.

35. "Consolidate Universal Social Health Insurance."

36. According to the fiscal data about government budgetary revenues and expenses, none of the Chinese mainland provinces had fiscal surpluses; in other words, all Chinese mainland provinces were in a fiscal shortage—it is just a matter of degree. The fiscal shortage in rich provinces such as Beijing, Shanghai, and Zhejiang was modest, less than 10% of their fiscal revenue; the shortage in the periphery provinces such as Xinjiang, Inner Mongolia, and Tibet, could be as high as 60% to 70% of fiscal revenue.

37. Note that Chinese local governments usually have extra-budgetary revenues and the rich localities have strong incentives to put money into the extra-budgetary account to hide it from the central government. The extra-budgetary revenues are not included in the official finance data that Figure 4 uses. The official finance data documents the central-to-local fiscal transfers and the budgetary revenues/expenses of central and local governments.

38. It is published annually by China Finance and Economy Press.

39. This categorization is approximate only. The central government's categorization of fiscal transfers changes over time. Even if we have data for each kind of fiscal transfers, the content (inclusion of items) of each kind is not identical or perfectly comparable

across years. Given the data of total transfers, tax rebates, and equalization transfers directly provided in the *Local Fiscal Statistics*, I computed the "other transfers" by subtracting tax rebates and equalization transfers from total transfers.

Chapter 5

1. Interview #22, with an official of municipal social insurance bureau, Wuhan city of Hubei province, May 23, 2012.
2. Interview #7, with an official of the municipal social insurance bureau, Shenzhen city of Guangdong province, June 29, 2011; Interview #23, with an official of the municipal social insurance bureau, Changsha city of Hunan province, May 25, 2012; Interview #22, with an official of the municipal social insurance bureau, Wuhan city of Hubei province, May 23, 2012; Interview #25, with an official of the municipal social insurance bureau, Shenyang city of Liaoning province, June 14, 2012; Interview #15, with an official of the municipal social insurance bureau, Chongqing city, April 16, 2012.
3. Interview #26, with an official of the municipal social insurance bureau, Dalian city of Liaoning province, June 18, 2012.
4. Interview #28, with an official of the municipal social insurance bureau, Kunshan city of Jiangsu province, July 10, 2012.
5. State Council, 2009, 2009–2011 Implementation Scheme of Deeper Medical and Health Reform (*guan yu shen hua yi yao wei sheng ti zhi gai ge de yi jian*), Beijing.
6. Several local officials of social welfare confirmed this during my interviews. Interview #28, with an official of the municipal social insurance bureau, Kunshan city of Jiangsu province, July 10, 2012; Interview #23, with an official of the municipal social insurance bureau, Changsha city of Hunan province, May 25, 2012; Interview #21, with an officer of the provincial social insurance bureau, Wuhan city of Hubei province, May 22, 2012.
7. Interview #8, with an official of the municipal social insurance bureau, Zhuhai city of Guangdong province, July 1, 2011.
8. Interview #2, with an official of the municipal social insurance bureau, Nanning city of Guangxi province, June 8, 2011.
9. Because duplicate enrollment is made on paper only, the county or city governments do not actually pay the subsidies due but cheat the upper-level governments (the provincial or even the central government), which have no idea about the true enrollment size, out of the subsidies for these enrollments.
10. Interview #13, with an official of the provincial social insurance bureau, Nanning city of Guangxi province, March 31, 2012.
11. Interview #9, with an official of the provincial social insurance bureau, Nanning city of Guangxi province, July 15, 2011; Interview #25, with an official of the municipal social insurance bureau, Shenyang city of Liaoning province, June 14, 2012; Interview #24, with an official of the municipal social insurance bureau, Harbin city of Heilongjiang province, June 11, 2012.

12. Interview #9, with an official of the provincial social insurance bureau, Nanning city of Guangxi province, July 15, 2011.
13. Interview #15, with an official of the municipal social insurance bureau, Chongqing, April 16, 2012; Interview #2, with an official of the municipal social insurance bureau, Nanning city of Guangxi province, June 8, 2011.
14. Interview #27, with an official of the municipal social insurance bureau, Kunshan city of Jiangsu Province, July 9, 2012.
15. Interview #5, with an official of the county social insurance bureau, Yuhuan county of Zhejiang Province, June 22, 2011.
16. Interview #25, with an official of the municipal social insurance bureau, Shenyang city of Liaoning Province, June 14, 2012.
17. Ministry of Human Resources and Social Security, *Overview of Urban Basic Health Insurance (2010)*, Beijing, 2010.
18. Interview #27, with an official of the municipal social insurance bureau, Kunshan city of Jiangsu Province, July 9, 2012.
19. Ministry of Human Resources and Social Security, *Overview of Urban Basic Health Insurance (2010)*, Beijing, 2010.
20. Recent Focus and Implementation Plan of Health Care and Medical System Reforms (2009–2011) [*yi yao wei sheng ti zhi gai ge jin qi zhong dian shi shi fang an*], State Council, 3/18/2009, retrieved from http://www.gov.cn/zwgk/2009-04/07/content_1279256.htm, August 22, 2017.
21. The number of months is calculated as $\dfrac{total\ surplus\ of\ health\ insurance}{average\ monthly\ expense\ of\ health\ insurance}$
22. Interview #11, with an official of the county social insurance bureau, Xing'an county of Guangxi Province, August 10, 2011; Interview #24, with an official of the municipal social insurance bureau, Harbin city of Heilongjiang Province, June 11, 2012.
23. Interview #1, with an official of the township social insurance bureau, Lidu township of Jiangxi Province, June 2, 2011.
24. Interview #24, with an official of the municipal social insurance bureau, Harbin city of Heilongjiang province, June 11, 2012; Interview #22, with an official of the municipal social insurance bureau, Wuhan city of Hubei province, May 23, 2012; Interview #26, with an official of the municipal social insurance bureau, Dalian city of Liaoning province, June 18, 2012; Interview #27, with an official of the municipal social insurance bureau, Kunshan city of Jiangsu province, July 9, 2012; Interview #12, with an official of the municipal social insurance bureau, Guilin city of Guangxi province, August 10, 2011.
25. Losing in the competition means not only losing an honor before fellow cities, but also losing a certain amount of award money distributed by the Ministry of Finance, which would have gone to local coffers.
26. Interview #6, with an official of the municipal social welfare bureau, Dongguan city, Guangdong province, June 27, 2011.
27. The health insurance premium for non-employees (including urban and rural residents) was set at 480 yuan/person, for which the local government subsidized 470

yuan/person, and individuals paid the remaining 10 yuan. The reimbursement rate was 100% for qualified medical expenses.

28. See, for example, a case study by two researchers at Chinese Social Science Academy: http://www.cn-health care.com/article/20170530/content-492781.html; an investigative report published by *Phoenix Weekly* on February 20, 2013 with a focus on the inclusive nature of Shenmu's health care reform, http://blog.sina.com.cn/s/blog_4b8bd1450102ec3r.html, accessed September 15, 2017; an op-ed published on May 18, 2009, by CCP-sponsored *Beijing News* that questioned the financial sustainability of Shenmu's "free" health insurance http://opinion.people.com.cn/GB/9315703.html, accessed on September 15, 2017; an article praising the attributes of equity and public goods in Shenmu's health insurance reform published in the CCP's official newspaper *Guangmin Daily* on March 31, 2011: http://theory.people.com.cn/GB/14287314.html, accessed September 15, 2017.

29. Guo was transferred to Yulin city of Shaanxi province to be the vice director of the municipal People's Congress. This is commonly considered a de facto demotion as congressional positions, especially at the local levels, have much less power and fewer resources compared to party or government positions.

30. Interview #15, with an official of the municipal social welfare bureau, Chongqing, April 16, 2012; Interview #23, with an official of the municipal social insurance bureau, Changsha city, Hunan province, May 25, 2012.

31. Interview #3 and #30, with a MoHRSS official, Beijing, June 16, 2011 and July 3, 2013.

32. MoH was reorganized named Commission of Health and Family Planning in 2013; it was further renamed National Health Commission in 2018.

33. Managing the social insurance program can significantly enhance the bureau's power through larger budgets, more personnel slots, and greater regulatory power (Duckett 2003; Hsiao 2007).

34. Finally in January 2016, the Center mandated the urban-rural integration of social health insurance (by merging URBMI and NRCMS) nationwide, announcing that the MoHRSS would take the lead in the integration and administer the integrated social health insurance program.

35. Interviews #3 and #30, with an MoHRSS official, Beijing, June 16, 2011 and July 3, 2013.

36. In the Third Plenum of the 18th Chinese Communist Party Congress in November 2013, the central leadership promised to create an "urban-rural integrated social welfare system" but it is not clear yet how the Center wants it to be done and what will be the specific arrangement or compensation for the vested interest groups.

37. Interview #14, with an administrator of the municipal social health insurance, Chengdu city, Sichuan province, April 13, 2012.

38. Most UEBMI funds are pooled at the city level; however, the UEBMI for provincial-level civil servants and state-sector employees is pooled at the provincial level; some URBMI and NRCMS funds are pooled at the city level and some at the county level.

39. Beneficiaries of UEBMI are entitled to having individual health expense (saving) accounts that can be used to pay for medicine and outpatient services. The funds in the individual health expense accounts consists of (part of) individuals' health insurance

premiums and government subsidies. The funds can accumulate and roll over if not spent by the end of a year, and they are for use by the designated individuals only.

40. Overview of Urban Basic Health Insurance (2010), Ministry of Human Resources and Social Security, Beijing, 2010.

41. Interview #17, with an official of the provincial social insurance bureau, Lanzhou city of Gansu province, April 20, 2012.

42. Overview of Urban Basic Health Insurance (2010), Ministry of Human Resources and Social Security, Beijing, 2010.

43. Interview #8, with an official of the municipal social insurance bureau, Zhuhai city of Guangdong Province, July 1, 2011.

44. An exception is that the party secretary of Shenmu county in Shaanxi province, Guo Baocheng, was transferred to another post (demoted in effect) due to his radical social welfare policy, such as free health care for all local *hukou* residents.

45. Interview #24, with an official of the municipal social insurance bureau, Harbin city of Heilongjiang province, June 11, 2012.

46. Interview #4, with an official of the city district social insurance bureau, Taizhou of Zhejiang, June 21, 2011; Interview #10, with an official of the city district social insurance bureau, Nanning city of Guangxi province, August 5, 2011.

47. State Council, *Decision to Establish Urban Employee Basic Health Insurance*, December 14, 1998.

48. Interview #25, with an official of the municipal social insurance bureau, Shenyang city of Liaoning Province, June 14, 2012.

49. In order to qualify for the no-premium benefit for health insurance after retirement, males need to pay health insurance premiums for no less than 30 years and females for no less than 25 years. See http://www.dongguan.gov.cn/cndg/notice/201611/ 63e12e6f7b73493db730c63d84acd471.shtml, retrieved on August 25, 2017.

50. See http://p.zs.gov.cn/citizen/website/info-news/detail/151;jsessionid=03B06C04C6 50129DEC16D4A10D33534A, retrieved on August 25, 2017.

51. As such, the Dongguan and Zhongshan cities' local discretionary rules on retirees' health insurance contribution are not sharply against the Social Insurance Law and thus are implicitly tolerated by the Center.

52. Interview #28, with an official of the municipal social insurance bureau, Kunshan city of Jiangsu Province, July 10, 2012.

53. Interview #13, with an official of the provincial social insurance bureau, Nanning city of Guangxi province, March 31, 2012; Interview #20, with an official of the provincial social insurance bureau, Hefei city of Anhui province, May 17, 2012. Similar complaints were found in media reports, for example, "Why Beijing Reformed GIS? Surging Medical Expense and Unbearable Fiscal Burden," http://view.news.qq.com/ a/20130115/000006.htm, accessed on September 16, 2017.

54. "Supplementary Health Insurance Is GIS Privilege," http://view.news.qq.com/a/ 20130115/000005.htm, accessed on September 16, 2017.

55. *Decision to Establish Urban Employee Basic Health Insurance*, State Council Document #44, PRC, 1998. In China, rules for personnel management of public-institute employees are similar to the ones for civil servants at the same administrative level.

56. "Supplementary Health Insurance Is GIS Privilege," http://view.news.qq.com/a/20130115/000005.htm, accessed on August 3, 2017.

57. In 2011, the health care subsidy for retired officials in Beijing was 3,300 yuan per month per person, 39,600 yuan per person for one year, http://www.sohu.com/a/116843897_184627, accessed on August 3, 2017.

58. "Health Reform for Central-Level Civil Servants: Transforming GIS to Social Health Insurance," http://finance.ifeng.com/news/macro/20120116/5457350.shtml, accessed on August 3, 2017; "Why Beijing Reformed GIS? Surging Medical Expense and Unbearable Fiscal Burden," http://view.news.qq.com/a/20130115/000006.htm, accessed on August 3, 2017.

59. "Nanjing Abolished GIS for Civil Servants, excluding Deputy Department Level and Above Officials," http://news.qq.com/a/20121211/000026.htm; "Discovering Ministerial Officials' Benefits: Biggest Welfare Difference Lies on Health Care," http://view.news.qq.com/a/20130115/000002.htm; "GIS: More Wasteful than Medical Speculators," http://www.sohu.com/a/116843897_184627, all accessed on August 3, 2017.

Chapter 6

1. Generally speaking, people without urban household registration (*hukou*) cannot join urban social health insurance designated for urban residents (i.e., URBMI); people without formal employment cannot join urban social health insurance designated for urban employees (i.e., UEBMI).

2. See, for example, "*Guowuyuan guan yu jian li chengzhen zhi gong ji ben yi liao bao xian zhi du de jue ding*" ("*Decision about establishing urban employee basic medical insurance*") (Beijing: State Council Decree #44, 1998). "*Guowuyuan guan yu kai zhan cheng zhen ju min ji ben yi liao bao xian shi dian de zhi dao yi jian*" ("*Directives about establishing urban resident basic medical insurance*") (Beijing: State Council Decree #20, 2007). "*Guan yu jian li xin xing nong cun he zuo yi liao zhi du de yi jian*" ("*Directives about establishing new rural cooperative health insurance*") (Beijing: Ministry of Finance, Ministry of Health, Ministry of Agriculture, 2003).

3. Local governments accounted for nearly 70% of all government spending. See Wong 2000.

4. According to the Social Insurance Law promulgated in 2010, social insurance should be pooled at (or above) the county or prefectural city level; within each of the pooling units (e.g., county, district, or city), social insurance is divided into at least three schemes corresponding to different levels of benefits: urban employee scheme, urban resident scheme, and rural resident scheme.

5. On the partially "federal" characteristics of China, see Weingast 1995.

6. This mechanism is the same for labor-inflowing and -outflowing regions. It seems more obvious in labor-outflowing regions, where mass labor outflows exacerbate population aging and place burdensome payment pressures on local social health insurance funds. However, the risk-magnifying mechanism applies to labor-inflowing

regions too, because the regions receiving mass labor inflows are heavily reliant on labor-intensive manufacturing and service sectors. With potentially high needs of medical service and threats of large labor outflows, local officials in the labor-inflowing regions prefer expansive risk pooling for social insurance to counter the increased social risk.

7. Chinese social health insurance programs consist of two types: urban and rural. Urban health insurance that mainly consists of UEBMI and URBMI is pooled at pre-fectural or provincial levels and managed by the local governments of the respective level; rural health insurance that mainly refers to the NRCMS is pooled at county or prefectural levels and managed by the respective county or prefectural governments.

8. They are compiled from *China Human Resources and Social Security Yearbooks* (2007–2010) and *China Health Statistics Yearbooks* (2007–2010). As the data for rural health insurance expenditures are missing in *China Health Statistics Yearbooks*, the generosity variable in the empirical studies of this chapter pertains to urban social health insurance only.

9. The reason for using 2007 as the starting year is because the URBMI program (so-cial health insurance for urban residents) was established in 2007; since 2007, the Chinese social health insurance has begun to cover all major social groups with three programs (URBMI, UEBMI, and NRCMS) co-existing nationwide.

10. Cluster analysis is a quantitative method that classifies objects into relatively ho-mogenous groups. The objective is to group n units into r clusters where r is much smaller than n. Each group identified by cluster analysis is as internally homogenous as possible, but as distinct as possible from all other groups. For more details of this method, see Lewis-Beck et al. 2004. For examples of using this method in compara-tive social welfare studies, see Rudra 2007; Gough 2001; Ragin 1994.

11. There are many procedures (or "stopping rules") to determine the number of clusters in a dataset. Milligan and Cooper have conducted a well-known study to distinguish between the many stopping rules and assess which criteria provide the most valid test for the existence of a cluster. Their experiment suggests that the Duda and Hart pro-cedure performs best in determining stopping rules. See Milligan and Cooper 1985; Duda and Hart 1973; Tidmore and Turner 1983.

12. Statistics show that 83.9% of migrants in mainland China are younger than 40 years old and many of them are between 15 and 29 years old. They migrate across regions mainly for jobs. See National Bureau of Statistics of China, 2010; Yu, 2008.

13. Interview #19 with a municipal official of social health insurance, Zhengzhou city of Henan province, May 14, 2012.

14. Interview #20 with a provincial official of social insurance, Hefei city of Anhui prov-ince, May 17, 2012.

15. Interview #21 with a provincial official of social insurance, Wuhan city of Hubei province, May 22, 2012; Interview #23 with a municipal official of social insurance, Changsha city of Hunan province, May 25, 2012.

16. Interview #16 with a provincial academy of social science official, Chengdu city of Sichuan province, April 17, 2012.

17. Ministry of Human Resources and Social Security, *Urban Social Health Insurance Report 2010* (2010 *quanguo chengzhen jiben yiliao baoxian qingkuang fenxi*), Internal materials.

18. Interview #6 with a municipal official of social insurance, Dongguan city of Guangdong province, June 27, 2011.

19. Interview #27 with a municipal official of social insurance, Kunshan city of Jiangsu province, July 9, 2012.

20. It seems informally "institutionalized" that the party secretaries who represent the provincial-level municipalities such as Beijing, Shanghai, and Tianjin are typically appointed into the Politburo of the central committee of the CCP. According to Saich (2011), of the Politburo members who have had provincial experience, 69% have worked in the coastal areas such as Beijing, Tianjin, and Shanghai.

21. *Xinhua News*, "New Policy for Severe Disease Insurance: Double Reimbursement above 50% of Medical Expense (*da bin yi bao xin zheng: di er ci bao xiao bi li bu di yu 50%*)," http://news.xinhuanet.com/health/2013-01/23/c_124267873.htm, accessed on May 30, 2013.

22. In my interviews with local officials of the other types of provinces, a few speculated that those privileged provinces are pioneers in social health insurance expansion, actively experimenting and proposing various reform initiatives or measures, because the more they [e.g., provinces like Ningxia in China's Northwest] spend, the more the Center makes transfers to them.

23. It is estimated that 60%–70% of government subsidies to URBMI and NRCMS programs in Ningxia province come from the central government.

24. Interview #18 with a provincial official of social insurance, Yinchuan city of Ningxia province, April 24, 2012.

25. Interview #2 with a municipal official of social insurance, Nanning city of Guangxi province, June 8, 2011; Interview #29 with a provincial official of social insurance, Nanning city of Guangxi province, March 15, 2013. A similar answer is found in Interview #24 with a municipal official of social insurance, Harbin city of Heilongjiang province, June 11, 2012.

26. Such a measure does not take intra-province migration into account. Hence, it is a "conservative" approximation of migration for a province.

27. For a robustness check, different measures of the key independent variables were used in the analysis. For example, the migration variable was broken down into two variables: labor outflow and labor inflow. Likewise, the fiscal resource variable was broken down into fiscal transfers and fiscal revenues, respectively. The findings from the regression results do not change when the alternative proxies or measures of the key independent variables were used.

28. Province is assigned a value from 1 to 4, depending on the applicability of a set of criteria. A value of 4 indicates a provincial governor who holds a provincial post while also serving in a central government position; a value of 3 refers to a provincial official with significant past service in central ministries; a value of 2 means a provincial official with significant service in other provinces; and a value of 1 suggests a provincial official with significant service in that province. The notion of BINT and its

coding were first used in Huang (1996). It was further used in Sheng (2010). The data for coding this variable are provincial governors' resumés, collected from *Zheng Tan Wang* (http://www.zt360.cn/jgzyjl/ljjl/), a government-sponsored media organization in Guangdong.

29. For panel or cross-section time-series data, the major concern is the contemporaneous correlation and heteroskedasticity in the error structure, which is normally corrected using panel-corrected standard errors (PCSEs). See Beck and Katz 1995.

30. For panel or cross-section time-series data, another concern is the omitted variable bias (OVB) derived from the unobserved year- or province-specific factors, and the most common way to avoid this bias is to use a fixed-effects (FE) regression.

31. As the results from PCSEs may not be reliable if serial correlation is present in the data, one-year lagged dependent variables (LDV) were included in some of the regressions as a robustness check. Some scholars suggest that we can think of FE and LDV as bounding the true effect of interest. See Angrist and Pischke 2008.

32. "The Rural-Urban Divide: Ending Apartheid," *Economist*, April 19, 2014, https://www.economist.com/news/special-report/21600798-chinas-reforms-work-its-citizens-have-be-made-more-equal-ending-apartheid, accessed June 2, 2015.

33. In an additional analysis, I included a variable for trade openness measured by the share of trade in GDP and found that the trade openness variable was statistically insignificant in all model specifications.

Chapter 7

1. "Labor market insiders" refers to employees who have formal employment relations or labor contracts with employers. By contrast, "labor market outsiders" are people who have no formal or stable labor relations or contracts, such as temporary, part-time, or student workers.

2. According to a 2005 China Urban Labor Survey, over 85% of Chinese domestic migrants were in the private sector, where the prevalence of labor contracts was lowest. The rate of informal employment (i.e., insecure or unstable employment without labor contracts) among all migrants was extremely high (Park and Cai 2011). Although it has been improved by the social insurance expansion, migrant and informal workers have lower rates of social insurance coverage than formal workers.

3. Scott Cendrowski, "China's Global 500 Companies Are Bigger then Ever—and Mostly State-Owned," *Fortune*, July 22, 2015, http://fortune.com/2015/07/22/china-global-500-government-owned/, accessed on April 23, 2019.

4. China Health and Nutrition Survey (CHNS) covers nine Chinese provinces that vary substantially in geography, economic development, public resources, and health indicators. The first wave of the CHNS data was collected in 1989 and seven additional panels were collected in 1991, 1993, 1997, 2000, 2004, 2006, and 2009. For more information about CHNS, see http://www.cpc.unc.edu/projects/china.

5. Social health insurance is the dominant type of health insurance in China. Chinese social health insurance is organized and managed by the government; it is also

promoted by the government through economic, administrative, and legal means. Other types of health insurance in China include commercial health insurance for individuals and company supplementary health insurance.

6. In this sense, the residency-based social health insurance in China is conceptually closer to the social transfers financed from general taxes that are commonly seen in Scandinavian welfare states, rather than the conventional social insurance models employed in continental European welfare states.

7. The Chinese mainland provinces with the largest numbers of tertiary hospitals include Guangdong (61), Liaoning (58), Beijing (48), Shandong (48), and Hubei (48). Except Hubei province, these provinces are in the eastern coastal part of China.

8. It is not uncommon for non-local patients to have to wait for more than one month before being admitted into the tertiary hospitals for in-hospital treatments or operations. See, for example, http://www.people.com.cn/GB/channel1/13/20000531/ 83280.html and http://www.cnhubei.com/news/xwhbyw/xwwc/201204/t2040529. shtml, accessed on October 22, 2016.

9. The China General Social Survey (CGSS) is an annual or biannual questionnaire survey of China's urban and rural households aiming to systematically monitor the changing relationship between social structure and quality of life in urban and rural China. For more information, see http://www.chinagss.org/.

10. These categories of employment sectors are state-owned enterprise or *SOE,* collective-owned enterprise or *COE,* private-owned enterprise or *POE,* foreign-owned enterprise or *FOE,* and *other.*

11. The main idea of the "divide by 4" rule is that one can take logistic regression coefficients and divide them by 4 to get an upper bound of the predictive difference corresponding to a unit difference in x. This upper bound is a reasonable approximation near the midpoint of the logistic curve, where probabilities are close to 0.5. At this point the slope of the logistic curve or the derivative of the logistic function is maximized. See Gelman and Hill 2006, 82.

12. The variable "prog" is multinomial, with "1" being "commercial or other health insurance scheme"; "2" being GIS or "government scheme"; "3" being UEBMI or "urban employee scheme"; "4" being URBMI or "urban resident scheme"; and "5" being NRCMS or "rural cooperative scheme." Because the urban resident health insurance, URBMI, was initiated in 2007, there is no case under this category in the 2004 CHNS sample.

13. The variable "urban hukou" is binary, with "1" representing urban *hukou* and "0" meaning having no urban *hukou.*

14. The variable "edu" is ordinary, with "0"= no regular education; "1"=primary school; "2"=middle school; "3"=high school; "4"=technical or occupational school; "5"=college; "6"=graduate school and above.

15. The variable "employsta" is categorical, with "1"=employed; "2"=unemployed or student; "3"=housekeeping; "4"=retired; "5"=other.

16. The variable "employown" is categorical with "1"=government or public institute; "2"=state-owned enterprise (SOE); "3"=collective-owned enterprise (COE); "4"=private-owned firms (POE); "5"=foreign-owned firm (FOE); "6"=other.

(FOE); "6"=other.

17. The variable "employsz" is ordinary with "1"="<20 employees"; "2"="20–100 employees"; "3"= ">100 employees."

18. Note that CHNS doesn't cover all Chinese provinces in sampling; all the privileging type provinces identified in Chapter 6 (Beijing, Shanghai, Tianjin, Xinjiang, Ningxia, and Qinghai) are not included in CHNS data.

19. Xinhua News Agency, 2002, "80% of Chinese Provinces Abolished Government Free Medical Care," http://news.xinhuanet.com/local/2012-12/14/c_114025198.htm, accessed May 19, 2017.

20. For more examples on the fragmented social insurance model promoted by the authoritarian welfare state such as Germany under Bismarck, Austria under von Taaffe, and France under Napoleon III, see Esping-Andersen 1990; Beck 1997; Rimlinger 1971.

Chapter 8

1. Similar concepts, such as authoritarian governments' "limited responsiveness" and "bounded representation" can be found in recent studies of Chinese politics. Among others, see Truex 2016; Meng et al. 2017, Distelhorst and Hou 2017.

2. Chen Jian, "*Hukou* Reform in Chengdu City: Peasant as an Occupation rather than Status," April 2, 2011, retrieved from http://www.xj.xinhuanet.com/2011-04-02/content_22440321_1.htm on December 2, 2016.

3. Within URRBMI, there are still multiple schemes with different contribution and reimbursement rates. Rural residents mostly choose the scheme with the lowest rates while urban residents mostly choose the one with the highest rates. Non-local people (migrants) are not eligible for URRBMI. In places where urban-rural integration takes place the pivotal criterion for claiming social benefits is the possession of local resident status, regardless of whether it is urban or rural; in these locations, the urban-rural integration of social insurance has transformed social cleavage from "the urban-rural divide" to the "within-without" divide (Shi 2012).

4. The Social Insurance Law, which took effect in 2011, broadly stipulates "the basic pension should be gradually pooled at the national level, and other social insurance should be gradually pooled at the provincial level."

5. See, for example, *Xinhua News*, 2013, "Further Integrating Social Security System for Urbanization [cheng zhen hua jin cheng zhong jia kuai tui jin she hui bao zhang zhi du xie jie yu zeng he]," http://news.xinhuanet.com/politics/2013-05/15/c_124715276.htm, accessed October 31, 2015; *Xinhua News*, 2013, "Urbanization Requires Eliminating Several Institutional Obstacles [cheng zhen hua gai ge xu jia kuai po chu xiang guan zhi du zang ai]," http://news.xinhuanet.com/2013-05/25/c_124763476.htm, accessed October 31, 2015.

6. The study found that about 60% of respondents who identified as belonging to the "upper middle stratum" of society had a positive view of their local government's performance. By contrast, 48% of those who identified as in the lowest stratum held a

positive view. "Compared to the working class, and especially workers in the state sector, China's middle class has a more positive assessment of perceptions of the rich-poor gap, trustworthiness of officials and government performance," the study said. "The middle class has the potential to become a social stabilizer" (Li et al. 2015, 212).

7. The data are available at http://www.adb.org/features/focus-social-protection-reducing-poverty-and-inequality, accessed April 16, 2014.

8. The breadth of social protection is computed as $\dfrac{\text{Total Actual Beneficiaries}}{\text{Total Intended Beneficiaries}}$.

9. The depth of social protection is computed as $\dfrac{\text{Total Expenditure}}{\text{Total Actual Beneficiaries}}$.

10. The SPI data measure stratification of social protection by income groups rather than by social status (e.g., urban/rural residency, employment sectors and status), but the finding based on the data that democracies have lower levels of stratification (or inequality) of social welfare than do non-democracies is not inconsistent with my argument about the Chinese case.

11. "Bahrain's King Gives Out Cash ahead of Protests," Reuters. February 12, 2011, retrieved from http://af.reuters.com/article/commoditiesNews/idAFLDE71A24Z20110211, accessed on January 5, 2017.

12. "Hard Choice for the Government," *The Economist*, January 20, 2011, retrieved from http://www.economist.com/node/17963303, accessed on January 5, 2017.

13. "Bahrain King in Saudi Arabia to Discuss Unrest," *New York Times*, February 23, 2011, retrieved from http://www.nytimes.com/2011/02/24/world/middleeast/24bahrain.html, accessed on January 5, 2017.

14. A growing body of literature has found that non-state actors (e.g., ethnic and sectarian organizations, family and friendship networks, faith-based organizations, and informal brokers) play important roles in influencing citizen access to social services (Cammett 2015; Cammett and MacLean 2014).

15. This opens up an interesting avenue of future research on social policy in authoritarian countries to explain intertemporal and cross-national variations of the stratified expansion of social welfare provision. Future research can also examine whether autocrats' trade-offs and strategy of balancing between elites and masses can be found in other policy areas.

References

Acemoglu, Daron, and James A. Robinson. 2006. *Economic Origins of Dictatorship and Democracy*. New York: Cambridge University Press.

Albertus, Michael. 2015. *Autocracy and Redistribution: The Politics of Land Reform*. Cambridge Studies in Comparative Politics. New York: Cambridge University Press.

Ang, Yuen Yuen. 2016a. "Beyond Weber: Conceptualizing an Alternative Ideal Type of Bureaucracy in Developing Contexts." *Regulation & Governance* 11 (3):282–298.

Ang, Yuen Yuen 2016b. *How China Escaped the Poverty Trap, Cornell Studies in Political Economy*. Ithaca, NY: Cornell University Press.

Angrist, Joshua D., and Jorn-Steffen Pischke. 2008. *Mostly Harmless Econometrics: An Empiricist's Companion*. Princeton, NJ: Princeton University Press.

Bates, Robert H. 1981. *Markets and States in Tropical Africa: The Political Basis of Agricultural Policies*. Berkeley: University of California Press.

Beck, Hermann. 1997. *The Origins of the Authoritarian Welfare State in Prussia: Conservatives, Bureaucracy, and the Social Question, 1815–70*. Ann Arbor: University of Michigan Press.

Beck, Nathaniel, and Jonathan N. Katz. 1995. "What to Do (and Not to Do) with Time-Series Cross-Section Data." *American Political Science Review* 89 (3):634–647.

Beramendi, Pablo. 2012. *The Political Geography of Inequality: Regions and Redistribution*. New York: Cambridge University Press.

Bian, Yanjie. 1994. *Work and Inequality in Urban China*. Albany: State University of New York Press.

Bian, Yanjie. 2002. "Chinese Social Stratification and Social Mobility." *Annual Review of Sociology* 28 (1):91–116.

Bian, Yanjie. 2009. "Urban Occupational Mobility and Employment Institutions: Hierarchy, Market, and Networks in a Mixed System." In *Creating Wealth and Poverty in Postsocialist China*, edited by Deborah S. Davis and Wang Feng. Stanford, CA: Stanford University Press.

Blaydes, Lisa. 2010. *Elections and Distributive Politics in Mubarak's Egypt*. Cambridge, MA: Cambridge University Press.

Boix, Carles. 2003. *Democracy and Redistribution*. Cambridge: Cambridge University Press.

Boix, Carles, and Milan W. Svolik. 2013. "The Foundations of Limited Authoritarian Government: Institutions, Commitment, and Power-Sharing in Dictatorships." *Journal of Politics* 75 (2):300–316.

Boone, Catherine. 1990. "The Making of the Rentier Class: Wealth Accumulation and Political Control in Senegal." *Journal of Development Studies* 26 (3):425–450.

Brown, David S. 2004. "Democracy and Human Capital Formation: Education Spending in Latin America, 1980–1997." *Comparative Political Studies* 37 (7):842–864.

Brownlee, Jason. 2007. *Authoritarianism in an Age of Democratization*. New York: Cambridge University Press.

Bueno de Mesquita, Bruce, Alastair Smith, Randolph M. Siverson, and James D. Morrow. 2003. *The Logic of Political Survival*. Cambridge, MA: MIT Press.

Bulman, David J. 2010. "China and the Financial Crisis." *Stanford Journal of East Asian Affairs* 10 (2):20–38.

Bulmer, Martin, Jane Lewis, and David Piachaud, eds. 1989. *The Goals of Social Policy*. London: Unwin Hyman.

Cai, Yongshun. 2002. "The Resistance of Chinese Laid-off Workers in the Reform Period." *China Quarterly* 170 (June):327–344.

Cai, Yongshun. 2006. *State and Laid-off Workers in Reform China: The Silence and Collective Action of the Retreated*. London: Routledge.

Cai, Yongshun. 2008. "Power Structure and Regime Resilience: Contentious Politics in China." *British Journal of Political Science* 38 (3):411–432.

Cameron, David. 1978. "The Expansion of the Public Economy: A Comparative Analysis." *American Political Science Review* 72 (4):1243–1261.

Cammett, Melani. 2014. *Compassionate Communalism: Welfare and Sectarianism in Lebanon*. Ithaca, NY: Cornell University Press.

Cammett, Melani, and Lauren M. MacLean. 2014. *The Politics of Non-State Social Welfare*. Ithaca, NY: Cornell University Press.

Cammett, Melani, and Aytug Sasmaz. 2016. "Social Policy in Developing Countries." In *The Oxford Handbook of Historical Institutionalism*, edited by Orfeo Fioretos, Tulia G. Falleti, and Adam Sheingate. New York: Oxford University Press.

Chan, Kam Wing. 1994. *Cities with Invisible Walls: Reinterpreting Urbanization in Post-1949 China*. New York: Oxford University Press.

Chan, Kam Wing. 2010. "Fundamentals of China's Urbanization and Policy." *China Review* 10 (1):63–94.

Chan, Kam Wing. 2012. "Migration and Development in China: Trends, Geography and Current Issues." *Migration and Development* 1 (2):187–205.

Chan, Kam Wing, and Will Buckingham. 2008. "Is China Abolishing the Hukou System?" *China Quarterly* 195 (September):582–606.

Charron, Nicholas, and Victo Lapuente. 2011. "Which Dictators Produce Quality of Governemnt?" *Studies in Comparative International Development* 46 (4):397–423.

Chen, Jidong, Jennifer Pan, and Yiqing Xu. 2016. "Sources of Authoritarian Responsiveness: A Field Experiment in China." *American Journal of Political Science* 60 (2):383–400.

Chen, Juan, and Mary Gallagher. 2013. "Urban Social Insurance Provision: Regional and Ownership Variation." In *Chinese Social Policy in a Time of Transition*, edited by Douglas Besharov and Karen Baehler. Oxford: Oxford University Press.

Chung, Jae Ho. 2000. *Central Control and Local Discretion in China: Leadership and Implementation during Post-Mao Decollectivization*. New York: Oxford University Press.

Chung, Jae Ho. 2011. Managing Political Crises in China: The Cases of Collective Protests. In *China's Crisis Management*, edited by Jae Ho Chung. London: Routledge.

Cook, Linda J. 2007. *Postcommunist Welfare States: Reform Politics in Russia and Eastern Europe*. Ithaca, NY: Cornell University Press.

De La O, Ana L. 2013. "Do Conditional Cash Transfers Affect Electoral Behavior? Evidence from a Randomized Experiment in Mexico." *American Journal of Political Science* 57 (1):1–14.

Deng, Yanhua, and Kevin J. O'Brien. 2013. "Relational Repression in China: Using Social Ties to Demobilize Protesters." *China Quarterly* 215:533–552.

Diaz-Cayeros, Alberto. 2006. *Federalism, Fiscal Authority, and Centralization in Latin America.* New York: Cambridge University Press.

Diaz-Cayeros, Alberto, Federico Estevez, and Beatriz Magaloni. 2016. *The Political Logic of Poverty Relief: Electoral Strategies and Social Policy in Mexico.* New York: Cambridge University Press.

Dickson, Bruce. 2016. *The Dictator's Dilemma: The Chinese Communist Party's Strategy for Survival.* New York: Oxford University Press.

Dickson, Bruce, and Maria Rost Rublee. 2000. "Membership Has Its Privileges: The Socioeconomic Characteristics of Communist Party Members in Urban China." *Comparative Political Studies* 33 (1):87–112.

Dillon, Nara. 2015. *Radical Inequalities: China's Revolutionary Welfare State in Comparative Perspective.* Harvard East Asian Monograph Series 383, Harvard University Asia Center. Cambridge, MA: Harvard University Press.

Distelhorst, Greg, and Yue Hou. 2017. "Constituency Service under Nondemocratic Rule: Evidence from China." *Journal of Politics* 79 (3):1024–1040.

Dixon, John. 1981. *The Chinese Welfare System, 1949–1979.* New York: Praeger.

Downs, Anthony. 1965. "A Theory of Bureaucracy." *American Economic Review* 55 (1/2):439–446.

Duckett, Jane. 2003. "Bureaucratic Institutions and Interests in the Making of China's Social Policy." *Public Administration Quarterly* 27 (2):210–237.

Duckett, Jane. 2004. "State, Collectivism and Worker Privilege: A Study of Urban Health Insurance Reform." *China Quarterly* 177 (March):155–173.

Duckett, Jane. 2011. *The Chinese State's Retreat from Health: Policy and the Politics of Retrenchment.* New York: Taylor & Francis.

Duckett, Jane. 2018. "International Influences on Policymaking in China: Network Authoritarianism from Jiang Zemin to Hu Jintao." *China Quarterly* 237 (1):15–37.

Duda, Richard O., and Peter E. Hart. 1973. *Pattern Classification and Scene Analysis.* New York: John Wiley.

Edin, Maria. 2003a. "Remaking the Communist Party-State: The Cadre Responsibility System at the Local Level in China." *China: An International Journal* 1 (1):1–15.

Edin, Maria. 2003b. "State Capacity and Local Agent Control in China: CCP Cadre Management from a Township Perspective." *China Quarterly* 173 (March):35–52.

Esping-Andersen, Gosta. 1990. *Three Worlds of Welfare Capitalism.* Princeton, NJ: Princeton University Press.

Esping-Andersen, Gosta. 1999. *Social Foundations of Postindustrial Economies.* New York: Oxford University Press.

Estevez-Abe, Margarita, Torben Iversen, and David Soskice. 2001. "Social Protection and the Formation of Skills: A Reinterpretation of the Welfare State." In *Varieties of Capitalism: The Institutional Foundations of Comparative Advantage,* edited by Peter Hall and David Soskice, 145–183. Oxford: Oxford University Press.

Fan, C. Cindy. 1997. "Uneven Development and Beyond: Regional Development Theory in Post-Mao China." *International Journal of Urban and Regional Research* 21 (4):620–639.

Flora, Peter, and Arnold Heidenheimer, eds. 1981. *The Development of Welfare States in Europe and America.* New Brunswick, NJ: Transaction Press.

Flora, Peter, and Jens Alber. 1981. "Modernization, Democratization, and the Development of Welfare States in Western Europe." In *Development of Welfare States in Europe and America*, edited by Peter Flora. New York: Routledge.

Forrat, Natalia. 2012. *The Authoritarian Welfare State: A Marginalized Concept.* Comparative-Historical Social Science Working Paper Series. Evanston, IL: Northwestern University.

Frazier, Mark. 2010 *Socialist Insecurity: Pensions and the Politics of Uneven Development in China*. Ithaca, NY: Cornell University Press.

Frazier, Mark. 2011. "Social Policy and Public Opinion in an Age of Insecurity." In *From Iron Rice Bowl to Informalization: Markets, Workers, and the State in a Changing China*, edited by Sarosh Kuruvilla, Ching Kwan Lee, and Mary E. Gallagher. Ithaca, NY: Cornell University Press.

Frazier, Mark W. 2004. "China's Pension Reform and Its Discontents." *China Journal* 51 (January):97–114.

Gallagher, Mary. 2005. *Contagious Capitalism: Globalization and the Politics of Chinese Labour*. Princeton, NJ: Princeton University Press.

Gallagher, Mary. 2016. *Authoritarian Legality: Law, Workers and the State in Contemporary China*. New York: Cambridge University Press.

Gallagher, Mary, and Baohua Dong. 2011. "Legislating Harmony: Labor Law Reform in Cotemporary China." In *From Iron Rice Bowl to Informalization: Markets, Workers, and the State in a Changing China*, edited by Sarosh Kuruvilla, Ching Kwan Lee, and Mary E. Gallagher. Ithaca, NY: Cornell University Press.

Gallagher, Mary, John Giles, Albert Park, and Meiyan Wang. 2015. "China's 2008 Labor Contract Law: Implementation and Implications for China's Workers." *Human Relations* 68 (2):197–235.

Gallagher, Mary, and Jonathan K. Hanson. 2009. "Coalitions, Carrots, and Sticks: Economic Inequality and Authoritarian States." *PS: Political Science & Politics* 42 (4):667–672.

Gandhi, Jennifer. 2008. *Political Institutions under Dictatorship*. Cambridge: Cambridge University Press.

Gandhi, Jennifer, and Adam Przeworski. 2006. "Cooperation, Cooptation, and Rebellion under Dictatorships." *Economics and Politics* 18 (1):1–26.

Gao, Qin, and Johanna Rickne. 2014. "Firm Ownership and Social Insurance Inequality in Transitional China: Evidence from a Large Panel of Firm Data." *European Journal of Social Security* 16 (1):2–25.

Gao, Qin, and Johanna Rickne. 2017. "Inequality in Social Insurance Participation and Generosity: Do Firm Characteristics Matter?" *Social Policy & Administration* 51 (5):755–775. doi: 10.1111/spol.12195.

Gao, Qin, Sui Yang, and Shi Li. 2012. "Labor Contracts and Social Insurance Participation among Migrant Workers in China." *China Economic Review* 23 (4):1195–1205.

Garay, Candelaria. 2016. *Social Policy Expansion in Latin America*. New York: Cambridge University Press.

Gelman, Andrew, and Jennifer Hill. 2006. *Data Analysis Using Regression and Multilevel/Hierarchical Models*. Cambridge: Cambridge University Press.

Gibson, Edward L. 2004. "Toward a New Comparative Politics of Federalism, Multinationalism, and Democracy: Beyond Rikerian Federalism." In *Federalism and Democracy in Latin America*. Baltimore: Johns Hopkins University Press.

Giles, John, Dewen Wang, and Albert Park. 2013. *Expanding Social Insurance Coverage in Urban China*. Policy Research Working Paper Series 6497. Washington, DC: World Bank.

Goldstone, Jack, and Charles Tilly. 2001. "Threat (and Opportunity): Popular Action and State Response in the Dynamics of Contentious Action." In *Silence and Voice in the Study of Contentious Politics*, edited by Jack A. Goldstone Ronald R. Aminzade, Dough McAdam, Elizabeth J. Perry, William H. Sewell Jr., Sidney Tarrow, and Charles Tilley, 179–194. New York: Cambridge University Press.

Gough, Ian. 2001. "Social Assistance Regimes: A Cluster Analysis." *Journal of European Social Policy* 11 (2):165–170.

Gu, Edward X. 2001a. "Dismantling the Chinese Mini-Welfare State? Marketization and the Politics of Institutional Transformation, 1979–1999." *Communist and Post-Communist Studies* 34 (1):91–111.

Gu, Edward X. 2001b. "Market Transition and the Transformation of the Health Care System in Urban China." *Policy Studies* 22 (3–4):197–215.

Gu, Edward, and Jianjun Zhang. 2006. "Health Care Regime Change in Urban China: Unmanaged Marketization and Reluctant Privatization." *Pacific Affairs* 79 (1):49–71.

Guo, Gang. 2007. "Retrospective Economic Accountability under Authoritarianism: Evidence from China." *Political Research Quarterly* 60 (3):378–390.

Guo, Gang. 2008. "Vertical Imbalance and Local Fiscal Discipline in China." *Journal of East Asian Studies* 8 (1):61–88.

Guo, Gang. 2009. "China's Local Political Budget Cycles." *American Journal of Political Science* 53 (3):620–631.

Haber, Stephen. 2007. "Authoritarian Government." In *Handbook of Political Economy*, edited by Barry R. Weingast and Donald A. Wittman, 693–707. New York: Oxford University Press.

Hadenius, Axel, and Jan Teorell. 2007. "Pathways from Authoritarianism." *Journal of Democracy* 18 (1):143–157.

Haggard, Stephan, and Robert Kaufman. 2008. *Development, Democracy, and Welfare States: Latin America, East Asia, and Eastern Europe*. Princeton, NJ: Princeton University Press.

Haggard, Stephan, and Robert Kaufman. 2016. *Dictators and Democrats: Masses, Elites, and Regime Change*. Princeton, NJ: Princeton University Press.

Harris, Kevan. 2013. "A Martyrs' Welfare State and Its Contradictions: Regime Resilience and Limits through the Lens of Social Policy in Iran." In *Middle East Authoritarianisms: Governance, Contestation, and Regime Resilience in Syria and Iran*, edited by Steven Heydemann and Reinoud Leenders, 61–80. Stanford, CA: Stanford University Press.

Harris, Kevan. 2017. *A Social Revolution: Politics and the Welfare State in Iran*. Oakland: University of California Press.

He, Baogang, and Stig Thogersen. 2010. "Giving the People a Voice? Experiments with Consultative Authoritarian Institutions in China." *Journal of Contemporary China* 19 (66):675–692.

Heberer, Thomas, and Rene Trappel. 2013. "Evaluation Processes, Local Cadres' Behaviour and Local Development Processes." *Journal of Contemporary China* 22 (84):1048–1066.,

Heclo, Hugh. 1981. "Toward a New Welfare State?" In *The Development of Welfare States in Europe and America*, edited by Peter Flora and Arnold J. Heidenheimer, 383–406. New Brunswick, NJ: Transaction Books.

Heilmann, Sebastian 2008. "Policy Experimentation in China's Economic Rise." *Studies of Comparative and International Development* 43 (1):1–26.

Herd, Richard, Yu-Wei Hu, and Vincent Koen. 2010. *Improving China's Health Care System*. OECD Economics Department Working Papers, No. 751. Paris: OECD. https:// doi.org/10.1787/5kmlh4v2fv31-en.

Heurlin, Christopher. 2016. *Responsive Authoritarianism in China*. Cambridge: Cambridge University Press.

Hodson, Randy, and Robert L. Kaufman. 1982. "Economic Dualism: A Critical Review." *American Sociological Review* 47 (6):727–739.

Hong, Ma. 1992. *Zhongguo Gaige Quanshu 1978–1991 (Handbook of Reforms in China, 1978–1991)*. Dalian: Dalian chubanshe.

Hossain, Shaikh I. 1997. *Tackling Health Transition in China*. Washington DC: World Bank.

Hsiao, William C. 2007. "The Political Economy of Chinese Health Reform." *Health Economics, Policy and Law* 2 (3):241–249.

Hu, Jintao. 2016. *Hu Jintao wen ji (Selected Works of Hu Jintao)*, Vol. 1. Beijing: People's Publishing House.

Huang, Xian, and Qin Gao. 2017. "Does Social Insurance Enrollment Improve Citizen Assessment of Local Government Performance? Evidence from China." *Social Science Research* 70 (February):28–40. doi: 10.1016/j.ssresearch.2017.11.001.

Huang, Xian, and Qin Gao. 2019. "Alleviating Poverty or Discontent: Impact of Social Assistance on Chinese Citizens' Views of Government." *China: An International Journal* 17 (1):76–95.

Huang, Xian, and Sung Eun Kim. 2020. "When Top-Down Meets Bottom-Up: Local Adoption of Social Policy Reform in China." *Governance* 33 (2):343–364.

Huang, Yanzhong. 2011. "The Sick Man of Asia: China's Health Crisis." *Foreign Affairs* 90 (6):119–136.

Huang, Yanzhong. 2013. *Governing Health in Contemporary China*. New York: Routledge.

Huang, Yanzhong. 2015. "International Institutions and China's Health Policy." *Journal of Health Politics, Policy and Law* 40 (1):41–71.

Huang, Yanzhong, and Dali L. Yang. 2004. "Population Control and State Coercion in China." In *Holding China Together: Diversity and National Integration in the Post-Deng Era*, edited by Barry J. Naughton and Dali L. Yang, 193–225. New York: Cambridge University Press.

Huang, Yasheng. 1996. *Inflation and Investment Controls in China*: Cambridge University Press.

Huang, Yasheng. 2008. *Capitalism with Chinese Characteristics: Entrepreneurship and the State*. New York: Cambridge University Press.

Huber, John, and Charles R. Shipan. 2008. "Politics, Delegation, and Bureaucracy." In *The Oxford Handbook of Political Economy*, edited by Donald A. Wittman and Barry R. Weingast. Oxford: Oxford University Press.

Hurst, William. 2011. "Rebuilding the Urban Chinese Welfare State." *China Perspectives* Number 2011 (2):35–42.

Hurst, William 2009. *The Chinese Worker after Socialism*. Cambridge, MA: Cambridge University Press.

Hurst, William, and Kevin O'Brien. 2002. "China's Contentious Pensioners." *China Quarterly* 170 (June):345–360.

Iversen, Torben. 2001. "The Dynamics of Welfare State Expansion: Trade Openness, De-Industrialization and Partisan Politics." In *The New Politics of the Welfare State*, edited by Paul Pierson, 45–79. New York: Oxford University Press.

Jeong, Jihyeon. 2014. "Welfare for China's Western Minorities." Annual Conference of Mid-West Political Science Association, Chicago, April 2014.

Jiang, Zemin. 2010. *Selected Works of Jiang Zemin*, Vol. 1. Beijing: Foreign Languages Press.

Karindi, Liisi. 2008. "The Making of China's New Labour Contract Law." *China Analysis* 66 (Winter):1–15.

King, Gary, Jennifer Pan, and Margaret E. Roberts. 2013. "How Censorship in China Allows Government Criticism but Silences Collective Expression." *American Political Science Review* 107 (2):326–343.

Knutsen, C. H., and M. Rasmussen. 2018. "The Autocratic Welfare State: Old-Age Pensions, Credible Commitments, and Regime Survival." *Comparative Political Studies* 51 (5):659–695.

Kornreich, Yoel, Ilan Vertinsky, and Pitman Potter. 2012. "Consultation and Deliberation in China: The Making of China's Health-Care Reform." *China Journal* 68 (July):176–203.

Korpi, Walter. 1983. *The Democratic Class Struggle*. London: Routledge and Kegan Paul.

Lake, David A., and Matthew A. Baum. 2001. "The Invisible Hand of Democracy: Political Control and the Provision of Public Services." *Comparative Political Studies* 34 (6):587–621.

Lampton, David. 1979. "The Roots of Interprovincial Inequality in Education and Health Services in China." *American Political Science Review* 73 (June):459–477.

Landry, Pierre. 2008. *Decentralized Authoritarianism in China: The Communist Party's Control of Local Elites in the Post-Mao Era*. Cambridge: Cambridge University Press.

Lardy, Nicholas R. 1998. *China's Unfinished Economic Reform*. Washington, DC: Brookings Institution Press.

Lasswell, Harold D. 1936. *Politics: Who Gets What, When, How*: McGraw-Hill.

Lau, Lawrence J., Yingyi Qian, and Gerard Roland. 2000. "Reform without Losers: An Interpretation of China's Dual Track Approach to Transition." *Journal of Political Economy* 108 (1):120–143.

Lee, Ching Kwan. 2007. *Against the Law: Labor Protest in China's Rustbelt and Sunbelt*. Berkeley: University of California Press.

Leung, Joe C., and Yuebin Xu. 2015. *China's Social Welfare*. Cambridge: Polity Press.

Levitsky, Steven, and Lucan A. Way. 2010. *Competitive Authoritarianism: Hybrid Regimes after the Cold War*. New York: Cambridge University Press.

Lewis-Beck, Michael S., Alan Bryman, and Tim Futting Liao, eds. 2004. *The Sage Encyclopedia of Social Science Research Methods*, Vol. 3. Thousand Oaks, CA: Sage.

Li, Cheng. 2005. "Hu's Policy Shift and the Tuanpai's Coming-of-Age." *China Leadership Monitor* (Summer 15). https://www.hoover.org/research/hus-policy-shift-and-tuanpais-coming-age.

Li, Hongbin, and Li-An Zhou. 2005. "Political Turnover and Economic Performance: The Incentive Role of Personnel Control in China." *Journal of Public Economics* 89 (9–10):1743–1762.

Li, Jianxin, Ren Qiang, Wu Qiong, and Kong Tao. 2015. *China Family Panel Studies [zhongguo min sheng bao gao]*. Beijing: Peking University Press.

Liberthal, Kenneth. 2004. *Governing China: From Revolution through Reform.* 2nd ed. New York: Norton.

Liberthal, Kenneth, and Michel Oksenberg. 1988. *Policy Making in China: Leaders, Structures, and Processes.* Princeton, NJ: Princeton University Press.

Liebman, Benjamin L., and Curtis J. Milhaupt, eds. 2016. *Regulating the Visible Hand? The Institutional Implications of Chinese State Capitalism.* New York: Oxford University Press.

Liu, Mingxing, and Ran Tao. 2007. "Local Governance, Policy Mandates and Fiscal Reform in China." In *Paying for Progress in China: Public Finance, Human Welfare and Changing Patterns of Inequality,* edited by Vivienne Shue and Christine Wong. New York: Routledge.

Liu, Yuanli, William C. Hsiao, Qing Li, Xingzhu Liu, and Minghui Ren. 1995. "Transformation of China's Rural Health Care Financing." *Social Science & Medicine* 41 (8):1085–1093.

Lou, Jiwei, and Shuilin Wang. 2008. *Public Finance in China: Reform and Growth for a Harmonious Society:* World Bank.

Lü, Xiaobo 2014. "Social Policy and Regime Legitimacy: The Effects of Education Reform in China." *American Political Science Review* 108 (2):423–437.

Lü, Xiaobo, and Elizabeth Perry, eds. 1997. *Danwei: The Changing Chinese Workplace in Historical and Comparative Perspective.* Armonk, NY: M. E. Sharpe.

Ma, Zhiming. 2010. "Chinese Employee Class: An Analysis Using a Three-Dichotomy Segmentation Approach." *Journal of Contemporary China* 19 (67):935–948.

Magaloni, Beatriz. 2006. *Voting for Autocracy: Hegemonic Party Survival and Its Demise in Mexico.* New York: Cambridge University Press.

Magaloni, Beatriz, and Ruth Kricheli. 2010. "Political Order and One-Party Rule." *Annual Review of Political Science* 13 (June):123–143.

Manion, Melanie. 1984. "Cadre Recruitment and Management in the People's Republic of China." *Chinese Law and Government* 17 (3):3–128.

Mares, Isabela. 2003. *The Politics of Social Risk: Business and Welfare State Development.* Cambridge: Cambridge University Press.

Mares, Isabela, and Carnes Matthew E. 2009. "Social Policy in Developing Countries." *Annual Review of Political Science* 12 (June):93–113.

Marshall, T. H. 1950. *Citizenship and Social Class, and Other Essays* New York: Cambridge University Press.

Meltzer, Allan H., and Scott F. Richard. 1981. "A Rational Theory of the Size of Government." *Journal of Political Economy* 89 (October):914–927.

Meng, Qingyue, and Shenglan Tang. 2010. *Universal Coverage of Health Care in China: Challenges and Opportunities.* World Health Report 2010, Background Paper 7. Geneva: World Health Organization.

Meng, Tianguang, Jennifer Pan, and Ping Yang. 2017. "Conditional Receptivity to Citizen Participation: Evidence from a Survey Experiment in China." *Comparative Political Studies* 50 (4):399–433.

Mertha, Andrew 2009. "Fragmented Authoritarianism 2.0: Political Pluralization in the Policy Process." *China Quarterly* 200 (December):995–1012.

Milligan, Glenn W., and Martha C. Cooper. 1985. "An Examination of Procedures for Determining the Number of Clusters in a Dataset." *Psychometrika* 50 (2):159–179.

Ministry of Finance. 1999. *Di Fang Cai Zheng Tong Ji Zi Liao.* Beijing: Zhongguo cai zheng jing ji chu ban she.

Ministry of Finance. 2000. *Di Fang Cai Zheng Tong Ji Zi Liao*. Beijing: Zhongguo cai zheng jing ji chu ban she.

Ministry of Finance. 2001. *Di Fang Cai Zheng Tong Ji Zi Liao*. Beijing: Zhongguo cai zheng jing ji chu ban she.

Ministry of Finance. 2002. *Di Fang Cai Zheng Tong Ji Zi Liao*. Beijing: Zhongguo cai zheng jing ji chu ban she.

Ministry of Finance. 2003. *Di Fang Cai Zheng Tong Ji Zi Liao*. Beijing: Zhongguo cai zheng jing ji chu ban she.

Ministry of Finance. 2004. *Di Fang Cai Zheng Tong Ji Zi Liao*. Beijing: Zhongguo cai zheng jing ji chu ban she.

Ministry of Finance. 2005. *Di Fang Cai Zheng Tong Ji Zi Liao*. Beijing: Zhongguo cai zheng jing ji chu ban she.

Ministry of Finance. 2006. *Di Fang Cai Zheng Tong Ji Zi Liao*. Beijing: Zhongguo cai zheng jing ji chu ban she.

Ministry of Finance. 2007. *Di Fang Cai Zheng Tong Ji Zi Liao*. Beijing: Zhongguo cai zheng jing ji chu ban she.

Ministry of Finance. 2008. *Di Fang Cai Zheng Tong Ji Zi Liao*. Beijing: Zhongguo cai zheng jing ji chu ban she.

Ministry of Finance. 2009. *Di Fang Cai Zheng Tong Ji Zi Liao*. Beijing: Zhongguo cai zheng jing ji chu ban she.

Ministry of Finance. 2010. *Di Fang Cai Zheng Tong Ji Zi Liao*. Beijing: Zhongguo cai zheng jing ji chu ban she.

Ministry of Finance, Ministry of Health, and Ministry of Agriculture. 2003. Guan yu jian li xin xing nong cun he zuo yi liao zhi du de yi jian (Directives about establishing new rural cooperative health insurance). Beijing: State Council

Ministry of Health. 2007. *China Health Statistical Yearbook*. Peking: Peking Union Medical College Press.

Ministry of Health. 2008. *China Health Statistical Yearbook*: Peking: Peking Union Medical College Press.

Ministry of Health. 2009. *China Health Statistical Yearbook*: Peking: Peking Union Medical College Press.

Ministry of Health. 2010. *China Health Statistical Yearbook*: Peking: Peking Union Medical College Press.

Ministry of Human Resources and Social Security. 2004. *China Human Resources and Social Security Yearbook*. Beijing: China Labor and Social Security Press.

Ministry of Human Resources and Social Security. 2005. *China Human Resources and Social Security Yearbook*. Beijing: China Labor and Social Security Press.

Ministry of Human Resources and Social Security. 2006. *China Human Resources and Social Security Yearbook*. Beijing: China Labor and Social Security Press.

Ministry of Human Resources and Social Security. 2007. *China Human Resources and Social Security Yearbook*. Beijing: China Labor and Social Security Press.

Ministry of Human Resources and Social Security. 2008. *China Human Resources and Social Security Yearbook*. Beijing: China Labor and Social Security Press.

Ministry of Human Resources and Social Security. 2009. *China Human Resources and Social Security Yearbook*. Beijing: China Labor and Social Security Press.

Ministry of Human Resources and Social Security. 2010a. 2010 National Urban Social Health Insurance Operations Report (2010 quanguo chengzhen jiben yiliao baoxian qingkuang fenxi).

Ministry of Human Resources and Social Security. 2010b. *China Human Resources and Social Security Yearbook*. Beijing: China Labor and Social Security Press.

Ministry of Human Resources and Social Security. 2011. *China Human Resources and Social Security Yearbook*. Beijing: China Labor and Social Security Press.

Ministry of Human Resources and Social Security. 2012. *China Human Resources and Social Security Yearbook*. Beijing: China Labor and Social Security Press.

Montinola, Babriella, Yingyi Qian, and Barry R. Weingast. 1995. "Federalism, Chinese Style: The Political Basis for Economic Success in China." *World Politics* 48 (1):50–81.

Muller, Armin. 2017. "Functional Integration of China's Social Protection: Recent and Long-Term Trends of Institutional Change in Health and Pension Insurance." *Asian Survey* 57 (6):1110–1134.

Mulligan, Casey B., Xavier Sala-i-Martin, and Ricard Gil. 2004. "Do Democracies Have Different Public Policies than Nondemocracies?" *Journal of Economic Perspectives* 18 (1).51–74.

Munro, Neil, and Jane Duckett. 2015. "Explaining Public Satisfaction with Health-Care Systems: Findings from a Nationwide Survey in China." *Health Expectations* 19 (3):654–666.

Nathan, Andrew J. 2003. "Authoritarian Resilience." *Journal of Democracy* 14 (1):6–17.

National Bureau of Statistics. 1999. *China Labor Statistics Yearbook*. Beijing: China Statistics Press.

National Bureau of Statistics. 2000. *China Labor Statistics Yearbook*. Beijing: China Statistics Press.

National Bureau of Statistics. 2001. *China Labor Statistics Yearbook*. Beijing: China Statistics Press.

National Bureau of Statistics. 2002. *China Labor Statistics Yearbook*. Beijing: China Statistics Press.

National Bureau of Statistics. 2003. *China Labor Statistics Yearbook*. Beijing: China Statistics Press.

National Bureau of Statistics. 2004. *China Labor Statistics Yearbook*. Beijing: China Statistics Press.

National Bureau of Statistics. 2005. *China Labor Statistics Yearbook*. Beijing: China Statistics Press.

National Bureau of Statistics. 2006. *China Labor Statistics Yearbook*. Beijing: China Statistics Press.

National Bureau of Statistics. 2007. *China Labor Statistics Yearbook*. Beijing: China Statistics Press.

National Bureau of Statistics of China. 1995. *China Population Statistics Yearbook*. Beijing: China Statistics Press.

National Bureau of Statistics of China. 1999. *China Statistical Yearbook*. Beijing: China Statistics Press.

National Bureau of Statistics of China. 2000a. *China Population Statistics Yearbook*. Beijing: China Statistics Press.

National Bureau of Statistics of China. 2000b. *China Statistical Yearbook*. Beijing: China Statistics Press.

National Bureau of Statistics of China. 2001. *China Statistical Yearbook*. Beijing: China Statistics Press.

National Bureau of Statistics of China. 2002. *China Statistical Yearbook*. Beijing: China Statistics Press.

National Bureau of Statistics of China. 2003. *China Statistical Yearbook*. Beijing: China Statistics Press.

National Bureau of Statistics of China. 2004a. *China Statistical Yearbook*. Beijing: China Statistics Press.

National Bureau of Statistics of China. 2004b. *China Statistical Yearbook for Regional Economy*. Beijing: China Statistics Press.

National Bureau of Statistics of China. 2005a. *China Population Statistics Yearbook*. Beijing: China Statistics Press.

National Bureau of Statistics of China. 2005b. *China Statistical Yearbook*. Beijing: China Statistics Press.

National Bureau of Statistics of China. 2005c. *China Statistical Yearbook for Regional Economy*. Beijing: China Statistics Press.

National Bureau of Statistics of China. 2006a. *China Statistical Yearbook*. Beijing: China Statistics Press.

National Bureau of Statistics of China. 2006b. *China Statistical Yearbook for Regional Economy*. Beijing: China Statistics Press.

National Bureau of Statistics of China. 2007. *China Statistical Yearbook*. Beijing: China Statistics Press.

National Bureau of Statistics of China. 2008a. *China Statistical Yearbook*. Beijing: China Statistics Press.

National Bureau of Statistics of China. 2008b. *China Statistical Yearbook for Regional Economy*. Beijing: China Statistics Press.

National Bureau of Statistics of China. 2009a. *China Statistical Yearbook*. Beijing: China Statistics Press.

National Bureau of Statistics of China. 2009b. *China Statistical Yearbook for Regional Economy*. Beijing: China Statistics Press.

National Bureau of Statistics of China. 2010a. *China Population Statistics Yearbook*. Beijing: China Statistics Press.

National Bureau of Statistics of China. 2010b. *China Statistical Yearbook*. Beijing: China Statistics Press.

National Bureau of Statistics of China. 2010c. *China Statistical Yearbook for Regional Economy*. Beijing: China Statistics Press.

National Bureau of Statistics of China. 2010d. Nong ming gong diao cha jian ce bao gao (Peasant-workers survey and report) edited by National Statistics Bureau. Beijing.

Naughton, Barry. 2007. *The Chinese Economy: Transitions and Growth*. Cambridge, MA: MIT Press.

Nee, Victor. 1989. "A Theory of Market Transition: From Redistribution to Markets in State Socialism." *American Sociological Review* 54 (5):663–681.

Nee, Victor, and Yang Cao. 1999. "Path Dependent Societal Transformation: Stratification in Hybrid Mixed Economies." *Theory and Society* 28 (6):799–834.

Niedzwiecki, Sara. 2018. *Uneven Social Policies: The Politics of Subnational Variation in Latin America*. New York: Cambridge University Press.

Nyland, C., R. Smyth, and C. J. Zhu. 2006. "What Determines the Extent to Which Employers Will Comply with Their Social Security Obligations? Evidence from Chinese Firm-Level Data." *Social Policy & Administration* 40 (2):196–214.

O'Brien, Kevin J., and Lianjiang Li. 1999. "Selective Policy Implementation in Rural China." *Comparative Politics* 31 (2):167–186.

Oates, W. 1972. *Fiscal Federalism*. New York: Harcourt Brace Jovanovich.

Oi, Jean 1992. "Fiscal Reform and the Economic Foundations of Local State Corporatism in China." *World Politics* 45 (1):99–126.

Oi, Jean C., and Zhao Shukai. 2007. "Fiscal Crisis in China's Township: Causes and Consequences." In *Grassroots Political Reform in Contemporary China*, edited by Elizabeth J. Perry and Merle Goldman, 75–96. Cambridge, MA: Harvard University Press.

Ong, Lynette H. 2012. "Between Developmental and Clientelist States: Local State-Business Relationships in China." *Comparative Politics* 44 (2):191–209.

Pan, Jennifer. 2015. "Buying Inertia: Preempting Social Disorder with Selective Welfare Provision in Urban China." PhD dissertation, Cambridge, MA: Harvard University.

Parish, William L., and Ethan Michelson. 1996. "Politics and Markets: Dual Transformations." *American Journal of Sociology* 101 (4):1042–1059.

Park, Albert, and Fang Cai. 2011. "The Informalizatino of the Chinese Labor Market." In *From Iron Rice Bowl to Informalization: Markets, Workers, and the State in a Changing China*, edited by Sarosh Kuruvilla, Ching Kwan Lee, and Mary E. Gallagher. Ithaca, NY: Cornell University Press.

Pei, Minxin. 2003. "Rights and Resistance: The Changing Context of the Dissident Movement." In *Chinese Society: Change, Conflict, and Resistance*, edited by Elizabeth J. Perry and Mark Selden. New York: Routledge.

Peng, Ito, and Joseph Wong. 2008. "Institutions and Institutional Purpose: Continuity and Change in East Asian Social Policy." *Politics & Society* 36 (1):61–88.

Perry, Elizabeth J., and Sebastian Heilmann. 2011." Embracing Uncertainty: Guerilla Policy Style and Adaptive Governance in China." In *Mao's Invisible Hand: The Political Foundations of Adaptive Governance in China*, edited by Elizabeth J. Perry and Sebastian Heilmann, 1–29. Cambridge, MA: Harvard University Press.

Pierson, Paul. 1996. "The New Politics of the Welfare State." *World Politics* 48 (2):143–179.

Przeworski A., M. Alvarez, J. A. Cheibub, and F. Limongi. 2000. *Democracy and Development: Political Institutions and Well-Being in the World, 1950–1990*. New York: Cambridge University Press.

Qian, Jiwei, and Ake Blomqvist. 2014. *Health Policy Reform in China: A Comparative Perspective*. Singapore: World Scientific Publishing.

Ragin, Charles C. 1994. "A Qualitative Comparative Analysis of Pension Systems." In *The Comparative Political Economy of the Welfare State*, edited by Thomas Janoski and Alexander M. Hicks. New York: Cambridge University Press.

Rehm, Philipp. 2016. *Risk Inequality and Welfare States: Social Policy Preferences, Development, and Dynamics*. New York: Cambridge University Press.

Remington, Thomas F. 2019. "Institutional Change in Authoritarian Regimes: Pension Reform in Russia and China." *Problems of Post-Communism* 66 (5):1–14. doi: 10.1080/10758216.2018.1450154.

Riker, William H. 1964. *Federalism: Origin, Operation, Significance*. Boston: Little, Brown.

Rimlinger, Gaston V. 1971. *Welfare Policy and Industrialization in Europe, America, and Russia*. New York: Wiley.

Rithmire, Meg E. 2015. *Land Bargains and Chinese Capitalism: The Politics of Property Rights under Reform*. New York: Cambridge University Press.

Rodrik, Dani. 1997. *Has Globalization Gone Too Far?* Washington, DC: Institute for International Economics.

Rosen, Stanley. 1990. "The Chinese Communist Party and Chinese Society: Popular Attitudes toward Party Membership and the Party's Image." *Australian Journal of Chinese Affairs* 24 (July):51–92.

Rudra, Nita. 2007. "Welfare States in Developing Countries: Unique or Universal?" *Journal of Politics* 69 (2):378–396.

Saich, Tony 2011. *Governance and Politics of China.* Basingstoke: Palgrave Macmillan.

Shambaugh, David L. 2008. *China's Communist Party: Atrophy and Adaptation.* Berkeley: University of California Press.

Sheng, Yumin. 2010. *Economic Openness and Territorial Politics in China.* New York: Cambridge University Press.

Shi, Shih-Jiunn. 2012. "Towards Inclusive Social Citizenship? Rethinking China's Social Security in the Trend towards Urban-Rural Harmonisation." *Journal of Social Policy* 41 (4):789–810.

Shih, Victor. 2004a. "Dealing with Non-Performing Loans: Political Constraints and Financial Policies in China." *China Quarterly* 180 (December):922–944.

Shih, Victor. 2004b. "Factions Matter: Personal Networks and the Distribution of Bank Loans in China." *Journal of Contemporary China* 13 (38):3–19.

Shih, Victor. 2007. *Factions and Finance in China: Elite Conflict and Inflation.* New York: Cambridge University Press.

Shih, Victor, Christopher Adolph, and Mingxing Liu. 2012. "Getting ahead in the Communist Party: Explaining the Advancement of Central Committee Members in China." *American Political Science Review* 106 (1):166–187.

Shih, Victor, Luke Qi Zhang, and Mingxing Liu. 2010. *When the Autocrat Gives: Determines of Fiscal Transfers in China.* Evanston, IL: Northwestern University Press.

Shirk, Susan. 1993. *The Political Logic of Economic Reform in China.* Berkeley: University of California Press.

Snyder, Richard. 1992. "Explaining Transitions from Neopatrimonial Dictatorships." *Comparative Politics* 24 (4):379–399.

Solinger, Dorothy J. 1991. "The Place of the Central City in China's Economic Reform: From Hierarchy to Network." *City & Society* 5 (1):23–39.

Solinger, Dorothy J. 1995. "The Chinese Work Unit and Transient Labor in the Transition from Socialism." *Modern China* 21 (2):155–183.

Solinger, Dorothy J. 1999. *Contesting Citizenship in Urban China: Peasant Migrants, the State, and the Logic of the Market.* Berkeley: University of California Press.

Solinger, Dorothy J., and Yiyang Hu. 2012. "Welfare, Wealth and Poverty in Urban China: The Dibao and Its Differential Disbursement." *China Quarterly* 211 (September):741–764.

Solinger, Dorothy J., and Ting Jiang. 2016. "When Central Orders and Promotion Criteria Conflict: Recent Urban Decisions on the Dibao." *Modern China* 42 (6):571–606.

Soskice, David. 1999. "Divergent Production Regimes: Coordinated and Uncoordinated Market Economies in the 1980s and 1990s." *Continuity and Change in Contemporary Capitalism* 38: 101–134.

Stephens, John D. 1979. *The Transition from Capitalism to Socialism.* New York: Macmillan.

Svolik, Milan W. 2012. *The Politics of Authoritarian Rule.* New York: Cambridge University Press.

Swenson, Peter. 2002. *Capitalists against Markets: The Making of Labor Markets and Welfare States in the United States and Sweden.* Oxford: Oxford University Press.

Tidmore, Eugene F., and Danny W. Turner. 1983. "On Clustering with Chernoff-Type Faces." *Communications in Statistics* A12 (14):381–396.

Tiebout, Charles. 1956. "A Pure Theory of Local Expenditures." *Journal of Political Economy* 64:416–424.

Truex, Rory. 2016. *Making Autocracy Work: Representation and Responsiveness in Modern China*. Cambridge Studies in Comparative Politics. Cambridge: Cambridge University Press.

Truex, Rory. 2017. "Consultative Authoritarianism and Its Limits." *Comparative Political Studies* 50 (3):329–361.

Tullock, Gordon 1987. *Autocracy*. Dordrecht, the Netherlands: Kluwer Academic.

Wahman, Michael, Jan Teorell, and Axel Hadenius. 2013. "Authoritarian Regime Types Revisited: Updated Data in Comparative Perspective." *Contemporary Politics* 19 (1):19–34.

Walder, Andrew G. 1995. "Career Mobility and the Communist Political Order." *American Sociological Review* 60 (3):309–328.

Walder, Andrew G., Tianjue Luo, and Dan Wang. 2013. "Social Stratification in Transitional Economies: Property Rights and the Structure of Markets." *Theory and Society* 42 (6):561–588.

Wallace, Jeremy. 2014. *Cities and Stability: Urbanization, Redistribution, & Regime Survival in China*. New York: Oxford University Press.

Wang, Yuhua. 2014. "Coercive Capacity and the Durability of the Chinese Communist State." *Communist and Post-Communist Studies* 47 (1):13–25.

Weingast, Barry. 1995. "The Economic Role of Political Institutions: Market Preserving Federalism and Economic Growth." *Journal of Law, Economics, and Organization* 11 (1):1–31.

Whiting, Susan H. 2004. *Power and Wealth in Rural China: The Political Economy of Institutional Change*. New York: Cambridge University Press.

Wibbels, Erik. 2005. *Federalism and the Market: Intergovernmental Conflict and Economic Reform in the Developing World*. New York: Cambridge University Press.

Wibbels, Erik, and John S. Ahlquist. 2011. "Development, Trade, and Social Insurance." *International Studies Quarterly* 55 (1):125–149.

Wintrobe, Ronald. 1998. *The Political Economy of Dictatorship*. Cambridge: Cambridge University Press.

Wong, Christine. 2000. "Central-Local Relations Revisited: The 1994 Tax Sharing Reform and Public Expenditure Management in China." *China Perspective* 31 (September):52–63.

Wong, Christine. 2009. "Rebuilding Government for the 21st Century: Can China Incrementally Reform the Public Sector?" *China Quarterly* 200 (December):929–952.

Wong, Joseph. 2004. *Health Democracies: Welfare Politics in Taiwan and South-Korea*. Ithaca, NY: Cornell University Press.

World Bank. 1983. *China: Socialist Economic Development*. Washington, DC: World Bank.

World Bank. 1997. *Old Age Security: Pension Reform in China*. Washington, DC: World Bank.

Xiao, Yang, and Yanjie Bian. 2018. "The Influence of Hukou and College Education in China's Labor Market." *Urban Studies* 55 (7):1504–1524. doi: 10.1177/0042098017690471.

Xie, Yu, and Emily Hannum. 1996. "Regional Variation in Earnings Inequality in Reform-Era Urban China." *American Journal of Sociology* 101 (4):950–992.

Yang, Dennis Tao, Junsen Zhang, and Shaojie Zhou. 2011. "Why Are Saving Rates so High in China?" NBER Working Paper National Bureau of Economic Research.

Yin, Jidong. 1997. *Zhongguo shehui baozhang yanjiu (Research on China's Social Security)*. Nanchang: Jiangxi gaoxiao chubanshe.

Yu, Lu. 2008. *Xin shi qi Zhongguo guo nei yi min fen bu yan jiu [Research of the Domestic Migration in Contempoar China]*. Shanghai Shanghai san lian shu dian.

Zhan, Jing V. 2011. "Determinants of Central-Provincial Fiscal Transfer: Equity, Bargaining or Efficiency?" *Comparative Economic & Social Systems [jingji shehui tizhi bijiao]* (6):73–84.

Zhang, Lufa, and Nan Liu. 2014. "Health Reform and Out-of-Pocket Payments: Lessons from China." *Health Policy and Planning* 29 (2):217–226.

Zhang, Zhihua, and Jorge Martinez-Vazquez. 2002. "The System of Equalization Transfers in China." *International Studies Program Working Paper*. Andrew Young School of Policy Studies, Georgia State University. Atlanta.

Zhao, Dingxin 2009. "The Mandate of Heaven and Performance Legitimation in Historical and Contemporary China." *American Behavioral Scientist* 53 (3):416–433.

Zhou, Xueguang. 2000. "Economic transformation and income inequality in urban China: evidence from panel data." *American Journal of Sociology* 105 (4):1135–1174.

Zhou, Xueguang. 2004. *The State and Life Chances in Urban China: Redistribution and Stratification, 1949–1994*: Cambridge University Press.

Zhu, Rongji. 2013. *Zhu Rongji on the Record: The Road to Reform: 1991–1997*. Beijing: Foreign Languages Press.

Zhu, Rongji. 2014. *Zhu Rongji on the Record: The Road to Reform 1998-2003*. Beijing: Foreign Languages Press.

Zhu, Xufeng, and Youlang Zhang. 2016. "Political Mobility and Dynamic Diffusion of Innovation: The Spread of Municipal Pro-Business Administrative Reform in China." *Journal of Public Administration Research and Theory* 26 (3):535–551.

Zhu, Yuchao. 2011. ""Performance Legitimacy" and China's Political Adaptation Strategy." *Journal of Chinese Political Science* 16 (2):123–140.

Zucco, Cesar Jr. 2013. "When Payouts Pay Off: Conditional Cash Transfers and Voting Behavior in Brazil 2002-10." *American Journal of Political Science* 57 (4):810–822.

Zuo, Cai. 2014. "Understanding Local Government Incentives in Welfare Provision in China." Mid-West Political Science Association Annual Conference, Chicago, April, 2014.

Zuo, Cai. 2015. "Promoting City Leaders: The Structure of Political Incentives in China." *China Quarterly* 224 (December):955–984.

Index

Note: Tables and figures are indicated by *t* and *f* following the page number

For the benefit of digital users, indexed terms that span two pages (e.g., 52–53) may, on occasion, appear on only one of those pages.

accumulation rate in health insurance pooling funds, 126, 128
administrative units, 34
agent-centered approach, 20–21, 23
aggregated government social spending, 20
agricultural outputs, 103, 107
All-China Federation of Trade Unions, 69–70
Arab Spring, 15–16, 199–200
Asian Development Bank (ADB), 199
authoritarian countries/leaders. *See also* central leaders; distributive strategy of the Center
  consultative authoritarianism, 22
  critical supporters in, 29–30, 31
  deliberate state policies, 165
  fragmented authoritarianism, 23, 67–68, 212n13
  one-party authoritarian countries, 15
  political economy literature on autocracies, 29–31
  purges in autocracy, 13, 29–30, 207n6
  social health insurance expansion, 160–62
  social welfare provisions in, 5–6, 11–15, 12*f*, 29–34
  stratified expansion of social welfare provisions, 27–28, 51–56, 56*f*
  summary of, 190–94
  terror in, 29–30, 201–2, 207n6, 207n7
  torture in, 29–30, 207n6
authoritarian resilience, 197–98

Bashar al-Asad, 199–200
beneficiary groups of social health insurance, 5–6, 9*f*, 10, 11*f*, 14
benefit distribution, 31–34
Bian Yanjie, 167–68
bureaucratic integration score (BINT), 153, 157
bureaucratic power, 23, 70, 134

cash transfer programs, 199–200
catastrophic diseases, 2

central leaders (the Center). *See also* authoritarian countries/leaders; distributive strategy of the Center; local motivation and responses; subnational social health insurance
  agency/authority of, 35–36, 39
  bureaucratic power, 23, 70, 134
  central-to-local fiscal transfers, 96–109
  control and accommodation of, 137–38
  cooptation by, 13, 29–31, 33, 41–42, 199–200, 207n6, 209n12
  establishment of social health insurance, 87–90
  interests and strategies, 39–46
  introduction to, 86–87
  Social Insurance Law, 94–96
central-local interactions, 13–14, 15–17, 39, 116, 132–33
central-to-local fiscal transfers
  by central leaders, 96–109, 136–37
  composition and trends of, 96–102, 97*f*, 98*f*, 99*t*, 100*f*
  determinants of, 101*f*, 102–9, 103*t*, 105*t*, 108*t*
  introduction to, 96–109
  local governments and, 48–49
  relations, 6, 15–16, 38–39, 132–33
  research design, 18, 203
  summary of, 109–10, 190–94
chemotherapy, 1
China General Social Survey (CGSS), 20, 167–68, 175, 178–79
China Health and Nutrition Survey (CHNS), 20, 169–70, 179–88, 180*t*, 181–82*f*, 183–84*t*, 223n4
China Household Income Project (CHIP) survey, 168
China Mobil, 164
China National Petroleum Corporation, 164
China's Budget Law, 104

Chinese Communist Party (CCP)
    central economic work conference, 92
    economic reform, 78–84
    health insurance benefits for, 168–69, 175–78
    introduction to, 3, 35, 37–38
    social protection commitment, 200
    Soviet-style development strategy, 60–61
    stratified expansion of social health
        insurance, 95–96
Chinese Communist Revolution, 163–64
Chinese Ministry of Public Security, 41–42
clientelistic transfer programs, 32–33
coastal manufacturing centers, 145–47
collective-owned firms, 83, 186–87
collectivized agriculture, 59–60
commanding heights economy, 164
Commission of Health and Family Planning, 70
community committees (*shequ zuzhi*), 88
computed tomography (CT) exam, 1
congressional politics, 13–14
consultative authoritarianism, 21–22
Cooperative Medical Scheme (CMS, *nongcun
        hezuo yiliao*), 59–61, 62–63, 71–72
cooptation by leaders, 13, 29–31, 33, 41–42,
        199–200, 207n6, 209n12
county-level units, 34, 148, 194–95
critical realignments, 29–30
critical supporters in autocracy, 29–30, 31, 207n6
cross-section-time-series (CSTS) regression
        model, 104–7
Cultural Revolution, 37–38

danwei-based welfare system, 57, 58–62,
        69–70, 129–30
decentralized multilevel governance
    introduction to, 5–6, 13–14, 17
    in social health insurance, 54–56, 56f,
        68–70, 84
    in social welfare, 47
    stratified expansion of social welfare, 35
de-collectivization reform, 62–63, 80–82
democracy, 13–14, 21, 27, 29, 198–99
democratization, 3–5, 15–16, 30, 190
demographic shifts, 49
Deng Xiaoping, 78–79, 137, 212n19
dependency ratio, 145, 152–56
Development Research Center (DRC), 63
dictator's dilemma, 32
differentiation and de-empowerment of
        working class, 166–67
Dillon, Nara, 163–64
discrimination in health care, 2, 207n2
distributive strategy of the Center

in autocracies, 30–31, 33, 34, 52, 55, 111–12
    introduction to, 15–17, 24–25
    lower cost of, 38
    overview of, 87
    structure of, 34
    supply-side perspective, 36–37
diversification of regional economies,
        24, 78–84
"divide and rule" strategy, 16–17, 31, 42, 54–55,
        161, 162–63, 190–91
domestic unemployment, 92–93
"double counting" in health insurance
        enrollment, 151–52
double reimbursement scheme (*er ci baoxiao*),
        130, 150, 222n21
dual type of social health insurance expansion,
        25, 51, 139–43, 143f, 147–48

East Asian "productivist" welfare regime,
        76–77, 77f
economic development
    expansion of social welfare and, 41, 68–69,
        91–93, 201
    fiscal transfer and 104–7
    local motivation, 113–15
    migrant workers and, 129, 137
    control variables, 153
    promotion of, 79–80, 112, 132
    regression analysis, 153
    reorientation to, 167
    structural changes, 73–78
economic growth
    cost of, 115
    human capital for, 12
    promotion of, 113, 165–66, 198
    social welfare expansion and, 21, 29, 40,
        41–43, 47, 84–85, 91–92
    structural changes, 73–78
economic openness, 74–76, 83, 84–85, 88,
        147–48, 164, 166–67
economic paradigm, 21
economic reform
    Central Committee and, 78–79
    danwei-based welfare and, 61–62, 84–85
    impact of, 208n9
    mass migration, 49, 137
    overview of, 57–58
    social health insurance and, 58, 95–96
    support for, 212n19
economy model, 37–38
education level (*edu*), 175, 179–80
electoral politics, 13–14, 21, 35, 200
elite-mass balancing, 14–15, 30, 32, 190–91

employer ownership *(employown)*, 179–80,
182*f*, 186–87
employer size *(employsz)*, 122, 166–67, 175,
179–80, 182*f*
employment-based health insurance, 2, 128–29,
169, 174–79, 176*t*, 177*t*
employment status *(employsta)*, 10, 122, 129,
175, 178–80, 186
ethnic minority autonomous regions, 44, 48–49,
51, 97–98, 99*t*, 141–43, 144, 149–51, 154*t*
European Union (EU), 49
expansion of social health insurance. *See* social
health insurance expansion
expansion of social welfare. *See* stratified
expansion of social welfare
experimental zones *(shi dian)*, 195–96
experiment-based policy initiatives, 22
export-oriented manufacturing, 128, 143–44
export-oriented market economy, 80–82

Falun Gong, 63–64
feedback effect, 164–65
fiscal decentralization, 25, 48, 111,
136–37, 190–91
fiscal transfers, 43–44, 46. *See also* central-to-
local fiscal transfers
fixed effects (FE), 153–56
floating population, 117–18
foreign-owned firms, 52–53, 93, 186–87,
214n12, 224n10
foreign trade, 79–80, 144
formal employment, 2, 90–91, 163, 175–78,
220n1, 223n1, 223n2
fragmented authoritarianism, 23,
67–68, 212n13

global financial crisis (2008), 76, 77–78, 92–93
government hierarchy, 167–68
Government Insurance Scheme (GIS, *gongfei
yiliao*), 59–61, 62–63, 94–95, 129–32,
170, 180–86
government responsiveness, 22
Great Leap Forward, 37–38
gross domestic product (GDP), 15, 73–76,
74–75*f*, 92, 103, 107, 147–48, 157
Guo Baocheng, 123

Hamad ibn Isa Al-Khalifa, King, 199–200
harmonious society *(he xie she hui)*, 3, 37–38,
91–92, 164, 215n23
health insurance. *See* social health insurance;
stratified expansion of social welfare;
subnational social health insurance

health insurance accounts (HIAs), 62
health insurance fund (HIF)
accumulation rate in, 126
introduction to, 62
deficits in, 93, 125–26, 127–28
demographic impacts on, 49
labor outflows, 144–45
management struggles, 71–72
payment pressures on, 49–50, 116–17,
220–21n6
reimbursement rate, 119–21, 150
surplus in, 116–17, 119–21, 120*f*, 148
Health insurance integration, 67, 124, 147–48,
194–97
Health Policy Authority, 72*f*
horizontal mobilization, 124–25, 135–36,
188–89, 197–98
Hu Jintao, 3, 35–36, 37–38, 63–64, 88–89,
91–93, 94–96
Hu Xiaoyi, 92–93
hukou (household registration)
fiscal transfer and, 102, 104–8
social health insurance enrollment and,
175–78, 179–86
introduction to, 1
migraiton, 80–82
urbanization, 82–83
NRCMS outpatient reimbursement and, 121
social health insurance expansion, 117–18,
122, 129, 150–51
stratified social welfare system, 163, 165–66
human capital, 12, 53, 76–77, 78, 167,
168–69, 180–86
hypotheses for empirical tests, 102, 139, 165,
166, 168

income redistribution, 130–32, 195
industrial-development-park district
(gongye kaifa qu), 115
industrial value-added/ profits, 40
industrialization, 21, 60–61, 78–79, 83, 144,
147–48, 162, 165
inequalities in social health insurance, 160–61,
169–74, 170*f*, 171*f*, 172*f*, 173*f*
informally employed people, 31, 174
institutional arrangements, 23, 200–1
insurrection threats, 30
interest group organizations, 27, 36–37
internal migration, 49, 81*f*, 83, 146*t*, 210n25
Iraq war, 33
Islamic Republic, 33

Jiang Zemin, 22, 37–38, 87, 88–89, 213n1

labor-inflowing/-outflowing regions, 49–50,
80–82, 210n25, 220–21n6
Labor Insurance Scheme (LIS, *laobao*), 59–61,
62–63, 70, 71–72, 163–64
labor-intensive manufacturing, 49–50, 76–77,
80–82, 143–44, 148, 210n23, 220n5
labor market status, 166–67, 168–69,
174–75, 179
labor mobility
in ethnic minority autonomous regions, 151
impacts on, 195–96
social health insurance and, 111–12, 117,
118, 123–24, 147–48, 156t
social risks and, 49, 51, 53, 137, 152–56
in status-quo type provinces, 151–52
lagged dependent variable (LDV), 104,
153–57, 223n31
laid-off workers, 83, 88–90, 96, 166–67
leader-centered paradigm, 22–23
left-wing parties, 21, 23
legitimacy fragility, 41–42
Leninist regimes, 41
Li Jing, 1–2
Li Keqiang, 118–19
Liberthal, Kenneth G., 67–68
local capture in social health insurance, 54
*Local Fiscal Statistics (di fang cai zheng tong ji zi
liao)* publication, 97f, 98f, 99, 100f, 101f,
103t, 203, 215–16n39
local motivation and responses
divergence of interests, 125–27
to health insurance expansion, 116–25
to health insurance stratification, 125–32
initiatives and experimentation, 121–25
introduction to, 111–12
protecting retirees, 127–28
protecting state employees, 129–32
protecting urban formal workers, 128–29
resistance and noncompliance, 116–21
for social welfare development, 113–15
summary of, 132–33
local political economies, 6, 25, 143–52
logistic regression results, 175, 177t, 183t, 184t
low-status groups, 10

macroeconomic evolution, 57–58, 74–76,
78, 84–85
mainland provincial units, 34, 102
Mao Zedong, 37–38, 59–61, 163–64
market economy, 48–49, 57, 80–82, 87, 160, 164,
167, 178–79
migrants/migration
economic reform and, 49, 137

social health insurance, 2, 128–29, 169, 174,
176t, 177t
internal migration, 49, 81f, 83, 146t, 210n25
mass migration, 30, 49, 121–22, 123–24, 137
province-to-province migration, 152–53
risk pooling and, 49–50, 137
rural-to-urban migrants, 4–5, 53–54, 80–82,
81f, 82t, 83, 117–18
military coups, 30
minimum living allowance *(dibao)*, 84, 89
Ministry of Human Resources and Social
Security (MOHRSS), 70–73, 92–93, 124
multidimensional conceptualization of social
welfare provision, 14, 20, 28, 193

National Development and Reform
Commission, 70–71, 209n14
New Rural Cooperative Medical Schemes
(NRCMS)
coverage of, 64, 64f, 171f
expansion of, 91, 117–18, 121
fragmentation of authority, 71–72
generosity of, 10, 11f, 54, 65–67, 170–72,
173–74
hukou (household registration), 181f,
184t, 195–96
insurance beneficiaries, 179–88, 183–84t
introduction to, 3, 64f, 64
outpatient reimbursement, 121, 152
integration, 121–25, 195–96
stratification of social health insurance and,
94–96, 169–74
Ningxia Hui Minority Autonomous Region,
149–51, 158
nomenklatura list, 36, 208n4
non-agricultural outputs, 82–83
non-democratic governments, 27, 41
nongovernmental organizations (NGOs), 19–20
non-working population, 3, 48, 95, 136–37

Oksenberg, Michael, 67–68
old industrial base *(lao gongye jidi)*, 83, 127–28
one-party authoritarian countries, 15
ordinary least squares (OLS) regression, 153
organizational proliferation, 13, 29–30,
207n6, 209n12
out-of-network hospital, 1
outpatient services, 61–62, 65–67, 119, 121, 130,
172f, 172, 218–19n39

parliamentary politics, 13–14
particularistic transfer programs, 32–33
partisan politics, 13–14, 21

party cadre responsibility system, 45
pay-out differences, 124–25
payroll-based social insurance, 169
peasant organizations, 29–30
People's Republic of China (PRC), 3
personal connections (*guanxi*), 2
personnel management, 43, 45, 46, 135–36
placating masses in social welfare provision, 33,
    41–43, 151
play-off strategy, 33, 37–38
police patrol (inspection tours), 46
Politburo members, 14, 222n20
political calculation, 18, 36–37
political capital, 168–69
political economy literature, 29–31,
    34–37, 57–58
political strategy for distribution, 13,
    29–34, 162–69
prefectural units, 34, 93
private goods, 29, 207n5
private-owned enterprises, 52–53, 77–78,
    186–87, 224n10
privileging type of social health insurance
    expansion, 25, 35, 51, 139–43,
    143*f*, 149–51
province-to-province migration, 152–53
provincial-level municipalities, 34, 51, 141, 151,
    153, 204, 222n20
public goods, 27, 29–30, 43, 47, 79, 136, 207n5,
    207n7, 212n11
public policy in democracies, 29
purges in autocracy, 13, 29–30, 207n6

redistributive grievances, 30, 208n2
red pockets payments, 1
re-employment services, 84
regime stability, 5–6, 11–12, 13–14, 30,
    31–32, 45, 46–47, 68, 124–25, 135–36,
    188–89, 193–94
regional economic diversification, 78–84, 144
regression analysis, 25, 102–9,
    152–58, 174–88
reimbursement rate of social health insurance,
    65–67, 116–17, 118–21, 130, 170–72, 171*f*,
    173–74, 217–18n27, 225n3
rent-seeking opportunities, 54, 113
residency-based social health insurance
    programs, 52–53, 54, 128–29, 169–72, 174,
    187, 224n6
retirees, protecting, 127–28, 164
riot threats, 30, 41–42, 188–89
risk pooling
    fragmentation, 49, 137, 160–61

migration and, 49–50, 137, 220–21n6
in social health insurance reform, 61–62,
    69–70, 71–72, 95–96, 130–32
social risks, 6, 17, 134, 137, 191
type of social health insurance expansion,
    50–51, 141–43, 143*f*, 144–47, 158*f*, 178,
    180, 187
risk-sharing mechanism, 32–33, 49, 53, 69–70,
    130–32, 137, 145, 148, 195
rural poor, 31, 33
rural-to-urban migrants (migrant workers),
    4–5, 37, 53–54, 80–82, 91, 93, 117–18, 148

SARS (severe acute respiratory syndrome)
    outbreak, 63
scientific development, 3, 37–38, 214n15
second-class citizens, 165–66
selectorate theory, 13, 29, 31, 207n5
self-employed people, 3–5
Seventh Five-Year Plan (1986-1990), 78–79
single-party authoritarian regime, 15, 33–34
16th Party Congress, 88–89, 91–92, 214n7
social health insurance. *See also* stratified
    expansion of social welfare; subnational
    social health insurance
    accumulation rate in pooling funds, 126, 128
    beneficiary groups, 3, 9–10, 9*f*
    coverage of, 6–8, 7*f*, 8*f*, 14–15, 17–18, 19,
      31–32, 50–51, 52–53, 60, 62–63, 65–67,
      66*f*, 88, 91, 116, 138, 139–43, 142*t*, 152–58,
      154*t*, 156*t*, 158*f*, 169, 170*f*, 191–92
    decentralization of, 68–70
    distribution of benefits, 179–88, 181–82*f*,
      183–84*t*
    double reimbursement scheme, 130, 150
    dual type, 25, 50, 51, 139–43, 143*f*, 147–48,
      158*f*, 187
    employment-based health insurance, 2, 63,
      128–29, 169–70, 174–79, 177*t*
    establishment of, 3, 87–90
    expansion of, 6–11, 62–67
    fiscal resources and, 48–49, 65, 136–37, 139,
      156–57, 156*t*
    fragmentation of, 70–73
    future direction of, 194–97
    generosity of, 7–8, 7*f*, 8*f*, 11*f*, 14–15, 18, 19,
      28, 50–51, 53–54, 138, 139–43, 152–58,
      156*t*, 158*f*
    hukou (household registration), 122, 129,
      150–51, 174–88, 177*t*, 181*f*, 183*t*, 184*t*
    inequalities in, 169–74, 173*f*
    introduction to, 1–6, 4*f*, 57–58
    local motivation and, 116–25

social health insurance (*cont.*)
  outpatient services, 61–62, 65–67, 119, 121,
    130, 172*f*, 172, 218–19n39
  pathways to, 58–67
  power structure of, 67–73
  privileging type, 25, 35, 40–41, 50, 51,
    139–43, 143*f*, 149–51, 158*f*, 178
  risk pooling type, 25, 50–51, 139–43, 143*f*,
    144–47, 158*f*, 178, 187
  socioeconomic conditions/status and, 19, 37,
    50, 94, 111–12, 138, 144, 152–58, 156*t*, 175,
    178–80, 187–88
  status-quo type , 25, 50–51, 139–43, 143*f*,
    151–52, 158*f*, 175, 180
  stratified expansion of, 6–11, 8*f*, 9*f*, 12*f*,
    14–15, 27–28, 56*f*, 86, 90–96
  summary of, 84, 159
  transition to, 61–62
  for urban formal employees, 87–90
social health insurance expansion
  distribution of benefits, 179–88, 181–82*f*,
    183–84*t*
  employment-based health insurance, 2,
    128–29, 169, 174–79, 177*t*
  inequalities in, 169–74, 170*f*, 171*f*, 172*f*, 173*f*
  introduction to, 6–11, 7*f*, 8*f*, 160–62
  social stratification as political
    strategy, 162–69
  summary of, 188–89, 190–94
Social Insurance Law, 44–45, 47–48, 94–96,
    125–29, 192, 215n28, 219n51,
    220n4, 225n4
social legislation, 18, 43, 44–45, 46, 47–48,
    135–36, 137–38, 192, 200–1
social management (*she hui guan li*), 164
social media, 2, 145
Social Protection Index (SPI), 199
social-rights-based welfare, 94, 196
social safety net, 42–43, 76, 95–96, 113
social status, 2, 10–11, 60–61, 168, 226n10
social stratification, 84, 162–69,
    188–89, 194–95
social welfare provisions. *See also* stratified
    expansion of social welfare
  alternative explanations for, 20–23
  in authoritarian countries, 3–6, 11–15,
    12*f*, 29–34
  expansion of, 4*f*, 15–18
  local motivation for, 113–15
  multidimensional conceptualization of, 14,
    20, 28, 193
  overview of, 23–26
  political economy of, 34–37

possible solutions for, 31–34
  research design of, 18–20, 19*t*
  strategy of, 37–39
  summary of, 190–94
  trade-offs with, 29–31
socioeconomic conditions/status
  employment-based social health
    insurance, 175
  introduction to, 10, 25
  regional variation of social health insurance
    and, 152–58, 156*t*
  social health insurance expansion and, 160–62
  social welfareexpansion, 50–51
  stratified social welfare system, 163
Soviet-style development strategy, 60–61
Special Economic Zones, 19, 137
stability maintenance (*wei wen*), 164
state-owned enterprises (SOEs)
  economic reform and, 58, 69–70, 109–10
  financial resource shortage of, 88
  introduction to, 4–5, 16–17
  privileging elites, 37, 40–41
  restructuring and layoffs, 76, 83–84, 89–90
status-quo type of social health insurance
    expansion, 25, 50, 139–43, 143*f*, 151–52
stratified expansion of social welfare
  agency in, 35–37
  in authoritarian China, 27–28, 56*f*
  in authoritarian countries, 29–34
  central leaders' interest in, 35–36, 38–46
  local leaders' interest in, 36, 39, 46–51
  distribution of benefits, 179–88, 181–82*f*,
    183–84*t*
  economic context of, 73–84
  employment-based health insurance, 2,
    128–29, 169, 174–79, 177*t*
  socioeconomic status, 163, 165–68
  inequalities in social health insurance,
    169–74, 170*f*, 171*f*, 172*f*, 173*f*
  introduction to, 6–11, 7*f*, 8*f*, 9*f*, 11*f*, 12*f*,
    14–18, 27–28
  local choices in, 50–51
  local constraints in, 47–50
  local motivations for, 46–47
  placating masses, 41–43
  political economy of, 34–39
  privileging elites, 40–41
  social health insurance and, 6–11, 7*f*, 8*f*, 9*f*,
    11*f*, 12*f*, 14–15
  strategy of, 37–39
  structure of, 34–35
  summary of, 51–56, 84, 188–89, 197–99
subnational politicians, 13–14, 194

subnational variation in social health insurance
distributive implications, 135–39
dual type provinces, 147–48
introduction to, 134–35
local political economy and, 143–52
privileging type provinces, 149–51
regional variation in, 139–43, 140*t*,
142*t*, 143*f*
risk-pooling type provinces, 144–47
status-quo type provinces, 151–52
supplementary health benefits, 122, 125–26,
130, 196–97

tax revenues, 40, 44, 73–76, 75*f*, 96–98
terror in autocracy, 29–30, 201–2, 207n6, 207n7
three representatives, 37–38
Three Worlds of Welfare Capitalism
(Esping-Andersen), 162
Tiananmen protest (1989), 15–16, 63–64,
166–67, 212n19
torture in autocracy, 29–30, 207n6
township-level units, 19–20, 34, 113–14, 118,
121, 139, 172–73
trade liberalization, 78–79

unemployment concerns, 3, 4–5, 48, 95, 136–37
universal *(quanmin)* coverage, 65–67,
188, 212n10
universal free health care *(quanmin mianfei
yiliao)*, 123
universalistic welfare, 38, 94, 122, 202
universalizing benefits, 5–6, 13, 27–28, 30,
86, 190–91
Urban and Rural Resident Basic Medical
Insurance (URRBMI), 124–25
Urban Employee Basic Medical Insurance
(UEBMI)
change in surplus for, 119–21, 120*f*, 126, 149*f*
coverage of, 62–63, 64–65, 66*f*, 91, 171*f*
establishment of, 62–63
integration, 195–96
beneficiaries, 169–70, 174–88, 181–82*f*,
183–84*t*
introduction to, 3
local non-employees and migrant workers in,
117–18, 129
MoHRSS, and, 71–72, 124
political motivation for, 93
state employees and urban formal employees
in, 128–32, 131*f*
generosity of, 10, 11*f*, 65–67, 127–28, 170–72,
171*f*, 172*f*, 173–74

stratification of social health insurance and,
94–96, 169–74
urban formal workers, 10, 86, 87–90, 93, 119–
21, 127–32, 172, 173–74, 179–89, 194–98
urban poor, 4–5, 31, 52–54, 58, 70, 130, 174
Urban Resident Basic Medical Insurance
(URBMI)
change in surplus for, 119–21, 120*f*
coverage, 64, 65*f*, 91, 171*f*
establishment of, 64, 65*f*, 71–72
expansion, 117–18
generosity, 10, 11*f*, 54, 65–67, 119, 170–72,
171–72*f*, 173–74
beneficiaries, 9–10, 170, 179–88,
181–82*f*, 184*t*
MoHRSS, 71–72
introduction to, 3
integration, 121–25, 195–96
stratification of social health insurance and,
94–96, 169–74
urban-rural divide, 25–26, 60–61, 79–80,
160–61, 194–95
urban-rural integrative development *(cheng
xiang tong chou fa zhan),* 124, 195–96,
218n34, 218n36, 225n3
urbanization
economic development and, 148, 153
economic integration and, 195–97
hukou (household registration),
165–66, 210n25
increases in, 82–83, 82*t*
regional diversity and, 84–85
social health insurance, 144, 153, 156*t*, 157

value-added, 40, 73

Wang Dongjin, 89
Wang Nan, 1–3
Weibo, 2
Wen Jiabao, 3, 22, 35–36
work-unit-based welfare provision, 42, 169
working-class, 29–30, 160–61, 166–67, 169,
225–26n6
World Trade Organization (WTO), 74–76,
80–82, 88–89

Xi Jinping, 22, 26

Yin Dakui, 65

Zhu Qingsheng, 63
Zhu Rongji, 22, 88, 89–90